URBAN CHURCHES, VITAL SIGNS

Urban Churches, Vital Signs

Beyond Charity Toward Justice

Nile Harper
and associates

WILLIAM B. EERDMANS PUBLISHING COMPANY
GRAND RAPIDS, MICHIGAN / CAMBRIDGE, U.K.

© 1999 Wm. B. Eerdmans Publishing Co.
255 Jefferson Ave. S.E., Grand Rapids, Michigan 49503 /
P.O. Box 163, Cambridge CB3 9PU U.K.

Printed in the United States of America

04 03 02 01 00 99   7 6 5 4 3 2 1

Library of Congress Cataloging-in-Publication Data

Urban churches, vital signs: beyond charity toward justice /
Nile Harper.
    p.   cm.
Includes bibliographical references.
ISBN 0-8028-4441-3 (pbk.: alk. paper)
1. City churches — United States — Case studies.
I. Harper, Nile.
BV637.U73   1999
277.3′0829′091732 — dc21   98-44943
CIP

Contents

96348

CONTENTS

Contents

Contents

Foreword

As a former Commissioner of the New York City Community Development Agency charged with administering the city's multimillion dollar Community Action Program, I read this exposition of the movement "Beyond Charity Toward Justice" with great appreciation. Acts of charity, service, and justice do indeed overlap, and there are no books that show the interaction and continuity better than *Urban Churches, Vital Signs: Beyond Charity Toward Justice*, by Nile Harper.

As a United States Congressman representing a Brooklyn constituency that is predominantly poor, and as a recent applicant for a Federal Empowerment Zone grant, I found my identification with the numerous stories of community redevelopment in this book greatly heightened. The vital signs set forth here and the stories of lessons learned offer great encouragement for many scarred veterans of the earlier "War on Poverty" to plan intelligently for new programs without some of the old blunders.

Faith-based organizations with a slow, steady, long-term commitment may promote and realize the ambitious vision of the architects of the Community Action Program, which was part of the earlier "War on Poverty." What the Economic Opportunity Act could not achieve through a political framework, urban churches may over several decades still accomplish.

Empowerment has now become an accepted, respectable concept sanctioned by forces all across the political spectrum. The church promotion of empowerment in impoverished communities can certainly contribute to urban redevelopment and church revitalization. The ultimate goal of justice helps to bring church and community interests together. One of the great blunders of many earlier Community Action Program agencies in the late sixties and seventies was their failure to seek more working partnerships with urban ministries. Some Catholic and Protestant inner-city church organizations discouraged such potential partnerships because of their overemphasis on charity and contempt for social action. On the other hand, political patronage purveyors and radical community opportunists often sabotaged collaborative efforts by vulnerable grassroots groups.

Today, greater balance and maturity between church and community leadership is evident. The ever-increasing burden of charity, coupled with political attacks on services for the poor, has helped to stimulate the new quest for justice. The achievement of justice requires the nurturing of people and the creation of a set of forces to form an environment favorable to social policy making that places a priority on meeting the needs of citizens at every economic level in our society. Faith-based organizations must be aware of and vigilant against the pitfalls their success may generate. The empowerment of the poor is still a threat to those already entrenched in power and privilege. Success may generate new political competition. Success may encourage opportunistic exploitation by new leaders from within the ranks of the poor. Churches with a realistic understanding of the limitations of human nature are in a better position to see and avoid these pitfalls.

The message of *Urban Churches, Vital Signs: Beyond Charity Toward Justice* that generates the greatest hope is that there are now enough faith-based urban projects under way, and enough institutional experience now in place, to withstand political backlash. The number and diversity of the stories witness to the strength of the movement. The likelihood is that these efforts will increase without alarming oppressive elements in the power structure. One can even dream, with some supportive evidence, that within the foreseeable future the movement toward justice will place more elected representatives in legislative and executive leadership positions who can take action to increase and preserve justice not only for the poor but for the whole society.

Major Owens, Congressman
The Eleventh District, Brooklyn, New York
The United States House of Representatives

Acknowledgments

Many persons in cities across the country have been helpful in assisting with contacts in churches and insight into urban ministry. They have graciously shared their knowledge of congregations engaged in creative ministries that move well beyond charity and toward increasing justice. We thank the following persons without whom this book would not have been possible:

- In New York City: Ann Barstow, Jan Orr Harter, Erynne Ansel, Robert Stone, Mae Gautier, David Dyson, Floyd H. Flake.
- In Baltimore: Herbert Valentine, Curtis Jones, Wy Plummer, Mark Gornik.
- In Washington, D.C.: Jane Asche, Lee Earl, Ronnie Lowenstein, Justus Reeves, John Steinbruck, Terri Thomas.
- In Atlanta: Eleanor Malone, Ed Loring, Lee Carroll, Kim Richter, James Davis, Ted Wardlaw, Carole Jean Miller.
- In Savannah: Henry Delaney, Otis Johnson.
- In Cincinnati: Duane Holm, Harold Porter.
- In Cleveland: Otis Moss, Craig Schaub, Dennis Paulson, Mylion Waite, Donald Stoner, Mae Gautier, Robert Stone.
- In Detroit: Charles Mabee, Kathryn Thoresen, Bill Hopper, Ronald Spann, Jim Perkinson, Peg Rosenkrands.
- In Chicago: Charles Dahm, Susana Vasquez, Richard L. Tolliver, Don Coleman.

- In Kansas City: Kirk Perucca, Sharon Garfield, Earl Able, Sylvia Wilson.
- In Houston: Kirbyjon Caldwell, Tina Moore, Joan White, Rudy Rasmus, Juanita Rasmus.
- In Denver: Peter Kjeseth, Solveg Kjeseth, Bruce Johnson, Luther Johnson, Cynthia Cearley, Glendora Taylor.
- In Portland: William Creevey, Janet Leatherwood.
- In San Francisco: Howard Rice, Glenda Hope, Frank Jackson, Penny Sarvis, and Roland Gordon.
- In Los Angeles: Cecil Murray, Jean Bihari, Mary Minor Reed, Mark Whitlock, Brent Wood, Charles E. Blake, Paul Turner, James Valerius.

Teaching colleagues and students at New York Theological Seminary, The Schools of Theology in Dubuque, and the Ecumenical Theological Seminary in Detroit have encouraged and helped shape this book. The writer expresses appreciation especially for the late Reverend Dr. Kendig Brubaker Cully, who was Dean of the Faculty and a teaching colleague at New York Theological Seminary, and to colleague and friend Reverend Dr. Charles Mabee, Director of the Master of Divinity Program at Ecumenical Theological Seminary in Detroit. The warmest word of gratitude goes to Judith Ann Harper, my wife, for her constant encouragement, manuscript editing, and commitment to the urban church research project.

Nile Harper

Introduction

History suggests that Christianity has been primarily an urban-oriented faith. Cities seem to have been symbolized with the cross inside a circle — the crossroads and market place contained within an enclosure. The enclosure may have been originally more for definition — an encirclement of sacred space — than for protection or defense. The city has been a place of ideas, creativity, and stimulating interaction. Indeed, some would define the city as the place of "transaction maximization." Some suggest that cities were first created to serve religion, as in ancient Egypt, and that priests were the first city officials. In religious life, cities have provided the context in which faith communities engaged the world in transformation by the grace of God's active spirit. The dynamic city suggests to the religious mind the ongoing creative activity of God among humankind.

People of the world are moving to the cities around the globe at an amazing speed. For better or worse, the rural populations are declining and the urban centers are increasing in density and absolute number. The places around the world where Christianity is growing the most rapidly are the great cities of the Asian Pacific, the cities of East Africa, and urban Latin America.

In the United States, after a season of decline, city-center churches are once again growing. Part of the recovery of urban churches is rooted in their reengagement of the creative talents of urban people in their struggle to transform life into humane community.

The purpose of this book is to tell stories of urban churches engaged in transformation. It seeks to give voice to the people and pastors of urban congregations that are doing creative things to live faithfully as Christians in the city. This is a book of hope. It is a collectivity of stories telling the ways in which churches are expanding God's justice, peace, and love in the world. It is written from the perspective that God is doing new and wondrous things in the world every day, and calling people through the churches to participate in the divine/human drama.

The methodology employed included site visits, interviews with pastors and church members, observation, and examination of church documents. After stories were written, they were read for factual accuracy by pastors or other designated readers.

This book is not an analytical study. It is not a survey or cross section of urban churches, nor is it a research into the relative well-being of urban churches. It is an affirmation that innovative, constructive, and faithful ministry is taking place in urban churches, and that this ministry is of such great importance to the life of American Christianity that it should be widely shared. The decade of the 1990s is a decisive decade for urban church redevelopment, revitalization, and reformation. There is evidence of this in almost every major city in the United States today. Not all, but many urban churches are:

- creating more culturally appropriate worship
- creating more inclusive, spiritually mature community
- nurturing faith that engages the challenges of city life
- reaching out to make global connections for peace and justice
- finding effective ways to nurture and mentor children and youth
- inventing constructive ways of redeveloping neighborhoods
- promoting the redevelopment of affordable housing
- enabling people to recover from destructive addictions
- strengthening family life spiritually, socially, and economically
- forming partnerships for resource development
- developing community-based schools.

The intention in compiling the book was to find urban churches that believe congregational life and social responsibility are necessarily interdependent. The kinds of churches sought were those that were creating meaningful worship, doing a good job of Christian education, and engaging the challenges of housing, health, employment, education, and family life. The churches selected illustrate creative ministries of redevelopment, social justice, and engagement with the tough challenges of urban life in city centers. The stories tell of big things done by congregations of all sizes, from 125 to 15,000 members. They are convincing testimonies that authenticity and effectiveness are a function not so much of size as of vision, faith, perceptiveness, and the capacity to take risks, change, and grow.

The book covers churches, pastors, and people in fifteen cities and twenty-eight congregations. Twenty-two of the stories were written by me, six by pastors (or, in one case, an elder) of the congregations. The stories are a witness to the good news of Jesus Christ alive among the people of urban America. There is tremendous diversity, energy, spiritual vitality, and faithful ministry taking place. We hope these stories will convey some of that strength to readers.

These are stories, not case studies. The stories are descriptive, attempting to listen for what we can learn. They are not intended as models. They are presented in the belief that the stories contain a wealth of ideas and possibilities for action, and in the hope that they will inspire readers to see possible connections with their own situations. The discussion questions at the end of the book are designed to help small groups think about their own church situations. We believe the best information can often come directly from pastors and others who have themselves been engaged in urban church life. They are the central actors in the stories of this book.

Nile Harper   April 1998

Vital Signs
in Urban Churches

Vital signs are indicators of life in the body. Urban churches are a significant part of the body of Christ. They have been through a season of distress and decline. In the past decade, there has been a redevelopment of strength and energy in a significant number of city-center congregations. While this is not true for the majority of urban churches, it is true for a substantial, creative minority. The vital signs that we report are symbolic of the improving health in a growing number of urban churches. These congregations constitute the nucleus of a movement that is evident in churches across the nation, large and small, across most denominations. The movement of spiritual revitalization and community redevelopment is taking place in African-American congregations, mainline churches, Roman Catholic parishes, and in evangelical fellowships.

An exciting rebirth is underway in many city centers across America. African-American churches are playing a significant role in this new life. Urban churches are being revitalized and reoriented to new ministries. Neighborhoods are being rebuilt; new housing is being constructed; businesses are being created; and new schools and community-based health care centers are being established. Communities are coming to new life and taking charge of their future.

Churches located in the heart of many urban centers are one of the most important sources for this renewal of American inner cities. From within the churches, and especially within African-American churches, there has emerged a passionate vision and push for redevelopment of city neighborhoods that is deeply rooted in religious faith and practical wisdom. In many older city-center neighborhoods, the churches are the only local institutions remaining that have credibility and connection to the people living there. Many urban congregations have a history and tradition of compassionate social service ministries among the poor, the oppressed, and the homeless. For more than a decade a variety of factors have come together to push, prod, and promote urban churches into a much more assertive, active, and creative role of leadership in community redevelopment. Faithful vision and spiritual power are at the center of the movement. The decline, decay, and deterioration of urban neighborhoods, especially in industrial cities, together with changing economic, political, and cultural circumstances, have contributed to the necessity for this new development. The people most impacted by these changes are organizing to respond creatively. Leadership has come from a variety of sources, but especially from among a generation of clergy and laity who believe change is possible, that the time is now, and the church must lead.

Congregations, pastors, religious communities, and local people have formed new partnerships among themselves and with other major institutions at local, state, and national levels to create a movement that has already produced significant accomplishments, made major improvements in the quality of urban life, and brought transformation to thousands of people and hundreds of neighborhoods. The vital signs are up and visible in many urban churches and communities. The religious factor in urban redevelopment and greater social justice in major cities is now widely noted, debated, and written about.[1]

---

1. Recent discussion of the vital involvement of faith communities in urban redevelopment can be found in the following publications: Joseph Klein, "Can Faith-Based Groups Save Us?" *The Responsive Community* 8:1 (Winter 1997/98); Kramnick and Moore, "Can the Churches Save the Cities?" *The American Prospect* (November/December 1997): 47-53; Henry Cisneros, *Higher Ground: Faith Communities and Community Building* (Washington, DC: U.S. Department of Housing and Urban Development, 1996); John Perkins, ed., *Restoring At-Risk Communities: Doing It Together and Doing It Right* (Grand Rapids: Baker Books, 1995); Elliott Wright, "Religious Institutions as Partners in Community Based Development," *Progressions* 8:1 (Winter 1995).

Vital Signs In Urban Churches

In visiting twenty-eight urban churches in fifteen major cities across the country, a number of vital signs of spiritual revitalization, dynamic redevelopment, greater inclusiveness, and wider justice were evident. These vital signs are indications of a movement that is changing the very nature of churches as well as their surrounding communities. Evidence of these vital signs are embedded throughout the stories of churches reported in this book. To alert the reader to some of the significant aspects of this movement toward revitalization, the following is a brief overview of a number of vital signs.

1. The most dynamic vital sign in urban churches is the increasingly vigorous and creative worship life taking place in a growing number of city congregations.

In many city churches, worship is spiritually powerful, culturally diverse, and directly related to mission. Renewed worship is designed to speak to the mind as well as the heart and soul. People are being educated to act from faith, hope, and love in order to bring compassion, new life, and justice into neighborhoods. The living Word of God is being proclaimed with vigor, is heard and embodied in urban churches in new ways. More and more urban churches are growing in vitality and numbers. This is good news for the churches. It is good news for people. It is good news for cities.

2. In city centers where congregations are vital and growing, church members and pastors are engaging in community-building in the neighborhoods.

People are creating community, within the congregation and within the neighborhoods, that is based upon significant, lasting, faith relationships. In almost every major American city today one finds churches that have come back from the dead. They learn to generate social cohesiveness, which brings stability, energy, and identity to city churches and their neighborhoods. The focus of such voluntary activity is most often the rebuilding of neighborhoods adjacent to churches.

3

These congregations understand city neighborhoods to be the field for mission involvement. Instead of organizing strategies that promote conflict, polarization, and confrontation, they focus now on creating community, forming partnerships, and building networks for the common good. Local leadership and ideas are encouraged and there is much less interest in looking to denominational sources for vision and strategy. Urban congregations are sponsoring, supporting, and giving leadership to local community organizations that are successfully rehabilitating neighborhood housing, constructing new affordable housing, creating new economic enterprises that put people to work, organizing community-based health care for persons and families that often have no medical care, and working to improve education in communities.

There is now wide recognition that churches can create and sustain human community better than almost any other urban institution. It is in the very nature of a faith-based body to generate the sense of belonging, trust, symbolic meaning, and capacity to care for one another that is so crucial to urban neighborhoods. Churches are intermediate-level communities that help people deal with the larger impersonal structures beyond the local neighborhood, and affirm individuals and families at the more personal level.

3. Urban churches, more than any other institution, are places where people of all ages — children, youth, young adults, older adults — can experience acceptance, affirmation, and encouragement, rooted in the unconditional love of God.

Congregations can demonstrate in their worship, education, and fellowship that people are valuable not for what they can do, but as persons. The continuing personal support, which urban churches create, can become the spiritual power that motivates people to take risks for justice and make sacrifices for the common good.

At the same time, however, new life has come as people in the church are brought together by church leadership to do the work of compassion, community rebuilding, and justice. Worship, Bible study, and pastoral ministry take on a deeper meaning and urgency as the result of engagement in the struggles for affordable housing, economic development, community health care, improved education, family life support, and the reduction of crime.

4

4. With this focus on community-building, many churches in city centers are taking leadership in creative ministries of redevelopment.

This is especially visible in a number of African-American churches, which have gone far beyond providing safety net social service. They are rebuilding whole urban communities, creating affordable housing, developing employment, providing community health care, and establishing good-quality schools. What begins as isolated acts of charity, individual actions of compassion, or programs of social service can develop under the power of God's spirit through creative leadership into very positive collaborative actions for systemic justice, which changes policy and structures that have oppressed people.

More and more urban churches have learned that authentic spirituality by its very nature includes doing the work of social justice. Believers are moving beyond individual deeds of compassion into the larger structures of society to powerfully shape the quality of human life in cities. This is taking place in churches of all sizes with different levels of human and financial resources. We see this in the 200-member New Song Community Church in Baltimore, in the 750-member Central Presbyterian Church in Atlanta, in the 2,500-member St. John's Methodist Church in Houston, and the 10,000-member First African Methodist Episcopal Church in Los Angeles. This is good news that needs to be widely shared, learned from, and celebrated.

5. As churches become more and more involved with social justice work, they have also become more politically aware and involved.

Political awareness has also come as connection to the liberation struggles in Latin America, the Middle East, Africa, and Asia has stimulated some urban churches to acts of solidarity, assistance, and support. The cosmopolitan nature of large cities provides opportunity for urban congregations to become aware of and enter into the struggles of people in other parts of the world. Often these experiences spur consciousness raising, promote stronger commitment to social justice, and stir spiritual growth in church members.

A number of urban churches have developed sophisticated networks for political action in support of resources for urban redevelopment. The needs and interests of people who have been oppressed, neglected, and underrepresented in government policy-making are now more adequately presented and heard. Creating a positive track record through community issue organizing and redevelopment projects helps attract political support. This is necessary to gain more resources for affordable housing, better schools, adequate health care, and economic development in city centers.

A number of national organizations have been formed to represent the interests of faith communities in Congress and federal government agencies. These important religious collaboratives (e.g., The Congress of National Black Churches, The Christian Community Development Association, the National Community Building Network, the National Congress for Community Development) are helping to articulate the hopes, plans, and initiatives of urban church people at the national level.

6. Urban church are working in partnership with the U.S. Department of Housing and Urban Development (HUD) in much greater numbers with a new spirit of mutual respect and collaboration.

This trend began in the 1980s in the Reagan and Bush administrations, and has been greatly enhanced during the Clinton administration. HUD Secretary Henry Cisneros created a special Office of Religious Organizations Initiatives to provide direct interaction with religious institutions as partners in the development of affordable housing in urban areas. The capacity of religious leaders to help urban communities identify their assets, do creative planning, and propose specific development projects is strongly affirmed by HUD. Partnership is now invited. The credibility of churches in urban neighborhoods is recognized and their participation in planning and development is officially encouraged and affirmed in Washington.

7. Increased community and justice work has led urban congregations to seek out a variety of resources with a new understanding that asset development and financial resources are potential spiritual power.

Human and economic resources are part of God's creation. Churches are learning to see the potential strengths of people and finding the potential economic assets in underdeveloped communities. It means envisioning what can be done with vacant land, old buildings, unemployed people, and creating new uses for untapped resources. A positive approach to older neighborhoods empowers people to take new actions for their own self-development.

Many urban churches have realized that resources for ministry must come from a whole metropolitan region, not merely from within the church or from one neighborhood. The practical development of metropolitan partners in ministry greatly strengthens city-center churches. They are creating networks of communication, financial support, technical skills, and political connections that are important for influencing policy, structures, and projects.

One resource that urban congregations are rapidly learning to use is the creation of nonprofit 501-C-3 corporations to utilize funding from foundations, businesses, government agencies, and individual donors who will not give to churches directly. Churches are learning how to compete successfully for financial resources along with other nonprofit organizations. There is a growing realization that urban churches should not be limited to doing only that which members can financially support by their giving. Good stewardship means using imagination to secure much greater resources from beyond the local community.

8. Urban congregations are generating new financial resources for faith-based community ministry by creating new businesses.

They are involved in a variety of business enterprises: owning and operating affordable housing, developing cooperative enterprises for construction, organizing community schools, forming job training and employment placement centers, operating restaurants, managing real estate, running bakeries and commercial catering services, making low-interest loans for starting small businesses, brokering home repair services, recording and marketing religious music CDs. The two common themes in all of these enterprises are that they strengthen local community life, and they put local people to work.

9. The creation of community development corporations (CDCs) by urban churches, and their positive record in promoting new housing, housing rehabilitation, and economic development has attracted strong interest and financial support from foundations.

There is growing support for CDCs from some of the most prestigious foundations, such as the Ford, MacArthur, Kresge, and Annie Casey, as well as the Lilly Foundation. Major foundations are interested in funding programs that demonstrate the capacity to enable people at risk to obtain education, develop job skills, foster economic enterprise, create stable families, and become self-supporting. Urban churches are developing resource links to these foundations.

A major channel for corporate economic support is the low-income housing tax credit program of the federal government. An entire industry has grown up around the sale and purchase of these tax credits. Most frequently, a syndicator such as the National Equity Fund (NEF) in Washington, D.C., arranges this. NEF organizes financial investors for affordable housing. The companies receive tax credits that can be applied toward their federal income tax. Community development corporations get loans and grants to construct affordable housing.

10. Many urban church–sponsored community development corporations (CDCs) have been significantly supported in their work to create affordable housing and advance economic development by the Local Initiatives Support Corporation (LISC).

In its first twenty years, LISC has raised nearly $2.5 billion from a variety of sources for use in grassroots community redevelopment. Over ninety-seven percent of this money is from private sources. LISC becomes the validating agent which corporate investors trust to make grants and loans to qualified community development corporations. The applications of CDCs must meet high standards and compete successfully among a large pool of project proposals. Many urban church-sponsored community development corporations have been supported and assisted in their projects for affordable housing, grassroots economic enterprise, and real estate redevelopment.

11. At the forefront of all this activity is a rising, new generation of urban church pastors who are skilled in organizing, creating partnerships, securing financial resources, and generating religious community.

They do all this with a focus on serving the deeper needs of urban neighborhoods. They understand the assets that are in urban communities and how to mobilize these human and physical assets to leverage larger outside investment in their areas. This generation of urban pastors is more politically sophisticated, more independent, and less denominationally oriented.

12. There is in many urban churches a kind of earthy wisdom about life in the human family. There is an appreciation of the family as an essential nurturing reality.

There is rich experience with diverse forms of family within the congregation. Mentoring — giving the gift of affirmation and discipline in a spirit of love — is widely practiced in urban churches that are redeveloping. Often it is this spiritual nurture that enables persons to turn their lives around and make new beginnings. Sometimes this is done in small groups, and sometimes in one-to-one relationships. Mentoring people-at-risk, with unconditional love, is taking place in every major city through evangelical ministries. There is a new appreciation of the capacity of faithful Christians to reclaim troubled urban youth and a strong emphasis on strengthening families.

13. A growing number of mainline urban churches are being revitalized by new members from diverse racial or ethnic groups.

New members are often attracted by changing patterns of worship, new leadership, vigorous community ministries, and strong spiritual life. These churches are finding ways to integrate personal and social justice ministries.

14. Emerging from this increasing diversity is a growing capacity in many urban congregations to deal with tough ethical decisions at the personal and social level.

Making ethical choices is more comprehensible in many urban churches because of the ongoing struggles embedded in the daily life and activity of the people themselves. There may be a deeper level of intuitive, empathetic, and creative understanding among urban church people about church decisions that involve risk, ambiguity, and the use of power.

15. There is a growing understanding that urban churches potentially have the human gifts that are most important for renewing and rebuilding urban communities.

These gifts are the intangible, but crucial, gifts of the spirit. They build trust, social cohesion, and human bonding, which results in a community that is strong enough to produce positive results for the larger neighborhood. This is what social scientists call "social capital." Social capital is the net gain of human energy, beyond what is needed for survival, coming from cooperative action that creates new goods and services needed by the larger community. It is the inner resource that lifts up new and indigenous leadership; it is the human asset that helps empower previously uninvolved people. It is the seedbed for new ideas; it is the social generator of new hope for a positive future.

In many urban churches the deep experience of suffering and oppression has sensitized people, given them unusual insight, created the capacity for inclusiveness, and forged the strength to have persistence. These are the gifts that enable people to engage in visioning, advocating, motivating, educating, organizing, developing, and affirming. It is from such faith-based gifts that powerful deeds come forth.

The special strengths of urban churches that are being renewed are numerous. Some of them can be recognized in this way: there is a positive turning away from a sense of dependence and disengagement toward affirmation of religious inner strength, identification of indigenous assets, local leadership, social cohesion through faith-based community, a new sense of empowerment, trust in the staying power of the church for the long-term, increased capacity for new partnerships, a deeper sense of human dignity and self-worth, a renewed practice of caring for one's neighbor, and confidence for shaping the future in a way that is more just and life-affirming.

New Song Community Church

The creation of a just community begins with small steps of personal compassion and moves toward larger, collaborative actions for systemic change. A vacant house is slowly rehabilitated by volunteers into a decent and affordable home for ownership. An opportunity for stable employment begins a career and breaks years of discouragement. A child's new determination against big odds turns into success in school and life. A physician's commitment to provide medical care for the uninsured becomes a growing health center. These are some of the areas of significant ministry described in the church's publication, *Small Changes, Big Differences.*[1]

New Song Community Church (Presbyterian Church in America) began in 1986 in the Sandtown-Winchester neighborhood on the west side of Baltimore as a new church development. This is a largely African-American area of the city with over fifty percent unemployment, median income of less than $10,000, decaying housing (over eight hundred boarded-up units), and very inadequate health and education services. Initial vision and leadership came from a small group — Mark Gornik, Allan and Susan Tibbels, Wy and Shirley Plummer, and Steve and Mary Smallman.

Mark Gornik has written about the start of the New Song Community Church, indicating that preparation included careful demo-

1. *Small Changes, Big Differences: Setting the Foundation of a New Community* (Baltimore: New Song Community Church, 1996).

graphic study of Baltimore's communities of need. The Sandtown area was identified as a place needing community redevelopment. Beginning as a circle of Christian friends, the founding families spent many months, after moving into the area, connecting with neighbors, meeting people in the community, on the streets, in the shops and local public schools. Their purpose was to become part of the community, to enter into its life and struggles before starting to organize a church. Gornik described their theology of incarnation as *listening* in a way that puts others first, *sharing* the world of their neighbors, *bonding* with the community, and *naming* where they lived *home*.[2] They began a house church with a commitment to be an interracial congregation focused on doing Christian community development. From this small beginning the New Song Community Church was born, nurtured, and developed into a lively congregation of over two hundred people, with an amazing diversity of creative ministries.

Worship and Christian Community

Currently, the Reverend Steve Smallman and the Reverend Wy Plummer are the co-pastors of the New Song Church. Both are talented worship leaders. Steve Smallman is a creative poet, songwriter, musician, and liturgist. Wy Plummer has a gift for strong preaching. These two pastors together with lay leaders have created a vital worship experience in the church that attracts not only people from the neighborhood but also from around Baltimore. Prayer, preaching, and singing are blended into a powerful service of praise and thanks to God. The proclamation of the good news of redemption in Jesus Christ is central to the worship. There is a profound sense of the presence of God's spirit in the lives of the congregation. The ministry of word and sacrament is focused on nurturing faith and commitment for serving God in all the arenas of personal life and the larger society.

The gathering of the community for worship on Sunday takes place in a renovated, older, three-story, residential building. The

2. Mark R. Gornik and Noel Castellanos, "How to Start a Christian Community Development Ministry," in *Restoring At-Risk Communities*, ed. John M. Perkins (Grand Rapids: Baker Books, 1995), 220.

church has chosen to put its resources into nurture, service, and community redevelopment instead of constructing a larger traditional church building. There is an atmosphere of warmth, informality, friendliness, and lots of human communication. Music plays an important role. Congregational singing is spirited. Electronic music brings vitality. Contemporary and traditional songs and hymns are used. The concerns of the people are shared. Prayer and witness integrate the realities of daily life with affirmation of God's providence, reconciling love, forgiveness, and calling to mission.

The church has created five non-profit corporations for affordable housing, education, community health care, Eden Job Placement, and Sandtown Music and Media Development. Currently the church is working to create yet another spin-off corporation to do economic development. So how has all this come about? Through a commitment to "living out the Gospel in the fullness of Christian community," says the Reverend Wy Plummer.[3] Involvement with human need in the neighborhood leads to engagement with the larger systems that profoundly shape people's lives.

Education

Beginning with the spiritual needs of people who gathered for Bible study and worship, New Song Church quickly saw the need to help children of the neighborhood with education. Instead of constructing a church building, the new congregation renovated an old, three-story, brick townhouse situated adjacent to a large intermediate public school. The profound needs of school children were evident. The first response was a preschool, and then an after-school tutoring program. This matured into a more substantial mentoring effort and a learning center. Then came a summer program for a hundred children. Next, the church created an Academy for Middle School Students, which has subsequently become a new public school. This is a full-day school with a commitment to academic excellence. Finally, there is a program of college scholarship aid for high school graduates to support postsecondary education. There are two goals: quality education within a Christian perspective, and investing in youth through

3. Wy Plummer, interview with author, Baltimore, 19 February 1997.

postsecondary level with the challenge for them to return to the community as future leaders.

As these educational initiatives have developed over a decade, many partnerships have been formed with people both inside and outside the community. Financial resources have been secured from other churches, foundations, businesses, participating families, and New Song Church members. A program of parent education has been one essential feature through which families are enabled to take a more positive, active role in supporting their children's learning.

The Middle School Academy builds on the close relationship with the public elementary school that is literally just a hundred yards away. It serves approximately one hundred students in a full-day school program. These are students whose families are committed to quality education with an academic focus that will get them ready for the college preparatory curriculum in high school. For a limited number of middle-school students there are significant scholarship opportunities to support enrollment in private, residential, prep schools. Many students who go through the tutoring, mentoring, and academy programs graduate from public high school and are able to compete successfully for admission and scholarships in good-quality universities and church-related colleges. They have learned positive work-study habits, the value of discipline, and achieved academic excellence.

Health Care

As the congregation became more engaged with families of school children the need for family health care emerged. A physician's willingness and determination to create health care for uninsured families provided the spark and the first initiative for what has become a major community health care center. The health center started in 1991 with Wednesday evening primary care for adults. Soon a Saturday morning pediatric clinic using volunteer doctors and nurses was added. As the need surpassed the limited services possible in the church facility, a vision for an expanded health care center facility was developed.

A vacant commercial building was acquired. In partnership with Habitat for Humanity and local volunteers, a commercial construction company building was completely renovated and brought up to code. Grants from foundations and the state of Maryland were vital. A key partnership with the Mercy Medical Center (a Catholic hospital in Baltimore) provided the medical staff and management. Now, over a thousand families are served annually.

The New Song Family Health Center provides access to quality, comprehensive pediatric and adult care regardless of ability to pay. The dignity of patients is affirmed and the strengths of the community are reinforced. Health education for families supplements the medical care program. A holistic approach is carried out. The board of the corporation includes church members, community people, medical professionals, and representatives from partner institutions. Funding comes from friends of the Center, partner churches, patient fees, gifts of professional service by doctors and other health professionals, government agencies, and the Mercy Medical Center of Baltimore.

Affordable Housing

The Sandtown Habitat for Humanity is a nonprofit 501-C-3 corporation organized as a Christian ministry in 1988. The Sandtown-Winchester community housing stock is architecturally and structurally sound. Most units are two- and three-story brick townhouses. Many are joined together in rows of townhouses. At the start of the project over eight hundred units were vacant and boarded up. Many families lived in substandard conditions and rented from absentee landlords. The New Song affiliate of Habitat for Humanity provided the organizing mechanism and volunteer labor. Local families became homeowners by investing three hundred hours of sweat equity in the remodeling work. The renovation was accomplished using private funding from churches, individuals, foundations, and businesses. The Enterprise Foundation has been a major partner in providing no-interest loans for construction financing.

Beginning in 1992, the project to rehabilitate one hundred homes in a twelve-block area was launched with the participation of former President Jimmy Carter. The goal was to completely renovate one hundred existing houses within five years. As of fall 1997, seventy-five units were completed and were owner-occupied. A major "blitz build" campaign in the summer months of 1997 helped to complete the project.

Four other key partners are the Baltimore City Department of Housing, which provided vacant houses for rehabilitation; the Baltimore Community Development Finance Corporation, which provided interest-free mortgages once the renovation was completed; the Neighborhood Design Center provided architectural guidance; and the Community Law Center provided legal aid in completing the transactions. The average cost per unit was $30,000 for renovation. This is about one-third of what commercial renovation costs. These cost reductions are due primarily to volunteer labor, gifts of some building materials, and no-interest financing. Homeowners who have invested three hundred hours of sweat equity qualify for long-term mortgages at no interest. Rehabbed houses are sold at cost. Mortgage payments go into a revolving fund that helps to finance other homes. The reconstruction project has brought a new spirit of vitality into the community. Other renovation projects have been inspired by the New Song effort. Some new housing is now under construction in the area. The outcome is a large-scale community redevelopment, and improvement in the quality of family life.

Employment

As a result of almost a decade of housing redevelopment, many people have learned skilled building trades and found their way into better paying, more stable construction jobs. Some began as volunteers, some as sweat equity workers, and still others as part-time paid helpers who learned technical skills. The great need for employment has been addressed by the New Song Church spin-off corporation called EDEN JOBS. This venture is an employment network with a full-time job developer working to establish an ongoing partnership with a number of businesses in the Baltimore metropolitan area. Continuous communication identifies employment opportunities and creates a positive connection with employers. Job seekers get three types of help at no cost: (1) one-on-one counseling, pre-job training, and attitudinal preparation; (2) employment referral for real jobs with a dependable business; (3) follow-up support and ongoing counseling for both the worker and employer. EDEN JOBS aims to place one hundred people a year in stable jobs.

"Good-paying jobs are a basic foundation for lasting community redevelopment," says Wy Plummer. "The continuing need to develop good income-producing businesses is one of our most difficult challenges."[4] One positive response to this challenge is the creation of Sandtown Records, which records and sells music CDs, sponsors a children's choir recording group — Voices of Hope — and stages concerts and celebrations. Another entrepreneurial effort in the planning stages is a Computer Training Center that will help area residents upgrade their job skills and improve employability.

What We Can Learn

Why has New Song Community Church been so successful? There are many contributing factors, including some of the following.

- *A holistic vision of mission.* The Christian ministry in the city center is an engagement with all the basic areas crucial to human life — spiritual, economic, education, health, and housing. The leadership of clergy — Mark Gornik, Wy Plummer, and Steve Smallman — has been crucial. The intentional decision to deal with basic needs of education, housing, health, and employment has strengthened the whole community and the congregation.
- *Planting an interracial team of pastors and their families in the neighborhood* provided strong leadership, showed serious intent, provided more skills, and modeled commitment to interracial community.
- *Not constructing a church building.* Constructing housing and health care facilities instead of a church building sends a powerful message of permanent commitment to serve people (the Church is primarily people) and indicates positive priorities.
- *Creative worship* with music, preaching, and liturgy that is meaningful and symbolically appropriate to people of the com-

---

4. Plummer, interview.

munity, and the creative talent of the clergy — especially of Steve Smallman — were important factors.

- *Creating nonprofit corporations with lay leadership.* The pastors did not try to run the community corporations. Each organization has a board of directors with wide-ranging membership. The five community-based corporations have greatly expanded the capability for securing gifts and grants from foundations, businesses, and government agencies.
- *Developing partnerships with the private and public sectors,* including business, foundations, churches, voluntary organizations, and government agencies led to the creation of a strong network to provide necessary skills, knowledge, and financial resources. They brought people with skills from beyond the area into redevelopment of the community.
- *Thinking regionally for resources* while acting locally for planning and ownership within the community has produced positive teamwork, energy, and real self-development.
- *The commitment of the Presbyterian Church in America* to long-term support of an interracial team of creative, skilled, and energetic pastors to do Christian community building was a wise decision.
- *The willingness to start small,* grow gradually, take a long-range view while having a vision for major transformation rooted in Christian faith and community contributed to success. Christian community development takes time, patience, and persistent work.
- *Making the most of a moment of opportunity.* Baltimore is clearly a city on the rebound with positive city government leadership and positive private sector leadership. The Sandtown-Winchester neighborhood has good housing stock ready for redevelopment and an under-employed population ready to be put to work. The potential was great. New Song Church provided the heart and soul to bring these potentials together for the good of the whole community.

Madison Avenue Presbyterian Church

Curtis A. Jones, with Nile Harper

As early as 1842, African slaves belonging to members of the First Presbyterian Church in Baltimore were involved in a Sunday School Mission Project in the church. Subsequently, they were allowed to sit in the balcony of the sanctuary for worship. This subservient relationship ended abruptly in 1848 when slaves sitting in the balcony attempted to vote during a congregational meeting. After being informed that they were not full members and could not vote, they walked out of the meeting. This event seems to have provided the momentum that led to the creation of the first black Presbyterian congregation in the state of Maryland in 1848. The new church was first named the Madison Street Presbyterian Church. It was founded according to tradition as a "Holy Protest," which affirmed that just and fair treatment between sisters and brothers in Christ was within the scope of reasonable expectation.[1] While this new church development was a kind of evangelism by default, it nevertheless began the life and work of Madison Avenue Church, which continues to manifest the strength of character and spirit of innovation that inspired the founders. Its members had a com-

1. William Britt, *Retrieving the Past: 1842-1997* (Baltimore: Madison Street Presbyterian Church, 1997).

The Reverend Dr. Curtis A. Jones is a Presbyterian minister and the Pastor of the Madison Avenue Presbyterian Church in Baltimore, Maryland. He is the President of the Baltimore H.O.P.E. community organization, President of the Presbyterian Black Caucus, and a leader in racial and ethnic church redevelopment.

mitment to education, self-development, economic ambition, and a sense of pride and confidence. The church developed a reputation for having a membership that was upwardly mobile, and became known as a black Presbyterian silk-stocking congregation.

During the 1950s, most of the Madison Avenue Presbyterian Church congregation lived within walking distance of the church. It was regarded as a community church. Housing in the area was very good. The public schools were of good quality. The streets were safe and clean. The surrounding area was a strong African-American community. During the 1960s, as the growing economy and expanding city brought new housing opportunities, many of the middle-class members moved away from the neighborhood. This outward movement brought about a decline in home ownership and less involvement of residents in maintenance of the neighborhood.

There was a corresponding decline in the quality of the local schools, an increase of street crime, and gradual deterioration of the quality of life in the community. The nature of the Baltimore economy changed from manufacturing toward information-age service businesses and life science technology. As this happened, much of the industry-based employment disappeared. Unemployment rose rapidly. Street crime, drug traffic, youth violence, and deterioration escalated in the older urban neighborhoods. This gradual drift continued through the decade of the 1970s and into the 1980s. In this context, the church lost members, and its witness was largely confined to Sunday worship and a neighborhood food basket program. By 1987, active membership was less than two hundred, and the congregation was becoming a gathering of older members; one-third of the members were over age sixty-five.

New Pastor and New Agenda

The Reverend Curtis A. Jones was called to be the pastor of the Madison Avenue Presbyterian Church in 1987. He came from a background of urban church ministry in Dallas, Texas. Jones began his work at Madison Avenue Church by making connections with the church leadership and the people of the neighborhood. He led the church governing body in a mission study, which resulted in a five-year Mission Plan that was adopted in 1987. The plan identified the strengths of the congregation and community as well as the needs of the church and the neighborhood. Three areas of mission emphasis were established in the plan:

1. education in the church and community;
2. economic development, especially housing;
3. church-based community organizing.

In 1988, the church established the Lillie A. Ross Child Development Center to be an overall agency for meeting some of the urgent education needs in the neighborhood. Lillie Ross, now in her nineties, was a longtime public school teacher and the first woman elder in the Madison Church. She is the honored matriarch of the congregation. The center is incorporated as a 501-C-3 nonprofit entity eligible for funding from a variety of sources, including governmental agencies. Over the years, the center has expanded its programming to include many significant efforts aimed at strengthening children, youth, and families in the neighborhood:

- the Lillie A. Ross Preschool has the goal of serving sixty children and their families
- the After School Program serves elementary and middle school children and their families
- the Adult Basic Education Program provides literacy ministry and programs to prepare persons to earn the General Education Diploma (GED)
- the Family Literacy Program is designed to promote positive learning reinforcement for the entire family group.

In support of these educational initiatives, an experienced social worker relates to families, helps them utilize other social agencies, and works to create community among socially and politically disenfranchised people in the Madison Avenue area. Several hundred children and middle school youth and their families are served.

The education programs are housed in a number of older townhouses that have been renovated in the neighborhood. Recently, classes in parenting and family life skills have been added. There is a staff of thirteen teachers and assistants (many from the neighborhood) relating to students, adults, and family groups through the work of the center.

After a decade of struggle, growth and development, the educational ministries of the Madison Church are moving forward. The plan is in place to develop an urban campus in a three-block area adjacent to the church building. Property acquisition is proceeding and has reached about two-thirds of the intended goal. Buildings within this area are being renovated into educational facilities. When completed, this $1.5 million complex will be known as the Madison Outreach Center. It is a visible symbol of community initiative and progress. The development of the outreach center has been done through the Madison Development Corporation, a separate 501-C-3 agency created by the church. Funding for the outreach center has come from a block grant through the city of Baltimore, general obligation bonds through the state of Maryland, and from income earned by the church's Housing Development Corporation.

The community education outreach has put the Madison Avenue Church visibly into the neighborhood. The lives of hundreds of families, youth, and children have been positively influenced. Church Christian education that is carried on within the congregation has been enlarged and given new vitality. Over one hundred younger members have joined the congregation. The presence of the church in the surrounding area has taken on new significance. The congregation has become more diverse, including older, longtime members; new members from the neighborhood; and others from the more affluent adjacent Reservoir Hill community, which is being revitalized.

The Church Rebuilds Housing

Turning a neighborhood around is a complex process that has many facets. One of the most basic needs around the Madison Avenue Presbyterian Church is to reverse the decline in housing. Beginning in 1986, the church created the Daniels Housing Corporation (named for the previous pastor) as an entity to reconstruct the old church parsonage into an income-producing apartment building for senior citizens. Curtis Jones inherited this project when he arrived in 1987. At that time it was an idea waiting to be carried out. The church struggled with this project, but finally completed it five years later. This was the first major housing victory for the church. Now called the Walker-Daniels Apartments, it is a symbol of community improvement and new hope. This success helped motivate the leadership to undertake a larger project to renovate adjacent buildings across from the church into forty-eight units of good-quality, low-income, apartment housing. This was a $5.5 million project that created a significant supply of affordable housing for seniors. It became a highly visible sign of the new spirit taking hold in the Madison Church neighborhood.

With these positive victories, the church and its pastor were encouraged to reach out to four other African-American Presbyterian churches in Baltimore to form a new development corporation called Baltimore Hope. The Presbyterian churches joining in this partnership for community improvement include Cherry Hill, Grace, Knox, Trinity, and Madison Avenue. They were encouraged and supported in this new effort by the Baltimore Presbytery, and especially by its Executive Presbyter, the Reverend Herbert Valentine. Each church has a subsidiary development corporation, and together they constitute Baltimore Hope, with enough presence to enter into a major redevelopment project. The most significant redevelopment to emerge through Baltimore Hope, in collaboration with other entities, is the Reservoir Hill Revitalization Plan, for renewal in an area of 3,200 households.[2] This redevelopment will be the work of a decade, and is being planned at a time when there is a sharp decrease in government funding for such projects. It is designed to attract private investment. Some of the key strengths that make the area excellent for redevelopment are:

- a large stock of sturdy, historic housing
- a choice location close to the city center
- access to Baltimore public transportation
- a good variety of housing types and sizes for families
- many community resources within the area and nearby.

Some of the challenges and issues facing the redevelopers:

- many absentee property owners and disengaged landlords
- very poor city sanitation services
- lack of a natural geographic integrating center

2. *Reservoir Hill Revitalization Plan* (Baltimore: Allison Platt and Associates, 1996).

- significant crime and perception of unsafe streets
- numerous deteriorating and uninhabited buildings
- significant sectors without any community groups
- inadequate automobile off-street parking areas
- generally bad conditions in alleyways and backyards.

Baltimore Hope (Hope is acronym for Housing and Outreach through Presbyterian Enterprise) has joined with the major citywide community organizing institution, B.U.I.L.D (acronym for Baltimoreans United In Leadership Development), the St. Ambrose Catholic Housing Center, and the Reservoir Hill Improvement Council to become a development collaborative. Together they have hired professional architects to work with the community in preparing the plan for urban revitalization. This plan, assembled in 1996, is now the basis for doing the detailed planning and securing of funds from outside investors to realize the full vision of a renewed city neighborhood. Property procurement is proceeding. Buildings are being purchased and land secured. The city of Baltimore is the largest owner, followed by the City Housing Authority. Their cooperation has been secured and, as the development progresses, the city will make significant transfers of property to aid the revitalization. Initial building renovation is underway and already some streets are showing the signs of new life, safety, order, and community vitality. You can feel the spirit of transformation taking hold as you walk in parts of the neighborhood. The foreword to the Plan draws together the larger vision in these words:

> The opportunity to initiate effective partnership ministries in Baltimore has never been greater. The media has presented a one-sided (negative) image of our city. . . . However, for each act of violent crime in the city there are hundreds of acts of compassion. . . . Our city represents both a difficult challenge and a tremendous opportunity.
>
> With a new vision congregations and communities can lift up a different image, and sing a new song. The creation of viable ministries in our communities has been the banner of the African American church. . . . The role of the church as a community builder and focal point for the sustenance of local identity is especially critical in neighborhoods that lack social stability.

24

> To achieve change, it is necessary to move beyond the more tra-
> ditional models. . . . Community can be defined as a group of peo-
> ple who understand that their destiny is bound up with one an-
> other. . . . Building community involves nurturing and challenging a
> group of people until they achieve a sense of wholeness and are em-
> powered to control their own future.[3]

The grassroots community planning that produced the citizen input
required for the planning process began in 1992, and continued four
years until the final plan emerged and was approved in 1996. This
master plan maps out the ways in which churches can embrace an
empowerment ministry in their communities. It helps historically
oppressed people move beyond the mental walls of survivalist thinking and become proactive. It helps community leadership to realize
there is very little power in advising, no dignity in begging, and no
hope in the status quo. The new paradigm enables them to become
partners, create coalitions of solidarity, and use power constructively
to reshape community life.

Church and Community Work Together

In adopting its five-year Mission Plan in 1987, the church affirmed
its commitment to join the citywide community-organizing project
called B.U.I.L.D. One of the significant accomplishments of
B.U.I.L.D was to mobilize low-wage workers to unite for negotiating
an agreement — A Social Compact — with the city of Baltimore.
Madison Avenue Presbyterian Church's pastor served as the president
of B.U.I.L.D during this time of challenging the city to affirm a higher
minimum wage. The city's ministers challenged Mayor Kurt
Schmoke to face up to the fact that over a twenty-year period tens of
millions of dollars of tax-supported civic renewal projects, mostly in
the downtown Harbor tourist area, had been carried out with no benefit to working people. The new hotels, stadium, convention center,
restaurants, and shops created mostly part-time, low-hourly-wage
jobs with no benefits and no opportunity for advancement. The prevailing hourly wage was $4.25 per hour. B.U.I.L.D forged workers into
a new negotiating unit called the Solidarity Sponsoring Committee.

3. Curtis Jones, foreword to *Reservoir Hill Revitalization Plan*, pp. vii-viii.

After a number of rounds of collective pressure, the mayor agreed with the workers that change was needed. He signed a Social Compact calling for a number of changes:

- a new minimum wage set at $6.10 per hour with subsequent increase up to $7.70 per hour
- recognition of the workers' negotiating organization — the Solidarity Committee
- requirement of every vendor who does contract business with the city to pay the new wage.[4]

The agreement was formulated as an ordinance passed by the Baltimore City Council and signed by the mayor in December of 1994. The Solidarity Committee subsequently formed an incorporated worker-owned cooperative so that it can formally negotiate directly with employers to guarantee worker wages. The Madison Church has learned from this experience about the power of organized solidarity to create positive change for the benefit of many. The church has also benefited from welcoming new members from the solidarity movement into its fellowship. The diversity of church membership has been strengthened and the congregation is more representative of the neighborhood population. The church and the community working together are a living reality at the level of daily economic experience. Viewed theologically, the spiritual power of reconciliation and transformation moves freely between the church and the community.

Another significant interaction between B.U.I.L.D community organizing and the Madison Church is in the area of improving education and community services for children. Children in the area are especially at risk in the hours after school and before working parents come home in the evening. Studies have indicated that 3:00-6:00 p.m. is the most dangerous time for children, with the greatest exposure to drugs, crime, violence, and sexual activity. Through B.U.I.L.D, church leadership sought cooperative relief from this negative situation for children. The Madison Church developed the first human resource authority for children in the city. The idea was to create a partnership with the local public school to extend the time

4. Baltimoreans United in Leadership Development, "The B.U.I.L.D Profile," 1994, pp. 5-8.

for the school to be open in order to create a safe environment for an educational, cultural, and recreational program. The problem was how to fund such a program and how to get the cooperation of the public school system. The challenge was to find a dependable, renewable funding source that would not be subject to the whims of the school board or the city council.

After research, study, and consultation through B.U.I.L.D, church leaders were able to bring forward a proposal to the state legislature to establish the Child First Authority. The legislature reacted favorably, passing a bill that officially created the Child First Authority. It authorized a small, but broad-based entertainment tax on tickets purchased for professional football and baseball games and other recreational entities. The funds gathered by the state are authorized for use by the Child First Authority. Local nonprofit groups, including churches, can create a partnership with a neighborhood public school to establish and operate an after-school program with educational and recreational components. The Madison Avenue Presbyterian Church presently operates a Child First Authority program in cooperation with the John Howard Elementary School in the church's neighborhood. The annual budget is in the range of $80,000. Over two hundred children in grades three through five are served. Another significant tie between the church and the community has thereby been established, and families are strengthened through their participation in the community after-school activity. Cooperation with the school has put church members and staff into helpful working relationships with teachers and parents.

The Church and Community Youth Ministry

In 1991, the Reverend Karen Brown was called by the Madison Church to be the associate pastor for the congregation, with special responsibility for youth ministry. The problem of finding summer jobs for youth is a persistent challenge. Summer brings time away from school and the opportunity for income-producing work. Some of the church youth approached the pastors and asked them to help find jobs. The pastors listened sympathetically and approached the request from the viewpoint "never do for people what they can do for themselves." They suggested that the youth consider creating a new business in which they could work for themselves. The pastors challenged them to stop thinking of themselves as employees, and see themselves as employers. The youth went to work on the challenge and with advice and counsel they came up with the plan to form an Afrocentric greeting card business. The Madison Church provided seed money for start-up of the business. The newly formed youth-owned business applied for a grant, to assist the capitalization, to two sources — the National Presbyterian Women and the Presbyterian Self-Development of People Fund. Grants were received and the business launched. The Umoja Greeting Card Company produced sales of over $100,000 during its first three years, and sales now exceed $150,000 for the past season. The company has been operating successfully for five years, expanding each year. The youth have earned and learned significant entrepreneurial skills. The youth ministry has grown and matured, and the youth have more respect for the church.

During the past decade the Madison Avenue Church has grown from under 200 to over 340 members. Even more important, the church has become a younger, stronger, and more active congregation. Its annual operating budget is just over $1 million for all its ministries, educational programs, and community outreach activities. There are thirty members of the church staff serving its overall ministry. The spiritual life of the church and the redevelopment of community life in the neighborhood have been significantly strengthened.

An effective strategy for urban ministry must assist a congregation to combine its energy and resources with those of the larger community for the good of the whole society. Outreach without spiritual conversion is merely well-intentioned social work that will not last for long. Religious activity without social outcomes is shallow spirituality that does not really affect daily living. The Madison Avenue Presbyterian Church seeks to live in the creative balance that unites deep spirituality and the struggle for justice.

The dynamic center of the church is in its worship. When we come together to pray, sing, listen to the word of God, praise the creator, confess and forgive, bring our offerings, celebrate the sacraments, and affirm one another in Christ, we are unified by God's grace. It is in worship that we find our marching orders for engaging in the struggles for justice. It is in worship that we find the direction and strength to move into the community to serve both friend and stranger. In worship we are embraced by God's love and we are enabled to embrace one another. In worship, old and young, child and parent, new members and longtime members, neighbors and strangers are brought together into the community of faith. And, we become Christ's disciples for Madison Avenue, for Reservoir Hill, for Baltimore, and for the world!

What We Can Learn

- Major community redevelopment often begins with small projects that build people's confidence and give valuable experience that becomes the basis for larger accomplishments.
- Seeing the assets of people and property, as well as the human needs, helps to create a positive starting point for faith-based community organizing.
- The collaboration of fifty congregations in B.U.I.L.D provided a strong base for developing people power sufficient to gain access to the city and state governments.
- The combination of older, long-term church members and younger new members, though difficult, provides a stronger base for doing the hard work of redevelopment.
- Skilled, long-term pastoral leadership is crucial for successful redevelopment of church and community.
- Creative funding that utilizes public and private resources beyond the limited giving possible in a small congregation is essential for redevelopment of the church and community.
- The use of multiple 501-C-3 corporations is helpful for securing wider funding. Getting competent guidance and professional counsel is wise and practical when planning multiple nonprofit development corporations.
- Affirming the interdependence of congregation and community, and engaging in the hard work of overcoming social and class difference is essential for substantial redevelopment.
- In urban church redevelopment, the skills most needed by a minister are those of transformative leadership — visioning, organizing, motivating, and active leading.

Allen African Methodist Episcopal Church

In November 1997, the Reverend Dr. Floyd H. Flake, United States Congressman from Queens, New York, announced that he would not complete his sixth term, saying to colleagues in the U.S. House of Representatives, "There is more important work to be done in the church." Flake is the pastor of the Allen African Methodist Episcopal (A.M.E.) Church in southeast Queens, New York City. He has also been the U.S. Congressman from southeast Queens for the past six terms (1986-98). Floyd Flake and the Allen A.M.E. Church symbolize the new assertiveness of urban congregations across the U.S. today. They know from experience that the way to rebuild a troubled neighborhood is for the church to take the lead, organize the people, plan the new community, become the developer, and partner with major government agencies and financial institutions to gain the funding and do the work. "The best role for the government," says Flake, "is to be a partner in the process [in which the church] takes a blighted urban community and turns it around."[1] That is just what the Allen A.M.E. Church has done in Queens, New York.

The Allen A.M.E. Church is a congregation of over 10,000 members where worship, Christian nurture, community redevelopment, and public service all go together. Flake emphasizes that the

---

1. Adam Cohen, "Feeding the Flock," *Time Magazine*, 25 August 1997, p. 47.

church is the center of rebuilding the community because it provides spiritual transformation, personal guidance, and a supportive
faith community. The church can create the trust, stability, and
network of relationships that are essential for turning the neighborhood around. This is not just idle talk. The Allen Church building itself is a symbol of the new vitality in the area. It is a new $23
million cathedral that includes the sanctuary for worship, education facilities, and church offices. It stands like a beacon of light in
the midst of the many challenges of life in New York City. It is not
surprising that its pastor prefers to be in this shining environment
instead of the dark halls of congressional office buildings in Washington, D.C. For the people of the Jamaica section of Queens, the
Allen A.M.E. Cathedral is a place of vision, spiritual power, and
personal and social transformation. It is a beacon of light for other
congregations in urban centers around the country. How did this
come about?

The church is named for Richard Allen, the African-American
spiritual leader, who freed himself from slavery in 1777, preached in
Methodist churches for many years, and in 1794 organized the Bethel
A.M.E. Church in Philadelphia. In 1816, Allen was elected the first
Bishop of the African Methodist Episcopal Church.[2] Allen was an
early promoter of freedom, education, self-development, and the abolition of slavery. His strong, self-reliant, faithful spirit is alive in the
Reverend Floyd Flake and the Allen A.M.E. Church today. The Allen
Church began in 1834 with a handful of people gathering for prayer
and Bible study in small homes in a rural area of Long Island called
Jamaica. They built their first church building — a small wooden
structure 18 feet wide by 30 feet long — in 1842. The building was
expanded to 30 feet by 40 feet in 1869, after the Civil War. After the
turn of the century, the congregation grew significantly with many
members migrating from the South. New York City expanded east-
ward to envelop the area. The church history indicates that there
were many peaks and valleys through the decades. There was financial hardship; there were acts of violence against the church. In 1944,
the church building burned down. In the 1960s, a new sanctuary was
built. In 1969, the church was firebombed. In spite of these adversi-

2. *Ebony History of Black America*, vol. 1 (Nashville: Southwestern Publishing Co., 1971), pp. 165, 171.

ties, the congregation continued to grow and to expand its program of Christian nurture and community service.[3]

Floyd Flake grew up in Houston, Texas, in a family of thirteen children. His father served in the army and was a janitor most of his life. There was a strong sense of discipline in the family. His mother was a housewife, faithful Christian, and active church member. Young Floyd grew up in the A.M.E. church and Sunday school. He was converted at age ten. By age fifteen he was preaching to youth groups, and at age seventeen he was president of the Texas Branch of the Richard Allen Youth Council of the A.M.E. Church. His pastor, the Reverend D. L. Dawson, and the Reverend W. D. Williams of the Wesley Chapel in Houston, helped him get a scholarship to Wilberforce University in Dayton, Ohio. He worked throughout his college years, holding two jobs and preaching on Sundays. He was educated for the ministry at Payne Theological Seminary in Ohio. He was an associate dean at Lincoln University from 1970 to 1973 while serving as pastor of the Second Presbyterian Church of West Chester, Pennsylvania. In 1973, he was called to be the Director of the Martin Luther King Center and Assistant Dean of Students at Boston University. There he eventually became Interim Dean of the Chapel. In 1976, he was called to become pastor of the Allen A.M.E. Church. His wife, Margaret McCollins Flake, who is an educator and minister, helped him found the Allen Christian School and became an assistant pastor at the church. Together they have provided leadership for the congregation that has grown from 1,200 members in 1976 to over 10,000 members in 1998.

A Cathedral Church for the Community

One can walk in any direction from the Allen A.M.E. Cathedral and find evidence of the good work done by the congregation in the surrounding community. There are new apartments, redeveloped buildings, new family duplex homes, a community social service center, cleaner and safer streets, a wonderful Head Start program, a church-sponsored community school for nearly five hundred students, thriv-

3. *The History of Allen A.M.E. Church* (New York: Allen A.M.E. Church, 1996), pp. 1-2.

ing small businesses, a church-operated transportation company, growing commercial enterprise, and a sense of community pride. The focal center of all this new life and community redevelopment is the worshipping congregation in the Cathedral on Sundays.

On Sunday mornings there are four services of worship — 6:30, 8:30, and 11:15 services fill the Cathedral, and there is a service of worship for youth in the Chapel at 11:15. The Reverend Flake preaches two sermons each week on a rotating basis between the three services. All services reflect a dignified but joyful spirit of praise and faith affirmation. Preaching is biblical in perspective and content. It is focused on teaching the congregation to be disciplined, responsible, and productive disciples of Christ. Flake, a former university dean, is both inspiring and didactic in his preaching. The spirit of worship is experiential and expressive as well as instructive and nurturing. Music is very important in carrying the spiritual content of the worship. There is vigorous congregational singing, and a mass choir fills the Cathedral with spirited anthems of praise and adoration, which evoke great response from the worshippers. The order of worship is a traditional A.M.E. service. The music, preaching, concerns of the community, congregational singing, and mission offerings bring lively, enthusiastic, and personal experience of God's presence into the worshipping community. Worship draws to a conclusion with the call to Christian discipleship, which affirms both personal salvation and the church's responsibility in the world. The Sunday worship bulletin is packed with announcements of the numerous ministries, meetings, prayer and Bible study gatherings, and community action involving church members during the week. The bulletin is a call to service and discipleship. The inner spiritual life and the outward journey of active involvement are joined together in the worship and work of the Allen A.M.E. Church.

Ministry Through Housing and Social Service

The Reverend Donald G. Ming was the predecessor of Reverend Flake. Ming started the planning and organization for a Senior Citizen Housing Project that Flake brought to completion. In 1978, the church organized Allen Housing and Development Corporation, and constructed the Allen Senior Citizen Housing Complex, which is a federally funded Section 8-202 apartment building. This was a land-mark event in the community. It signaled that the church was serious about redeveloping the neighborhood. This $12 million, 300-unit apartment facility was built on urban renewal land. The majority of the senior residents are not members of the church. The facility provided safe, secure, comfortable living space, and it was a visible symbol of transformation.

From this beginning in senior housing the Allen Church has gone on to develop many other types of affordable housing for citizens in the wider community. The Allen Neighborhood Preservation Corporation, created in 1978, has engaged in rehabilitating vacant houses, assisted owners in upgrading and remodeling their homes, acquired property for new housing development, and managed the 30,000-square-foot Multi-Service Center constructed by the City of New York.[4]

The Preservation Corporation has gone beyond renovation and rehabilitation of existing houses to sponsor more than 170 units of affordable new housing. For example, in 1985 sixty-two new family houses were built on land provided by the City of New York. All of these homes were for non–church member residents of the community. The duplex family houses are affordable homes for which the church helps buyers to qualify. This is scatter-site housing that has helped to renew and stabilize neighborhoods. None of the new houses were sold to church members. Construction, financing, and sales were all handled through the nonprofit corporation that is separate from the church. The neighborhood understands the integrity of the church-sponsored, community-based redevelopment program. "Church sponsored, non-profit community corporations do not preach the gospel," says Flake, "they bring life to it every day of the week."

Along with the several housing corporations and the educational endeavors, the Allen Church sponsors more than half a dozen other nonprofit corporations that engage in direct service delivery to persons and families with particular needs. All of these services have grown out of the basic commitment to assist people to become more independent and self-determining. The church mission statement ex-

4. *The History of Allen A.M.E. Church* (New York: Allen A.M.E. Church, 1996), p. 3.

presses this insight: "The revitalization of the community surrounding the church was not only accomplished by building structures, but by building social infrastructures. Both physical and social service structures are necessary to realize the wholeness and self-sufficiency [of people]."[5] The most visible symbol of social service is the South Jamaica Multi-Service Center. This building demonstrates the new partnership between the church and the government. It houses the following:

- a Head Start school (federally funded)
- the Women, Infants and Children Program
- a pre-natal counseling for teen mothers program
- a community renewal program (state funded)
- the Affordable Housing Program, City of New York
- a walk-in health clinic, City of New York
- a mental health and counseling center

All of these services are surrounded by the presence of the Allen Church congregation, which provides an ongoing welcome, support groups, and numerous opportunities for people to connect with a strong, permanent base of belonging.

Ministry Through Education

One of the most significant ministries of transformation in the urban neighborhood is the Allen Christian School. The church had always had a strong commitment to Christian education, but Reverend Flake encouraged the church to expand its vision to include the operation of a school for children of the community who were not being well served by the public schools. From his personal experience in Houston and from his work in Boston and New York he saw that most African-American children were not getting the quality of education that would enable them to gain entrance into college. Reading and math skills were substandard. Academic aspiration was stifled. Dropout rates were high. Many public schools were not safe. They tended

5. "Role of Ministry in the Allen A.M.E. Church," Allen A.M.E. Church Mission Statement, 1996, p.2.

to have low expectations for students. Teachers were often prevented by a variety of conditions from creating the educational environment necessary for the positive nurture of children at risk.

Flake formed a church education task force, made up of church members who were teachers and administrators in the New York City public school system, to advise him. They knew the difficulties faced by children in the urban schools. When in 1977 Flake asked them to consult, they thought he had in mind the creation of a tutoring program. They were surprised when he proposed creating a weekday school, kindergarten through eighth grade, open to the community. There were long and heated discussions. There was debate about public vs. church-sponsored education. There was concern about the cost and how a school could be funded, especially since the church had just been through an expensive building program for a new sanctuary. Flake asked the task force five fundamental questions:

1. Do we believe good, quality education is essential?
2. Do we believe the children of our community are getting quality education?
3. Do we have the capability and the will to create a school of educational excellence?
4. Does our Christian faith motivate us to take the risk and make the investment to create a school?
5. What action steps should we take?

The task force realized that inequality of educational opportunity was, in fact, a denial of basic civil rights for African-American children.[6] After much study, discussion and prayer, the church education task force joined with Flake in recommending that the church construct a school building and create the Allen Christian School to provide opportunity to children at risk for excellence in education. A campaign for church and community resources, together with borrowing, enabled the congregation to form the Allen Christian School Corporation, construct a new $4 million school building, and open the school in 1982.

The school has grown to an enrollment of nearly five hundred students. The school is a church-sponsored Christian school open

6. Floyd Flake, interview, April 1998.

to students from the community without regard to church affiliation. The Reverend Elaine Flake has played a significant leadership role as the school's education director. A majority of the students come from families who are not church members. Families pay tuition of $3,400 annually. There is a scholarship program. Families prize the opportunity for their children to become students at Allen Christian School. High schools in New York City eagerly recruit Allen students. Academic excellence and the nurture of Christian faith are the keystones of the Allen Christian School. Over 96 percent of its graduates are attending or have graduated from postsecondary education. Since its opening in 1982, more than a thousand students have graduated. A significant number have returned to work and serve in the community.

Of course, the story of the school is not all easy successes. The early years were a struggle. Flake says, "My wife, Elaine, and I turned our home into a giant grant-writing establishment. The dining room table was filled with a constant stream of paper from the never-ending quest for funding sources." The school's board and staff worked tirelessly and sacrificially. However, from 1982 to 1985, church membership more than doubled, growing from two thousand to over five thousand members. The greatly expanded membership provided a much larger base of support for the growing educational program. Education at all levels, including the new school, was the key to growth and self-development of people in the church and the community. "When people in the community saw that we were serious about their needs," says Flake, "they then began to trust the church." From that point in time, people and groups began to seek out the church, to join its community ministries, and to invite its partnership in development projects.

Flake has emphasized the importance of lay leadership in the early projects of housing and education. Church members who are teachers, government workers, civil servants, police, social workers, homemakers, and small business owners, together with others from the community, provided ongoing efforts required to complete many of the development projects and educational programs. As the church grew and its social ministries became larger, new members were attracted who brought talent in business administration, legal skills, and financial management. In the beginning, lay leadership and the pastor did it all. Today, leadership is a combination of lay volunteers and professional staff, with guidance from the pastor. Flake is assisted in ministry by fifteen clergy colleagues and a large, capable administrative and support staff. There is in the fullest sense of the word a "team" ministry in this large and complex church.

Ministry Through Political Service

In 1986, United States Congressman Joseph Addabbo, who represented the Southeast Queens district, died. A special election was called to fill the unexpired term of office. Many people and groups in the district urged Floyd Flake to stand for election to Congress. The encouragement came from friends inside and outside the Allen Church. After prayer, consultation, and discussion, the decision was made to go ahead and seek the office. This decision changed the way in which Flake would carry out his ministry for the next eleven years.[7] The official Democratic Party opposed the effort of Flake's supporters. It took a court struggle to get him on the ballot. The party ran a candidate against Flake. The people in the neighborhoods turned out in force and number, electing Flake, who entered the Congress in January 1987. He won five more re-elections, three of which were contested campaigns in which the Democratic Party ran candidates against him in the primary election. In his final election, Flake won over 80 percent of the vote and enjoyed bipartisan support. In retrospect, looking back over eleven years of political service, Flake says, "We are all children of God and we are all citizens of the country. The political process is part of God's world and is an arena for ministry, if we remain faithful." The years of commuting back and forth weekly between Washington and New York City opened new doors for service to the church and the community. Serving in the U.S. Congress enabled Flake to play a role in helping to bring systemic change through shaping legislation to assist the embattled urban areas across the nation. Among the many legislative efforts during the decade, Flake mentions just a few as standing out.[8]

---

7. Being in Washington, D.C., four to five days a week opened up the opportunity to delegate more responsibility, develop greater lay leadership, and create a more substantial professional staff.

8. Floyd Flake, interview, April 1988.

- The Banking Enterprise Act of 1991, which gave incentives to encourage lending institutions to invest in urban areas. It helped to start a substantial reinvestment in city centers impacted by poverty and decaying infrastructure.
- The Community Renewal Act of 1995, which gave a more prominent role to voluntary community development institutions. It recognized faith-based organizations as legitimate partners in urban redevelopment and opened up greater opportunity for 501-C-3 nonprofit agencies.
- The Welfare Reform Act of 1996, which established the authority for state governments to use "Charitable Choice" in contracting with religious organizations as vendors for delivery of social services along with secular social service agencies. Churches can now seek state funding directly to operate social services.

As Flake indicates, most faith-based communities are more personally interested in the well-being of people in need of social services. Furthermore, when churches get involved in assisting people they tend to provide a more dependable support network and a commitment to recovery that is more stable and long lasting. The success of the many church-sponsored, community-based programs in the parish area around Allen A.M.E. Church seems to support this positive evaluation. It is significant to note that during the eleven years that Flake served in Congress the Allen Church strengthened its commitment to redevelopment of its neighborhood community and the church membership grew from five thousand to over nine thousand. The church continued to expand its program of spiritual nurture, worship, pastoral care, and Christian education. It continued its strong emphasis on teaching, preaching, and helping persons mature in discipleship. At the same time it expanded its efforts in economic development, housing, social service, and improvement of education.

After his twenty-two years as pastor of the Allen A.M.E. Church, eleven years of political service in Congress, and a lifetime in urban ministry, it is significant that Flake now chooses to use his free time since leaving Congress to promote the development of church-sponsored schools in cities around the country. He says, "The cutting edge in the ongoing civil rights struggle today is the inequality of public schools for minority group children." It is a matter of basic justice denied. Hundreds of thousands of minority group children are being denied their civil rights through inferior and unequal public schools. Flake now devotes nearly 50 percent of his time to speaking in African-American churches in urban areas to stimulate the formation of church-sponsored schools. He says, "Churches have unused classrooms in cities where children are not getting even a good basic education. Churches can and should start schools to help overcome inequality and enable children to gain access to mainstream opportunity. There is a growing movement to do this and I want to help promote it."[9]

Flake is also writing a book, *The Way of a Bootstrapper,* which will include some autobiographical material. It will also serve as a motivational tool to inspire others to work diligently in the pursuit of excellence in spite of their fears and challenges.

What We Can Learn

- Strong, visionary, skilled pastoral leadership is at the center of this creative urban church.
- Having a big vision for ministry in the community that goes well beyond traditional patterns has helped attract new members.
- Strong lay leadership was cultivated by the pastor and provided the human resources for many of the diverse enterprises of the church.
- A strong commitment to self-development through education has enabled much of the growth in the Allen A.M.E. Church.
- An entrepreneurial spirit and the capacity to take thoughtful risks, reach beyond the conventional, and serve a wider public helped expand the base of support for new ministries.
- An incarnational theology — embodiment of the gospel — through service and systemic justice has enabled the church to bring great spiritual strength to its ministries.
- Seeing and responding to the great human needs of the south-

9. Floyd Flake, interview, April 1998.

east Queens area created credibility for the church in the community.

- A commitment to educational excellence in the Allen Christian School has provided a way of creating a new generation of leadership for the church and community.
- The Allen A.M.E. Church is an example of good balance between pastoral, prophetic, and priestly, between personal spirituality and systemic justice.
- The pastor's experience is an example of how political action can enhance and strengthen a congregation when it grows out of fundamental issues of civil rights and basic issues of justice.

The Lafayette Avenue Presbyterian Church

David W. Dyson

The Lafayette Avenue Presbyterian Church in the Fort Greene section of Brooklyn, New York has always had a passion for justice. Organized in 1857, at a time when the issue of slavery dominated the national debate, the church called Theodore Ledyard Cuyler, a militant abolitionist, as its founding pastor. Robert Todd Lincoln, the eldest son of the president, came north from Washington to break ground for the new church, carrying a special shovel from his father (this shovel still hangs on the wall of the church library). Though old friends, the Reverend Dr. Cuyler would press President Lincoln relentlessly on the issue of emancipation, both before and during the Civil War. The church was known from the outset as a "temple of abolition."

In 1872, Cuyler, himself now a famous preacher, arranged for what would become a most famous event. He invited Sarah Smiley, a Quaker preacher, to be the first woman ever to preach from a Presbyterian pulpit. The congregation took this in stride and supported it. Not so the local Presbyterian authorities, who brought Cuyler up on "heresy" charges and accused him of holding a "promiscuous assembly" (promiscuous because a woman was preaching). The debate raged for days on the front pages of the *Brooklyn Eagle* and *Harper's*

The Reverend David W. Dyson is Pastor of the Lafayette Avenue Presbyterian Church in Brooklyn, New York. He is the organizer and director the People of Faith Network, a voluntary association for justice in the workplace. He is an experienced labor organizer, author, and lecturer.

Weekly. Cuyler held firm and eventually the church authorities only issued a censure, and backed down on the heresy charges. But Lafayette Avenue Church was forever destined to be in the forefront of the social justice struggles of the day.

By the early 1970s, Lafayette Avenue Church was well on its way to being a multiracial, multicultural congregation, a phenomenon not reflected in the stately interior of the sanctuary. A young Pratt Institute artist, Hank Prussing, was commissioned to paint a giant mural around the upper balcony, reflecting the diversity of the community and the church. Prussing went out into the streets and took photographs of the neighborhood people and activity, which he used in painting the massive swirling sea of community life titled, "Mighty Cloud of Witnesses," a phrase from the letter to the Hebrews. To this day, people come into the church to find their parents', grandparents', and children's images in the great mural.

The Fort Greene section of Brooklyn, which is home to the church, is a tree-lined, brownstone neighborhood just across the river from the canyons of Manhattan. It is home to many musicians, actors, writers, and artists who have fled the higher rents of the more expensive Manhattan. The congregation is two-thirds black and one-third everything else, as is the neighborhood. Theodore Cuyler started the church in 1857 with 140 members. After his thirty-year pastorate, Lafayette Avenue boasted twenty-three hundred members. But the church went through the classic urban transformation in the 1930s and 1940s when the white and the wealthy moved out of the city and took their church membership with them. In recent years the church has managed to defy the national trends and is a growing, multiracial, multicultural, mid-sized (350 members), middle-class inner-city church with a strong gospel foundation; outstanding music (including one of the best gospel choirs in the city); a full menu of education programs and social service projects; "More Light" status (Presbyterian designation for full acceptance of gays and lesbians into leadership and ordained status in church); and a high profile in the community. Many new members "discover" Lafayette Avenue Church after attending a worship service, a concert, or one of the many community programs at the church. Lafayette Avenue has been most successful in attracting those who have been alienated by more traditional church models.

Economic Justice

Like most churchgoers, the eyes of people at Lafayette Avenue Church tend to glaze over when they hear talk of economics from the pulpit. In the United States economy it seems that things are always going up and down — housing starts are up while soy futures are down, the dollar is rising against the peso but falling against the yen. But two economic trends have caught the attention of the people in the pews at Lafayette Church: (1) the growing disparity between rich and poor, and (2) stagnant wages of workers.

The United States now has the largest income disparity between rich and poor of any industrialized nation in the world. Ireland is a distant second. One in five children in the United States now live at or below the poverty line. With the new welfare legislation and lack of jobs to help offset it, the number may one day be one in four. These are the families that most Americans don't see. More billionaires, fewer in the middle class, and more desperately poor is hardly the biblical vision of the reign of God. "Lord, when did we see thee hungry, or thirsty, or naked?" (Matt. 25:44).

The second economic trend of concern is stagnant wages. The wages of working families in the United States have been stagnant or declining (in real dollars) since the mid-1970s. In more and more Lafayette Avenue Church families, two spouses work instead of one, and some work two or even three jobs. Add this to the anxiety about layoffs, downsizing, and capital flight and you have more and more churchgoers looking for a word about economic justice from the scriptures. After all, more than any other subject, Jesus talks about the sin of self-righteousness and the love of money. More than any personal or sexual indiscretions, Jesus talks about equity for the poor. More than idolatry, apostasy, hypocrisy, or indolence Jesus talks about greed and false pride. Jesus forgave adulterers (the woman at the well), he forgave the blasphemer, he forgave Peter's denial and Thomas's doubt. But when he entered the Temple and saw the moneychangers swindling the poor, that is when his blood ran hot, his whip came down, and he declared, "You have made it [the Temple] a den of robbers" (Luke 19:46b).

In 1975, the salary of a corporate chief executive officer (CEO) was thirty times the salary of one of their average workers. In 1995, the CEO salary was 145 times as much! Because of the nation's phi-

44

losophy on trade, taxes, immigration, and foreign competition, and the growing concentration of corporate power, we are quickly moving toward a two-tiered society. The descendants of American pioneers who fled the tyranny of aristocracy and two-tiered societies in Europe are finding themselves moving steadily toward two economically separate and unequal populations within the nation.

This is a new economic phenomenon. At no other time in our history have median wages for breadwinners fallen for more than two decades. Never before have American workers suffered real wage reductions at the same time the per capita domestic product was increasing. Within a global economy in full swing with trade barriers dropping everywhere, the supply of cheap labor in the Third World has a profound effect on First-World wages. The people at the Lafayette Church are experiencing this very economic marginalization.

This perspective rarely finds its way into the "family values" debate. As the one-earner, middle-class family becomes rare, as children need ever more costly education and health care, as the cost of raising a family rises as sharply as earnings plunge, parents are spending more of their time working to provide the needed money and less time on the nurture and guidance of their children. Parents spend forty percent less time with their children than parents did thirty years ago. Despite the conventional wisdom, traditional families are being destroyed not so much by misguided social welfare programs as by a global economic system that has no more loyalty to families than it does to countries.

In 1997, while the national press was in a feeding frenzy about the booming economy and the record gains on Wall Street, the question Lafayette Avenue Church was dealing with was whether or not the boom on Wall Street was trickling down to Main Street or whether it merely exacerbated the concentration of the wealth in fewer and fewer hands.

"Concern" Changes to "Action"

The "last straw" for the Lafayette Avenue Church came in 1994. Newt Gingrich was *Time* magazine's Man of the Year. He was the foremost spokesman for the "Contract for America." His allies in the religious right and the Christian Coalition followed with a "Contract for the American Family." After a careful reading, church members were stunned to find that in discussing the momentous problems facing American families, not once did the "Contract" mention poverty, racism, or the global economy as contributing factors.

Within ten days of the *Time* magazine article, a group of progressive evangelicals, led by Reverend Jim Wallace of the Sojourners Community in Washington, D.C., issued a statement called, "The Cry for Renewal." They observed:

> With the ascendancy and influence of the Christian Right in party circles, the religious critique of power has been replaced with a religious competition for power. . . . Recently, the increased influence of religion in politics has too often made our political debate even more divisive, polarized, and less sensitive to the poor and the dispossessed. We are deeply concerned about the subversion of prophetic religion when wealth and power are extolled rather than held accountable, and when the gospel message is turned upside down to bring more comfort to those on the top of society than to those on the bottom. . . . To abandon or blame the poor for their oppression and affirm the affluent in their complacency would be a moral and religious failure, and is no alternative to social policies that have not succeeded. We must revive the lapsed virtues of personal responsibility and character, and repent for our social sins of racism, sexism and poverty.[1]

This was a rallying cry for those concerned members of the Lafayette Avenue Church who wanted to have a voice that could be effective in influencing the global economy. They realized that they, a moderate-sized congregation, could not do this by themselves. To be effective they needed to reach out and join with other congregations.

What was needed was a network which connected clergy and lay people in local congregations across the country to formulate campaigns around economic justice issues. These are the people who are in the front lines of moral and political response to the religious right. These are the people who are able to organize letter writing, phone calls, and demonstrations in support of justice issues. The key to any successful organizing is a network of activists who can be mobilized — not just a mailing list. A number of experienced pastors and lay

---

1. Call For Renewal, "Cry for Renewal: Biblical Faith and Spiritual Politics" (Washington, D.C.: Call for Renewal, 23 May 1995).

leaders in New York City had enough names in their address books to start a good network. With the blessing and involvement of the concerned and committed people of the Lafayette Avenue Presbyterian Church, the People of Faith Network was born in 1994. The network is a combination of hundreds of church people and others across the country. Using letter writing and phone communication, the network is able to quickly produce a substantial expression of opinion focused on a carefully selected issue. From the discussions of the founding group, the name — People of Faith — came about naturally. As we dialogued and debated we would say, "People of faith should . . . ," "People of faith ought to . . . ," "People of faith could . . . ," and before long we simply called ourselves People of Faith.

People of Faith developed around two basic organizing concepts: congregations and campaigns. *Congregations* are where the people are gathered and where religious faith is engaged for justice. Congregations have committees, sessions, and boards of people who are on the line, in the trenches, who feel the crunch of unjust policies and trends. Activists in congregations can mobilize sometimes only a handful of people, but when multiplied by thousands of congregations around the country they can form a mighty army for justice. *Campaigns* are the mechanism to move issues into visibility. The Bible tells us that without a vision the people perish. But without a vehicle, the vision has no wheels. Campaigns are those vehicles. Every successful advance in American social justice was connected to a campaign, be it abolition, child labor, labor rights, civil rights, racial justice, or women's rights. People learn best about social and economic inequity through active participation in campaigns that are geared to realistic objectives that can be accomplished by public action.

Campaign One: Sweatshops and The Gap

As the People of Faith Network was developing, an opportunity fell into our lap. Word came to us in New York from friends in Central America about the terrible conditions in a maquiladora factory (a factory where only labor is added to the production process) in El Salvador that is used by several United States clothing companies. Many of the hundreds of young girls working in the plant were underage, some as young as thirteen. The factory was brutally hot, the drinking water was dirty, the supervisors were sexually abusive, the girls were allowed only two short bathroom breaks a day, and many were forced to take birth control pills. Even with all this, the most unpopular feature to the girls was "forced overtime." When a big order came in it often meant twenty-hour shifts, from seven in the morning until three the following morning. Many girls went to work to make money (very hard to accomplish at fifty cents an hour) so that they might complete high school in night classes. With forced overtime, if they went to class and refused to work the long shift, they were fired and placed on a computerized "black list" shared with other companies. They would never work again in the garment industry, which was often the only employment game in town.

Working with trade union and human rights activists, we raised these deplorable conditions with executives of The Gap, a major United States clothing company using the Mandarin International Factory in El Salvador. They denied all the charges and said they checked the plant regularly. A war of words raged, but the evidence was mounting — against The Gap. Getting nowhere in our discussions with the company, we mailed out an appeal to our People of Faith Network, still in its infancy. As a result pastors, rabbis, priests, nuns, and lay people — consumers all — contacted The Gap, wanting to know why the company couldn't police its own subcontractors. One rabbi on the West Side of Manhattan got frustrated after writing two letters and receiving double-talk replies. In a third letter, written in December of 1995, Rabbi Rolando Matalon, leader of the large B'Nai Jeshrun congregation and a survivor of Argentina's Civil War, wrote The Gap that if they were not forthcoming with plans to change their corporate policy with regard to these factories, he would announce to his congregation that holiday shopping at The Gap was a violation of Jewish ethical law. That letter was one of hundreds, but it was a beauty. Two weeks later, senior Gap executives were on a plane to New York, not to meet with the captains of industry, but to meet with clergy. After much preliminary negotiating, we met together with The Gap officials, not at the University Club, not at a fancy New York hotel, but in the parlor of the house of Dr. Paul Smith, pastor of the First Presbyterian Church of Brooklyn.

At this historic meeting, an agreement was signed that called for the strict compliance of subcontractors with The Gap corporate code, the rehiring of workers fired for union activity, and the implementation of a team of independent human rights workers on the ground in El Salvador to watchdog conditions in the plant and to give the young seamstresses someone they can speak to without fear of reprisal. It is very hard for American church people to comprehend the complex problems of global economy. But here was one company, The Gap, that we knew, and we could speak to them. We were not a special interest group or labor union. We were their customers, and spoke with the authority of people of faith from all across the country. Robert Reich, United States Labor Secretary at the time, called The Gap settlement a watershed agreement. Encouraged by the success of the People of Faith Network in improving the working conditions of hundreds of young women in El Salvador, we were ready to respond again when we learned of unjust treatment of workers in Central America by other companies. It was not long before another sweatshop nightmare came to our attention.

Campaign Two: Kathie Lee Gifford Clothing

The National Labor Committee in Support of Worker and Human Rights in Central America does the best research on working conditions in Central America. Knowing of the People of Faith Network's successful work with The Gap, our friends at the National Labor Committee shared with us reports from Honduras of a factory, with a terrible record of labor abuses, that made clothes for big United States companies. As we sifted through the list of clothing labels from the shop, one leapt out at us — a big smiling picture of TV talk show host Kathie Lee Gifford. Ms. Gifford endorsed a line of clothes for the giant Wal-Mart chain. What particularly caught our attention was a line on the bottom of the clothing tag that read, "A portion of the proceeds from the sale of this garment will be donated to various Children's Charities." Children in Honduras (some as young as twelve) were working in horrible conditions and for low wages to produce Kathie Lee Gifford clothing so that Ms. Gifford could then donate some of her profit to children's charities in the United States! To us it represented the global economy truly gone mad. Charles Kernaghan, Director of the National Labor Committee, wrote two letters to Ms. Gifford drawing the issue to her attention and offering to work with her to clean up this problem. Weeks passed with no reply.

But the issue exploded into the limelight when a congressional committee investigating the use of illegal Third World sweatshops called Charles Kernaghan to Washington to testify. Kernaghan mentioned several United States firms in his testimony, but the press picked up on the Kathie Lee Gifford story. By that evening it was on the wire services across the country and on the network news.

The next day, Kathie Lee Gifford threw her now-famous crying fit on her national morning TV show. First, she said the information was untrue and that she would sue. People of Faith clergy wrote to her offering to help mediate the dispute. Then, as the press dug deeper, and the details of the sweatshops were confirmed, Ms. Gifford changed her line. She said she didn't know about the abuses and, anyway, she was concerned about children in *this* country. Less than two weeks later a sweatshop was discovered in *this* country, on the West Side of Manhattan, making Kathie Lee Gifford clothes. The workers, mostly Central American immigrants, had not been paid in two weeks. In an attempt at damage control, Kathie Lee's sportscaster husband, Frank Gifford, showed up at the New York factory with envelopes filled with hundred-dollar bills looking for the workers. It was one of the saddest spectacles of the whole affair. But then things began to change.

People of Faith mobilized its network, asking for letters to Ms. Gifford urging her to work with religious and human rights groups to clean up the sweatshops instead of continuing the fight in the press. Hundreds of letters were sent. Mobilizing grassroots cooperative action across the country helped to bring the issue to political visibility and create a sense of urgency.

The National Labor Committee brought fifteen-year-old Wendy Diaz from Honduras to New York. She is a young Honduran woman who had worked in the factory, sewing Kathie Lee clothes, since she was thirteen. Wendy was an orphan and supported herself and two younger brothers on wages of thirty-eight cents an hour. Kathie Lee Gifford, it was learned, made ten million dollars on her clothing line, which was more money than she made from her TV show. A New York newspaper reporter found that ten percent of it went to Ms. Gifford's own charities — Cody and Cassidy House.

Wendy Diaz was asked to testify before Congress, and won over everyone who heard her. The press asked her what she wanted to do while she was in the United States. Wendy said she wanted to meet

50

face to face with Kathie Lee Gifford to tell her personally of the reality for the thousands of young girls working in the Honduran factories. A meeting was arranged, at the residence of New York's Cardinal O'Connor, between Wendy Diaz and Kathie Lee Gifford, with representatives of People of Faith, the National Labor Committee, and the Union of Needletrade, Industrial and Textile Employees (UNITE) present. Ms. Gifford described how hard this incident had been on her family. Wendy explained that Kathie Lee was not the "victim" here. The victims were the girls locked into the Honduran maquiladora low-wage system sewing clothes for Wal-Mart and making Ms. Gifford rich. It was an electric moment of truth.

After the meeting, Ms. Gifford signed an agreement to combat child labor and sweatshops here and abroad. Ms. Gifford has, in fact, become the "national poster girl" against sweatshops, receiving several awards and appearing with President Clinton to launch a new White House Task Force to prevent sweatshop labor — a pernicious by-product of the new global economy. Here is an example of people of faith working for systemic justice through cooperative action and putting a human face on the issue.

Campaign Three: The Disney Corporation

In 1997, People of Faith started a letter-writing campaign targeting the Disney Corporation for the horrific conditions at the offshore factories producing its children's clothing. The first campaign mailing produced thousands of letters from parishioners, clergy, and students. A second mailing was followed by demonstrations in six major cities: New York, Minneapolis, Chicago, Los Angeles, San Francisco, and Washington, D.C. These demonstrations helped to get the Disney issue into the media and into public awareness.

The Disney Corporation initially refused to answer specific allegations, but within months acquiesced to two of three demands. The company closed its operation in Burma (a country dominated by an aggressive military regime), and ended contracts with Thai factories employing children. But the company made no concessions on its operations in Haiti. Disney refused to require that its subcontractors pay more than the Haitian minimum wage of twenty-eight cents an hour, a wage which does not even cover the cost of food for a single adult, much less a family. Disney came under heavy scrutiny on this issue by institutional shareholders at its annual shareholders' meeting in Anaheim, California, in March 1997. The national Methodist and Presbyterian Churches introduced shareholder resolutions demanding that Disney raise wages at its Haitian operation and that the company limit the astronomical salaries paid its top executives, including Michael Eisner.

After the Disney campaign, People of Faith co-sponsored a Conference on Independent Human Rights Monitoring, attended by 125 consumer, labor, and corporate organizations to discuss the future of the campaign against sweatshop labor. A key point of discussion was whether the movement against global sweatshops should hold fast to the demand that indigenous human rights monitors be given access to factories to inspect conditions. One week later, President Clinton and leaders from the apparel industry announced their own voluntary corporate "code of conduct." The agreement called on United States clothing retailers to require that their offshore contractors limit the workweek to sixty hours and not hire children under age fourteen. The voluntary code does not set minimum wage levels, establish the right to organize unions, or require access to the factories by independent human rights monitors. How many United States companies will comply with this limited, voluntary code is still unclear.

People of Faith remains active in the coalition of organizations developing international strategy in this justice arena. Our involvement demonstrates the power that local church members can bring to economic justice conflicts. Conversely, The Gap, Wal-Mart, and Disney campaigns have illuminated the growing impoverishment of American and Third World workers and their families — especially young women workers — and brought this to the attention of a new religious-based constituency in the United States. This is a justice issue that touches all consumers and many workers. But sweatshop labor is not the only active concern of People of Faith.

Health Care

A campaign focus that was not anticipated but became a priority was the effort to stop privatization of public hospitals. Downsizing New York City's public hospital system is a stated priority of Mayor

Rudolph Giuliani's administration. Early in 1996 he announced the sale of Coney Island Hospital to an out-of-state, for-profit company. The Coney Island Hospital was the first of four public hospitals that were to be sold. Nowhere in the plans was there any provision for the poor and the uninsured who use the city's public hospitals as their only access to health care.

Working within a broader community and labor effort — the Coalition to Save Coney Island Hospital — the People of Faith Network played a key role in mobilizing clergy and laity city-wide to meet, send letters to city and state officials, and join demonstrations. Two citywide breakfasts were held with elected officials of city government. A mailing list of five hundred affected churches, synagogues, and mosques was developed. Three Sunday letter-writing events were organized. Pastors at one hundred churches asked their members to sign cards or letters after worship services. In December 1996, the Coalition had a major win when the New York State Supreme Court stopped the hospital sale outright. The court found that the New York City Administration violated contract and public hearing procedures required by the New York City Charter. Though the city appealed the court's decision, it now appears increasingly unlikely that the privatization will go through. Again, people of faith inspired citizen action for justice and demonstrated how the processes of democracy can work for the collective good. Clergy and laity from the hospital's immediate vicinity have continued to meet monthly to monitor the situation and be ready for the city's next move. In March 1997, we sponsored a community forum on state and national health reform issues. To make the need for reform more urgent for politicians, we organized a Sunday letter-writing event at twenty-five churches the following month.

People of Faith's social and economic justice work has succeeded beyond our greatest expectations. It confirmed our basic belief that an enormous, untapped potential exists for local clergy and church members to become active participants in social and economic justice work. Each People of Faith campaign has succeeded, in some measure, in encouraging new clergy to come forward, and in generating coverage in denominational and secular media. Currently there are two thousand congregations in the People of Faith Network, and it is growing rapidly. Our passion for this ministry is born of the concern that we are becoming a nation of diminishing expectations, numb to realities that seem beyond our control. But the moment we abandon hope, we are lost. The moment we turn cynical or turn inward, we give up. We can never stop asking, "Lord, when did we see you hungry, or thirsty, or naked?" People of Faith, and the participating members at the Lafayette Avenue Presbyterian Church, have created a mechanism for small and middle-sized congregations to have a voice. It is a vehicle with which to slay giants. It is Christian faith moving beyond charity toward justice.

What We Can Learn

- A local congregation can think and act globally for justice.
- The market economy is directly influenced by global forces, and these forces are not beyond the reach of citizens when they unite in common action.
- Religious faith is a powerful motivation that can move people into positive, cooperative action for justice.
- To act effectively for economic justice it is necessary to work in broad-based alliances, to have a clear focus, and to use the media.
- Enabling groups of people to change their socioeconomic situation rather than simply adapt to it is crucial for social justice.
- Helping people and groups to think and act systematically is essential for creating a more just society.
- Greater distributive justice is usually a relative improvement and rarely a complete transformation.
- Often, issues of large significance arise out of what may appear at first to be local concerns, e.g., New York City and the clothing industry. Look for wider connections.
- Electronic communication can greatly expand the range and speed of network organizing.
- The local congregation can be the incubator for social justice campaigns of national and international significance. Thinking globally and acting locally promotes spiritual depth and creates the human connections necessary for justice.

Jan Hus Presbyterian Church: From Ethnic Ministry to Ministry for Justice

Ann L. Barstow

In 1997 the Jan Hus Presbyterian Church and its pastor received a signal honor. The national Presbyterian Peace Fellowship presented to them its annual Peace-Seeker Award at the denomination's General Assembly meeting in Syracuse, New York. The church was honored for its outstanding work with New York City's homeless, solidarity work in El Salvador and Haiti, participation in the campaign to close the military School of the Americas, and leadership in the denomination's gay rights movement.

This is the story of the long evolution that led to the current outstanding ministries of the church.[1] Founded over 120 years ago on Manhattan's East Side by Czech immigrants, the congregation constructed in 1885 a five-story church building that included a sanctuary, an apartment for the pastor, a fellowship hall, and a kitchen. The church flourished in its early decades as an ethnic community and spiritual home for first, second, and third generation Czech Americans. They named their church for the Czech pastor, reformer, and

---

1. The author expresses her appreciation to the following persons who provided firsthand accounts of their experience in the Jan Hus Church: Erynne Ansel, Tom Driver, Mae Gautier, Rose Luchart, Jan Orr-Harter, and Robert J. Stone.

Anne L. Barstow is an author, historian, national board member of the Witness for Peace organization, and Elder at the Jan Hus Presbyterian Church in New York City. She is a worker for peace and justice in Central America and in the Presbyterian Peace Fellowship.

martyr, Jan Hus (1369-1415). The church shared a lively sense of the Hussite call for simplicity in life and extravagance in response to the needs of people.

Alongside their new sanctuary the congregation constructed a six-story community center in 1915 which provided space for short-term housing for new immigrants, English language classes, job skill training, children's programs, music, art, a dance hall, recreational facilities, and a dental clinic. Embedded in their faith was a call to build community and to integrate both spiritual and practical responses to human need. In the early decades the mission of the church was focused on helping the immigrants. There was a strong emphasis on supporting the Czech cultural presence in the city. As late as 1970 the church still offered a worship service in the Czech language as well as in English. By that time most of the Czech community had relocated outside Manhattan, leaving behind a small and struggling congregation.

The first non-Czech pastor, the Reverend Brent Fisher, was called in 1972 to lead the existing group to begin more outreach into the changing neighborhood. It was not easy. Fisher revived the community center by bringing in a preschool for children from other countries. It was difficult for the congregation to learn to share their space with others, but they did begin to do this. A breakthrough came in 1975 when the Jan Hus Church joined with three other groups to sponsor a senior nutrition program called the Yorkville Luncheon Club. At the last minute, New York City officials rejected the site proposed for the program. On the following Sunday, after worship, the Hussite congregation gathered, discussed the situation, and decided to offer their sanctuary for the daily senior meal program. They did this even though it meant taking out the nearly one-hundred-year-old church pews. Old Jan Hus, the reformer, would have been proud of them. The senior meal club was an immediate success, serving hot meals five days a week to the neighborhood's elderly, including about one hundred homebound seniors. This service continues to this day. In spite of the new outreach initiatives the congregation continued to decline. There was a brief period when it did not have a regular pastor.

New Pastor Brings New Focus

In 1979 a new minister, the Reverend Robert J. Stone, was called to lead the congregation. Stone moved into the pastor's apartment in the church building, and began working with the church session and making contacts in the community. Stone pressed the church to open its building to the community even more and to reach out to the growing young adult population in the East Side neighborhood. He convinced the church governing body to rent meeting space to one Alcoholics Anonymous (AA) group. This was successful, and within a few years there were more than fifty AA groups meeting every week in the church. A variety of other self-help and twelve-step groups began to meet in the building. A professional theater company, Chicago City Limits, was invited to rent space in the building, and they did. This was the renewing of a community theater tradition in the church and proved to be successful. The rental activity produced income for the church and brought more people into the building.

An early emphasis in Stone's ministry was on renewal of the Sunday worship service. A new choir director, Matt Jones, a talented African-American musician and former civil rights organizer for the Southern Christian Leadership Conference, was hired. He brought new vitality to the music program, enlarged the choir, diversified the repertoire, and helped to invigorate the congregational singing. At a later time, under a different director, choir concerts with orchestra accompaniment were added. Worship was enhanced by increased congregational participation, including reports of mission activity, prayers for concerns of the people, and a new benediction sung by the people in the Czech and English languages.

Action for Peace and Justice

Robert (Bob) Stone, a conscientious objector to World War II and a longtime peace and justice activist, along with his wife, Mae Gautier, began to introduce a new focus on peace education and action, which was part of the Presbyterian denominational emphasis. This emphasis included support for nuclear disarmament and education about oppression in Central America. The peacemaking program was difficult for the remaining Czech members of the church to accept in light of their ties to Europe and their strong anticommunist feelings. The story of the transformation of the church into a leader in the peace and justice movement is not an account of liberalism among the laity. It is, instead, a story of vision and leadership by two ministers — Robert Stone and his successor, Jan Orr-Harter — who led the church in the 1980s and 1990s.

In the early 1980s a major antinuclear movement was building across the country. Bob Stone convinced the church to offer space in the building as a headquarters office for the New York Downstate Nuclear Freeze Campaign. As a result, much of the famous June 1982 antinuclear protest was planned in the old billiard room at Jan Hus Church. Following that event the church helped enlist neighborhood people for a massive petition, signature-gathering campaign and presented New York's two senators with thousands of petitions calling for an end to the arms race. Hundreds of people carried these signed petitions into the offices of Senators D'Amato and Moynihan. Some church members were among the half-million people who thronged Central Park for the 1982 demonstration which helped to put the Nuclear Freeze Campaign firmly on the national political agenda.

Responding to this active witness, the congregation began to come around. When Mae Gautier asked for volunteers to go by bus to a nationwide rally in Washington, D.C., to promote the nuclear freeze, four church members (all older women) volunteered. The women, one of them using a walker, marched at the front of the protest line wearing "Jan Hus Peacemaker" hats. Their experience became a positive influence when shared with the congregation back in New York. The church became more willing to support the Sanctuary Movement, offering church space for Central American refugees to stay overnight while they were journeying on the "overground railway" north to Canada. In the 1980s this was risky action during an era when the federal government strongly opposed such activity. The depth of commitment to pursuing peace in Central America can be seen in the ninety-one-week-long protest which two church members, Mae Gautier and Erynne Ansel, helped to organize. Their group of peace witnesses gathered once each week for nearly two years outside the U.S. Mission to the United Nations in New York to protest against the United States support for the Contra War in Nicaragua.

At about this time, Bob Stone began an important connection for the Jan Hus Church when he got in touch with Bill Green, the

U.S. congressman for the East Side Manhattan district. After Stone and Gautier went with a New York City Presbytery delegation to Nicaragua at the height of the Contra War, they reported to Congressman Green about the U.S.-funded violence they had seen and heard first-hand in Nicaragua. Green listened and, as a result, did further research of his own. He broke with his Republican colleagues to vote against the next appropriations bill, which funded the Contras — the antidemocratic forces in Nicaragua. Following Green's vote the Jan Hus Peacemakers Group joined others from the district in a parade in front of Green's office, passing out flyers praising the congressman's courageous vote against funding for military action by the Contras.

Meanwhile, the pastor was bringing a new constituency into the church — a younger and more diverse group of members. He initiated a program of small mission groups through which people gathered to study social justice issues and liberation Bible study. People learned that with religious faith goes commitment and responsibility to work for justice at home and around the world. Stone initiated a Resident Ministry Project in which young adult interns, through the Presbyterian denomination's internship program, came to live at Jan Hus Church. They held jobs in the city, lived in the Church House, and gave ten hours a week in volunteer service to the church. A folk music coffeehouse was created. This reinforced the growing young adult outreach of the church. Although most of the people who participated in these new community-oriented programs did not join the church, some did and others became part of the constituency touched by the church.

Change did not come easily in the Jan Hus Church. There was struggle and storm. A price was paid. Some members left in anger, others drifted away. But other new members came in with conviction. The congregation remained small, but the members who were open to change and to witness for social justice increased. The redevelopment of the church had begun when Bob Stone retired as pastor in 1987. He had opened the church up to the community, changed the worship, and led the congregation into positive actions for social justice and peacemaking. A foundation had been laid upon which the next pastor would build.

A New Generation of Leadership

When the Reverend Jan Orr-Harter accepted a call to be pastor in 1988, she did not face opposition to her ardent dedication to work for justice. Continuing the small-group approach, Orr-Harter taught that discipleship depends on an inward-outward dynamic — one strengthens one's faith to work for justice out in the world, and then one is driven by the injustice of society to strengthen one's faith. She learned about the reforms of Jan Hus of Bohemia in democratizing his church, and of the energetic early Czech immigrants to New York who lived the inward-outward journey in creating their church as a community center. She believed that a new ministry could grow out of this historic past, and bear fruit. And it has done so.

A new congregation of mostly young adults, although others are included, has formed around this new focus. Over half of the session members are under age forty. The church's music and style of worship changed to reflect this younger constituency. The community center grew, until now there are over one hundred self-help groups using the church space.

A new set of priorities began to emerge. For example, some much-needed church building repairs were put off; only those parts of the building in immediate use were repaired. This decision enabled Orr-Harter to invest church funds in programs for the homeless — not to provide shelter, but to train them for jobs. The church also became part of a consortium of churches and synagogues to offer a hot meal each night to indigent people. A number of homeless people, in turn, served the church, helping out in various capacities as paid workers. Some homeless persons and those who attended twelve-step groups began to join the church, bringing greater diversity, new insights, and different needs into the worship.

International Justice Perspective

Of long-lasting importance were the trips that a number of members made to El Salvador and Nicaragua, beginning in 1991, leading to the establishment of a long-term commitment to a Salvadoran refugee village, called Rancho Grande. For many years pictures of the martyred Salvadoran Archbishop Oscar Romero and the people of Rancho

Grande stood on the altar at Jan Hus, and the congregation prayed for them every Sunday. With the help of one member's deep commitment to the people of El Salvador, the church managed to raise considerable sums of money and material aid to assist the people of Rancho Grande in establishing small farms and rebuilding their village after the civil war in El Salvador. This partnership is continuing with a new focus on women's literacy education.

The church's commitment to Haiti began when two persons, who had followed closely the Haitians' brutal struggle for democracy in 1991-94, joined the congregation. In 1996, through members who joined two Witness for Peace delegations to Haiti, the church made connections with an elementary school in one of the poorest sections of Port-au-Prince. Organized by a pastor on the thinnest of shoestrings, the school was struggling to stay open. Jan Hus members agreed to pledge extra money to pay the salaries of the teachers. Books, supplies, and toys were also provided. Following up on its tradition of working to educate members of the U.S. Congress, the church held a "Haiti Night" complete with Haitian food, drumming, and a rousing speech by Congressman Major Owens of Brooklyn.

Orr-Harter also established a connection with the district's new congresswoman, Carolyn Maloney. When the church invited Maloney and her staff to a luncheon to learn about the church's work in Central America, the other guests were members of the Salvadoran rebel party, the FMLN. The Salvadorans told Maloney about the U.S.-funded violence that had driven them from their homeland. The church offered its contacts as a resource that Maloney could call on, and she has done so, in regard to the Haitian crisis and other issues.

Jan Hus Church contributes to the peace movement through its support of the Campaign to Close the School of the Americas, known as SOA Watch. Two members were arrested at Ft. Benning, Georgia, in the huge demonstration there against the School of the Americas (SOA) in November 1997. Two carloads of "Hussites" traveled to Washington, D.C., in the spring of 1997 to join a protest by SOA Watch on the steps of the Capitol Building. In addition, three church members participate in the national board of the Presbyterian Peace Fellowship, which Jan Hus helps by mailing out its newsletter. (The church pays those enrolled in its homeless job-training program to do the mailings. This job contributes to their progress toward entering the workforce.) Still another door opened through the connections one member had with Oxfam America. Now the church participates in the annual Oxfam fast, fundraising, and hunger education program.

Seeking Justice in the Wider Church

In the early 1990s Jan Hus Church began welcoming gay and lesbian laity and clergy. The church offered its pulpit for new voices to be heard. The congregation elected gay and lesbian lay people to its session, although this contravenes the national church rules. One of the church mission groups is an AIDS-support group. When in 1996 the Presbyterian Church (U.S.A.) General Assembly adopted Amendment B, which forbids ordination as clergy, elders, or deacons to anyone either not celibate or not married to a person of the opposite sex, Orr-Harter and the Jan Hus Church session went into action. They hired a United Church of Christ minister to work out of Jan Hus Church organizing "Presbyterian Welcome," a program of support for gay and lesbian ordination in the Northeast region. Celebrations of that work have been held at Jan Hus Church. A number of churches in New York City Presbytery have participated. On the front door of Jan Hus Church, members have nailed theses from ninety-five churches across the country that are protesting against Amendment B.

The church deliberately lives out its commitments to these causes. To be loyal to its understanding of what Jesus would do, it breaks Presbyterian Church law by electing gay and lesbian elders, just as it broke U.S. law to support Salvadoran refugees. When new members join, they are specifically asked if they support the historic Czech proto-protestant teaching to welcome into the church people who have been humiliated and marginalized. When the congregation elects and ordains officers, members are specifically given the opportunity to follow the Presbyterian rule to exclude persons on the basis of their sexual orientation. To date, no one has chosen to exclude anyone. The church has included this cause in its liturgy, just as it included the Salvadorans on its altar. The passage of Amendment B by the Presbyterian denomination was announced on Maundy Thursday, 1997. At the Maundy Thursday service that year, Jan Hus members nailed pink triangles to the cross in the sanctuary. The triangles will stay there until Amendment B is removed from the law of the Presbyterian Church.

The church has grown and has become reborn. People join Jan Hus *because* of its social witness and openness to diversity. It has attracted a number of dedicated administrators who have put these beliefs into practice. It took the ministries of two determined, clear-thinking clergy, willing to educate laity in small groups, to accomplish this change. A new church has come into existence. Out of respect for its Czech heritage, the benediction is still sung in Czech, new members are taught the story of the historical Jan Hus's revolt against the medieval Catholic Church. The members believe that in fifteenth-century Jan Hus there is a good precedent for their own revolt against injustices.

The church is clear about its priorities. Rather than renovating the building, the homeless and aged are fed, Central Americans and Haitians are supported, the gospel is preached, and justice is demanded. Although it has about 140 members, five thousand people a week use the church for self-help groups, meals, counseling, job training, friendship, peacemaking, and other services. The congregation worships with joy, everyone praying and sometimes even dancing. They are peace-seekers, but perhaps even more, in this day and time, they are speaking and acting for justice.

What We Can Learn

- Historic ethnic tradition can either hinder or help the generation of commitment for new ministries. While working with the tradition is not an easy path, it is worthwhile.
- Congregational redevelopment is never easy; it comes at a price. Some members leave, others join. Some valuable traditions are lost but new ones are created.
- Small mission study/action groups can help members in a church undergoing transition to see a new vision and work through the struggles of change, especially if they are structured to seek consensus and to honor dissent.
- Thoughtful adaptation of liturgy, music, and congregational participation across generational lines is one of the keys to congregational redevelopment.

- The creative use of church building space can be a positive means of engaging the neighborhood community.
- Seeking out and welcoming persons who are rejected by other congregations not only broadens the base of membership, but enables the members to learn the meaning of a truly inclusive Christianity.
- Welcoming the younger generation into the leadership and governing body of the congregation helps to attract new members and builds up the church.
- Engagement with the wider world beyond the parish helps to open up new vision for ministry within a congregation, energizes its worship, and gives it new insight into scripture.
- Commitment to social justice tends to grow from engagement, struggle, and suffering as well as from prayer and reflective thought. Moving to appropriate action for justice involves both intentional risk-taking and intelligent organization.

Luther Place Memorial Lutheran Church

The Reverend John Steinbruck, pastor of Luther Place Memorial Lutheran Church for over twenty-seven years, sees biblical hospitality as the basis for the ministry in this historic congregation, located just six blocks from the White House, at Thomas Circle and Vermont Avenue. The ancient tradition of welcoming the stranger and remembering that we are all sojourners in the land is the basis for hospitality in the church. Luther Place Church under the leadership of John Steinbruck has extended this ancient biblical understanding into a fully developed expression appropriate for contemporary society. They have done this by moving from compassion toward social systems that enable persons to be transformed and find new life.

The church, begun in the post–Civil War era, was for many decades the flagship Lutheran congregation in the center of Washington, D.C. It was surrounded by fine brownstone townhouses where business and professional families lived. After World War II, new suburbs developed outside of the District of Columbia and families moved out. The area began to change. Outrage over the assassination of Dr. Martin Luther King, Jr., and centuries of racism brought turbulence to Washington, D.C. As white flight increased, the black population grew and the parish area changed. The 1960s brought the peace movement and resistance to the Vietnam War into the streets around the church. In the 1970s there was a growing counterculture youth movement in the neighborhoods around the church. "Luther Place became enveloped with protest demonstrations bringing an atmosphere of fire, smoke, tear gas, police, National Guard, and armed clashes — all leaving a void that was filled by urban migrants, street hustlers, drug pushers, addicts, and prostitutes mixing with tourists, commuters, neighborhood residents, and churchgoers,"[1] says Steinbruck. Church membership declined and the population of street people grew. The response of the church over the past quarter century has been one of evolutionary development. It has moved from apathy, denial, resistance, being overwhelmed, giving charity, doing social service, and, finally, toward creating a systemic approach for human and institutional transformation.

In the winter of 1972, the consciousness of the congregation got a jolt when a Sunday edition of the *Washington Post* newspaper came out with a front-page photo and caption showing the front steps of a nearby church where a homeless man had frozen to death. The Parish Council that had been reluctant to open the church to the growing numbers of poor and homeless now responded to the pastor's advocacy for giving hospitality. Steinbruck frankly admits that for several years after the church opened up to the neighborhood people, "We were just overwhelmed. There were street people everywhere in the church. We did not really know what to do with them or for them."[2] Attempts to be compassionate, to provide shelter, food, and some basic care were difficult because the numbers of people coming were too large to handle. The church had to learn to set limits, become more disciplined, and focus its work. There was a great need to go beyond the soup kitchen and the night shelter.

> The late 1960s and the early 1970s were periods of testing for the congregation, from without and within. . . . Over a period of many months in 1970-1972, the congregation agonized over its reason for being. . . . While a significant number opted for "suburban security and stability," a strong and dedicated remnant stayed to provide a viable core willing to seize the time in God's name.[3]

One key to the situation was the church property. The sanctuary and adjacent brownstone buildings, a total of 37,000 square feet of

1. John Steinbruck, interview with author, Washington, D.C., 3 February 1997.
2. Steinbruck, interview.
3. Steinbruck, "Luther Place — A Church as Hospice," in *Luther Place Memorial Church, a Church as Refuge/Sanctuary* (Fall 1983): 3.

space, covered about a city block and a half. It provided the prospective physical place where strategic interventions could be helpfully made in the community. After the early experience of trying to meet too many needs, the decision was made to focus specifically on reaching out to homeless women. There were a number of shelters for men. Some shelters took both men and women, but the women did not feel safe in these places. There were no shelters for women, exclusively, in D.C. This decision led the church into developing a complex of wraparound, life-changing initiatives that have transformed the lives of hundreds of women. What emerged was a pioneering effort recognized in Washington and beyond as unique and trendsetting.

A Continuum of Care

The wraparound concept of spiritual recovery, health, life skills, employment training, and housing is the unique contribution of the interreligious N Street Village. This approach, developed in the 1970s, is now expressed in a series of interrelated programs and affordable apartments housed in a newly dedicated $17.9 million building across from Luther Place Church. The housing portion, Eden House, offers fifty-one affordable apartments (1-3 bedrooms), and the adjoining wing, Promise Place, offers programs that enable residents to acquire the tools for independent living. The Night Shelter is housed on the fourth floor of Luther Place Church.

Bethany Women's Center offers a daytime program for homeless women and serves as a place for intake screening, where women get a hot meal, a welcome off the street, initial counseling, and assessment of needs. If women are abusing alcohol or drugs, they must agree to take the first steps to recovery by attending three meetings a day as well as a meeting with the addiction counselor. Most women must agree to a psychiatric evaluation to further determine need. This is a crucial stage where decisions are made about who can be helped — those who will accept help and accompaniment, which is a prerequisite for entrance into the continuum.

The Luther Place Shelter is exclusively for women, offering dinner, nighttime sleeping, bathing and laundry facilities, and breakfast. To be admitted to the shelter women must be sober and not using drugs.

The Harriet Tubman House and Sarah House are residential care communities for women who have been admitted for treatment of their substance abuse addiction. To stay in these treatment communities women must commit to the house rules, stay off drugs, meet regularly with staff, and attend house meetings and Narcotics Anonymous and/or Alcoholics Anonymous meetings daily. In these communities there are life skill classes, including cooking and money management. Women are expected to work. There is a program to enable women to earn high school education equivalency. Women may live in this supportive community for up to two years. There is a long waiting list for applicants. The conclusion of this transforming process sends women into one of three streams: (1) entry into Eden House, (2) finding their own apartment in the neighborhood, or (3) placement in the Raoul Wallenberg or Carol Holmes section of Promise Place, which provides permanent residences for formerly homeless women who have mental disabilities and/or are in recovery and need to be in a long-term, supportive community.

We met some of the women in the Bethany Center dining room. Edyth is thirty-three, an African-American woman who has come through recovery from drug and alcohol addiction. Now she is the supervisor of the food service and dining room for the daytime program. She has attained three goals cherished by the women in the continuum program: recovery from addiction, stable employment, and independent living.

Mary is about forty. She grew up in a military family, suffered abuse and the consequences of frequent family moves. She left her family as a young adult, became homeless and addicted. Now she is seeking entry into the recovery program. She is talkative and cheerful. There is a spirit of hope in her presence. Reading the newspaper, she comments intelligently about a story describing sexual abuse of children in the D.C. area. Her tone suggests this is something she knows about from personal experience.

Joan is in her mid-thirties. She suffered at the hands of an abusive husband for many years and finally left him. She has been away for several months and is staying with a sister. She has an alcohol problem and wants to get into the recovery program. She comes to the Center for food and friendship, hoping to get into the program.

Rachel is in her mid-sixties. She has been homeless for many years. She is talkative and friendly, considers herself a member of the church, and sings in the Sunday choir. She identifies herself as a painter. There are several of her pictures hanging in the Center dining room. She wants to become a resident in the new apartment building for older women.

Martha is a well-dressed woman in her fifties. She is a church member. She lives in an apartment near the church. On Sunday afternoons she patrols the neighborhood, conversing with women and inviting several to come in for Sunday lunch. Martha has come through the recovery program and is now living independently, but staying in close touch with the center and sharing its "good news" with others. She has been through a lot, including abuse as a child, alcohol addiction, and homelessness. Her recovery is remarkable.

At the Sunday lunch with the women, we are reminded of Jesus sharing at the table with friends and strangers. Sharing food is an opportunity for sharing love. That is happening at Luther Place in the Women's Center in ways that are transforming.

Creative Funding: Public and Private Partnership

The entire Luther Place hospitality-recovery-housing complex known as Eden House/Promise Place is the outcome of twenty years of work and an $18 million capital fund campaign. The Luther Place Church realized that to make the kind of creative, comprehensive, and systematic program that was needed it would be necessary to tap many sources of funding and develop numerous partnerships. The campaign enabled renovation and new construction to create ninety-one units of living space and treatment facilities adjacent to the church. The design and construction of these facilities was carried out over a decade.

The congregation of 350 members gave over $3 million; $5.5 million was secured through the National Low Income Tax Credit Law. Because this was a pioneering, experimental project creating a continuum of services, a special congressional appropriation of $5 million was approved, which included an element of study and research. In addition, gifts and grants were secured from foundations, businesses, congregations near and far, and from individuals. The Jewish community strongly supported the campaign with substantial gifts.

The staff of the hospitality-recovery-housing complex consists of forty-five persons. Over twelve hundred volunteers undergird the total ministry. The director of the Women's Treatment and Recovery Program is the Reverend Betsy Hague, an ordained Episcopal clergyperson and a licensed psychiatric social worker. She says, "This continuum has grown out of doing a 'Band-Aid' ministry into a ministry of justice and transformation. By the grace of God, deliberate decision, and hard work we have become a community of recovery and new life."[4]

A Regional Church with A Big Vision

In the process of twenty years of learning, the Luther Place N Street Village has gathered a significant degree of expertise. The church has advocacy committees that have given testimony in Congress for changing the government's policy for the homeless. The staff and members of Luther Place speak from an experience in which there is a recovery rate of seventy percent of the women who enter these programs. For success to be lasting, homeless persons and others accustomed to poverty have to learn a new way of life. That takes time, lots of effort, money, a supportive community, and professionally skilled leadership. A total commitment is needed. John Steinbruck believes this is evangelism — good news — which means exemplifying the presence of God: "We seek to glorify God's name by bearing witness in body, mind, soul, and spirit to the transformation that faith in action can make in everyday life."[5] This message, and the technical skills needed to make it reality, have been widely shared with many sister institutions and in the United States Congress.

Another creative response to the upheavals of the seventies at Luther Place was the formation of the national Lutheran Volunteer Corps. It enables youth and young adults from across the nation to come to Washington, D.C. (six other cities as well) and give volunteer service through the church in various ministries. College and post-college volunteers serve in the Women's Recovery Program, Hospitality Center, the Church Education Program, government agencies, the

4. Betsy Hague, interview with author, Washington, D.C., 3 February 1997.
5. Steinbruck, interview.

Housing Program, and other justice efforts. The program has developed over the years on a national scale. The commitment to a year of service provides an experience through which hundreds of young people have been inspired to enter service vocations.

Other volunteer programs have benefited Luther Place, including VISTA volunteers, student volunteers from Georgetown University, and theological student volunteers from several seminaries in the D.C. area. Nearly one-half of all volunteers are students, both graduate and undergraduate. Luther Place has become a teaching church through its mentoring of volunteers, many of whom find their way into professional vocations serving the human needs of society.

Another part of the Luther Place work and witness is commitment to renewing the wider neighborhood. As so often is the case in neighborhoods across the land, the immediate neighborhood was flooded with false rumors regarding the new building. Much work went into meeting with the neighbors, allaying their fears, and promising to keep the façade of the five townhouses that had comprised the N Street Village. The bottom line of such "NIMBY" (not in my back yard) action was much unfair litigation and needless pain. Using historic preservation and any other legal action they could think of, the project was delayed, resulting in unneeded expenditure of funds for legal assistance. Finally victorious, the building stands and the neighbors have come around, and now have a stake in preserving this new, beautiful structure in their neighborhood. Invited in, some have begun to befriend the residents and to affirm the purpose of the program. By staying in the neighborhood, buying a number of older buildings, renovating, and doing new construction, Luther Place has helped bring stability. By creating affordable, low-income housing, the church has helped keep socio-economic diversity in the area and moderated the compulsive historical preservationists. Gaining this victory has required a large investment of time, energy, money, expertise, and the willingness to take the long-term view. Being a good citizen in the complex urban environment is not an easy task. But doing what is right and good has its own rewards.

Luther Place regards itself as a work in progress. Its ministry is an ongoing, evolving, unfinished challenge. One of the things the congregation has learned is the value of telling its own story widely and often and well. The church circulates a periodic newsletter to over eight thousand friends. It has made friends with the local news media and cultivated the newspapers for getting its story out into the D.C. region. The pastor, church members, and staff are engaged in public interpretation of their ministry as a regular part of their work. The benefits of such intentional proclamation have been numerous. There have been financial gifts, skilled volunteers, new members, and a wide range of support from other organizations eager to do a good, new thing. The net result is the perception, and the reality, of a new climate of stability, equity, and justice in the area around the church.

What We Can Learn

- Churches of modest size can bring a big vision for systematic transformation into reality.
- The partnership of private and public institutions can produce the financial resources needed for large-scale development projects.
- Leadership involves creating a series of interdependent relationships between the church and a wide variety of potentially interested parties.
- Large-scale projects that have systematic impact usually have social and personal costs in addition to financial costs. Some members leave. Serious new members come in. This kind of ministry is not for everyone.
- The opportunity to work for gospel-based social justice is a powerful motivation for bringing skilled volunteers into projects that are well-defined and innovative.
- The struggle to bring systemic justice is long, hard, and ongoing. The likelihood of long-term success is greatly enhanced when the new reality is well-institutionalized with clear policies, skilled leadership, and adequate financial resources.
- The vitality of an urban church can be greatly strengthened through commitment to and engagement in a long-term ministry toward systemic justice.
- Once a clear commitment has been made to a ministry of justice and transformation, priorities tend to be set in support of the central vision. This is an enabling necessity as well as a boundary-setting and limiting reality.
- Commitment to a major ministry of social justice has signifi-

cant influence on other aspects of church life and worship. It may take a decade (or at least a substantial time) for these new realities to be integrated.

- Capable pastoral leadership and the willingness of a congregation to change are crucial factors in successful urban ministry.
- Long-term pastoral commitment and creative imagination are essential to lasting success in this type of ministry.

The Shiloh Baptist Church

In April of 1862, during the Civil War, the United States Congress enacted a law that emancipated slaves within the District of Columbia. Thousands of black people from adjacent slave states fled into the District seeking sanctuary during the ensuing months. Among these men and women were several hundred who left Fredericksburg, Virginia, just before an impending attack by the Confederate army. Many of the refugees from Fredericksburg belonged to the Shiloh Baptist Church — an all-black congregation in Fredericksburg. When they settled in Washington, D.C., they longed for their church, which had been the center of life for them. The written history of the Shiloh Baptist Church in Washington indicates that first a Sunday school was organized, then friends began holding prayer meetings in homes, and finally a small group decided to organize a church. In September 1863, in the home of freed slave Henry D. Peyton, twenty-one persons met to form the Shiloh Baptist Church of Washington, D.C. The new church received immediate affirmation from three other Baptist churches, all white, in Washington. Before the end of September of 1863 the new church had been formally recognized and a new minister, William J. Walker, was ordained to serve as the first pastor of Shiloh Baptist Church in Washington.[1]

1. Evelyn Brooks Higginbotham, "From Strength to Strength: History of Shiloh Baptist Church of Washington, D.C., 1863-1988," in *From Strength to Strength: A Journey of Faith*, edited by Madlyn W. Calbert (Washington, D.C.: Shiloh Baptist Church, 1989), 25-28.

Out of the struggle, strife, and dislocation of the Civil War was born a new congregation devoted to the worship of God, nurture of faith, creation of supportive community, education, and social welfare. That original commitment to social solidarity, education, and cooperative action continues today in a greatly expanded fashion. During the 135 years of its life, Shiloh Baptist Church has grown from the original handful of charter members to a large congregation of over four thousand members.

Shiloh Baptist Church has a long history of organized commitment to a ministry of extensive social service and economic development. This emerged clearly during the years of the Reverend J. Milton Waldron, who served from 1907 to 1929. Waldron was a progressive thinker, theologian, and capable organizer who reflected the influence of the social gospel movement. He developed the concept of the institutional church, which emphasized ministry to the total person — spiritual, physical, economic, and social — and created programs to meet a full spectrum of human need. Prior to coming to Washington, Waldron was the pastor of Bethel Baptist Church in Jacksonville, Florida, where he organized strong self-help programs in the African-American community. The programs included a preschool and kindergarten for children, a night school for adults to gain literacy, and classes for women in cooking and sewing. He led a boycott of the public transport system in Jacksonville in response to the racial segregation laws of the city. More significantly, he played a key part in organizing the Afro-American Life Insurance Company, which became the largest black-owned business in Florida and has continued through the decades successfully. Waldron was a cofounder, with W. E. B. DuBois, of the Niagara Movement, a predecessor of the NAACP, in 1905 as an institutional expression of the struggle for civil rights.[2]

Waldron's ministry at Shiloh brought a heightened awareness of the struggle for social justice. He brought Shiloh Baptist Church into active involvement in improving the living conditions of poor and homeless people. He led this effort at many levels, including interventions with local and federal government. A day nursery and child care center was established in 1914; academic coaching classes were opened for high school students in the early 1920s; special worship

2. Higginbotham, 45-46.

services for the deaf were created and have continued to the present; and campaigns to improve housing conditions for the poor and homeless were a continuing emphasis. Waldron strengthened the civil rights focus of his ministry at Shiloh Church by being one of the founders of the NAACP in 1909. It is within this strong tradition of seeking social justice that the Shiloh Church stands today as an example of a congregation that goes beyond charity toward creating justice in society at large.[3]

The Reverend Henry C. Gregory III was the fifth senior minister in a line of significant, long-term pastorates enjoyed by Shiloh Church over its 135-year history. Gregory built upon its very significant heritage and created strong initiatives in four areas: family life education, economic development, improvement of education, and community building. He attracted numerous new members and volunteer professional people from the D.C. area, in addition to a talented regular staff.

Centrality of Family Life

Gregory affirmed early in his ministry the centrality of spiritual life for everything which the church does. The church, he taught, is an intergenerational bonding, and the family (in all its forms) is the primary means of socialization. It is in and through this broad understanding of family that Gregory led the church in its educational, economic, and social ministries that touched all age levels.

A concrete symbol of this approach to ministry was the construction of a new Family Life Center, a $5.2 million complex dedicated in 1982, to house a wide variety of education and human self-development programs. The Family Life Center stands adjacent to the sanctuary and includes facilities for adult education, family life classes, counseling, health care, job training, employment referral, and teen activity. The Heritage Hall is a large multipurpose area that is used for worship, school assemblies, education, large congregational dinners, and weekday groups. The center also houses a bookstore, a library, staff offices, and the Tuning Fork Restaurant, which offers a menu of healthy foods. The center hosts many community

3. Higginbotham, 52.

meetings and is a hub for developing partnerships with a wide variety of community organizations. There is a gymnasium, a commercial-quality kitchen, the Chapel of Hope, and a senior citizen center. The credit union has a long history going back a number of decades. It has evolved over the years from serving basic needs toward serving larger goals for capital investment in home ownership and small business development. It serves the wider Shiloh family and neighborhoods adjacent to the church. The focus is the empowerment of people to be productive and responsible members of church and society through individual and family life.

One of the most interesting programs that is intentionally designed to create a more just society is the Male Youth Enhancement Program. This project speaks directly to the deep needs of young black men by linking youth at risk with responsible, mature men who become friends, mentors, and role models. It includes specific education on health issues, physical fitness, character development, academic tutoring, and personal identity. The project has attracted funding from the Ford Foundation.

The Math and Science Learning Center is directed by a professional educator. It includes a computer laboratory for greater mastery of advanced mathematics and science. The program is planned in co-ordination with public school curriculum. The purpose is to strengthen the learning skills of young students and help them prepare for higher education. Parents are involved with their students so that there is reinforcement through the home. The Carnegie Foundation assisted the program by an initial grant.[4]

The FLC Employment Training Program provides numerous seminars and workshops for employment readiness, job skills, and referral relationships with employers. A career conference introduces people to new opportunities in public and private sector employment. A very specific part of the job training program is the Tuning Fork Restaurant and the Food Catering Service which are businesses inside the Shiloh Church. These enterprises hire young men and women, and provide on-the-job training in all aspects of the food/hospitality business, including marketing and management. This is an arena of wide opportunity in the Washington, D.C. region. It is a good example of entrepreneurial initiative in a market with large growth potential.

4. Justus Reeves, interview with author, 6 February 1997.

Economic Development in the Neighborhood

In 1991, the Reverend Wallace Charles Smith became the senior minister of the church. Under his leadership, the congregation committed to a focus for ministry, centering on:

1. renewal of self-development of people in the context of African-American history and culture;
2. renewal of understanding the psychosocial problems that surround families in the changing neighborhood around the church;
3. renewal of action for economic development in the neighborhood.

The Shiloh Economic Development Corporation was formed in the mid-1990s in response to needs in the changing neighborhood around the church. The downtown D.C. area is being gentrified. Young professionals and developers are buying up older townhouses, renovating them, and selling them at three to four times the original purchase price. This trend drives out lower-income people and often destroys their fragile hold on economic stability. Shiloh has a long and dynamic record of intervention on behalf of lower-income families. In the 1930s the church reached out with food, clothing, prayer, and pastoral care. In the 1960s the church bought a number of houses in the adjacent blocks around the church and provided low-rent housing to families and persons of limited income. In the 1990s the church, through the economic development corporation, has taken leadership in forming a plan for the immediate neighborhood: acquiring property; planning apartment housing; and facilitating a mix of small business, community services, and affordable housing. The church is an anchor of renewal and stability in the community.

The church works in cooperation with city and federal agencies. Partnerships with several banks and lending institutions have been formed through years of work and cultivation. The focus is on creating stable neighborhoods, promoting human community networks, enabling long-time residents to stay in the area, and establishing important supporting businesses and services. Neighborhood redevelopment is a source of new jobs and investment in the economic advancement of the parish area. These accomplishments do not come easily. Patience, persistence, and partnerships are required. There is entrenched opposition, competition for limited resources, and a variety of obstacles to overcome. But this is a church that has always affirmed — "We Shall Overcome." Reverend Smith sums up the deep commitment, "Vision is a dream with goals and a timetable."[5]

Shiloh's commitment to the larger community is dramatically embodied in the fact that the church does not put its own institutional needs above its engagement in community redevelopment. In 1991, a fire gutted the interior of the historic sanctuary. Instead of pouring all its financial resources into an immediate rebuilding campaign the church took time to carefully determine what kind of new sanctuary would best serve the community. In addition, it moved ahead with plans for housing and economic development. Worship was moved into the spacious Heritage Hall within the Family Life Center building. This created the opportunity to try new ideas in the services of worship.

At the time of writing this story, 1997, the rebuilding of the sanctuary was underway but not completed. Over six years after the fire, the Shiloh Church was moving ahead in its expanding involvement with neighborhood redevelopment and reconstructing its worship facility together. The church is a community of faithful people in mission and in worship. The two are interrelated. The new worship space is being created within the context of the old building. The outer facade has been kept. The new sanctuary will provide for worship in the round with the congregation gathered around the word and sacraments. There will be easier access for handicapped and older persons. The space is designed to greatly enhance music and communication. These good results are the fruit of patient planning, lots of consultation, and commitment to serving the community first and rebuilding the sanctuary second.

Shiloh Baptist Church in the Community

Another challenging event in the life of the church reveals how the spirit of Shiloh Church is incarnate in the local community. When the Washington, D.C., Board of Education decided to build a new ele-

5. Wallace C. Smith, from a sermon preached in Shiloh Baptist Church.

mentary school adjacent to the church, half of a large city block of property — most of which was owned by the church — was taken by the process of eminent domain. The church lost parking area, neighborhood housing, valuable buildings, and property for its own expansion. Some members saw this as a blow to the church, which had worked for years to obtain and use the property for ministry. Instead of seeing this as a loss and allowing anger to flourish, the pastor led the congregation to see the new public school as an opportunity for ministry.

A partnership was developed with the new Seaton Public School. The church offered the use of its gymnasium for school athletic programs, and its buses for use by the school for field trips. The church invited the school to hold its annual Academic Honors Banquet, which recognizes outstanding students, in the Heritage Hall. The church invited the school principal to serve as a board member for the Shiloh Family Life Center. The congregation adopted the school and affirmed its educational mission in the community. In partnership together, tutoring and mentoring programs were jointly developed. Today, many of the public school teachers are members of Shiloh Church, and the common good for the larger community is being advanced cooperatively.

The church does all the traditional things you would expect of a large congregation located in the city center, and more. The Shiloh Human Services Center provides personal counseling, operates a basic reading literacy program for adults, makes referral for employment, provides pre-employment training, gives emergency food and financial assistance, aids in finding affordable housing, provides temporary housing, advocates for people with a variety of agencies, and reaches out to senior citizens, homeless people, battered women, and abused children. The Shiloh Human Services Center actively fosters partnerships with cooperative service programs, including the D.C. Association for Community Service, the D.C. Summer Program for Youth, the Child Immunization Program, the Zachaeus Health Clinic, and the Program for Care of Diabetic Persons. The church has operated a program of child development since 1948, with a focus on early childhood needs for health and preschool preparation.

The Economic Development Corporation in recent years has greatly extended the systemic outreach of Shiloh Church through its community redevelopment activity. Older and vacant buildings on the principal streets adjacent to the church are being purchased and renovated for affordable housing and to create a wraparound series of community-oriented businesses and services. A senior citizen apartment building is planned. A grocery store, barbershop, and restaurant are underway. It is all part of a commitment to take back the neighborhood and make it a positive place for people.

While constantly developing new ways to embody Christian presence and transformation in the city center of Washington, D.C., Shiloh Baptist Church is making significant contributions to global mission. The congregation has an ongoing partnership with ministry in half-a-dozen countries in Africa. In the past century, over forty-five persons from Shiloh Church have served as missionaries and as fraternal and technical workers in Africa, the Caribbean, and Latin America. "The church has benefited from having many international members, and has responded by creating mission partnerships with churches in Nigeria, Liberia, Sierra Leone, and Ghana in Africa; with churches in Haiti, Cuba, and Nicaragua in Central America; and in Russia," says the Reverend Justus Reeves, associate pastor.[6] In addition, there has been mission interaction with churches in China, Korea, and Taiwan. The themes of spiritual and social transformation have an international and ecumenical character at Shiloh. The congregation continues its journey from slavery to freedom, and beyond self-development toward justice and global interdependence.

What We Can Learn

- Large, established congregations with long traditions can mature and develop new patterns of ministry that are creative and responsive to challenging and changing circumstances.
- It can be helpful to extend and build on earlier history, where possible, when seeking to do new forms of ministry.
- Listening to and actively engaging the local community when seeking to extend into community-based ministries is vital for long-term success.
- Creative pastoral leadership engages talented and committed staff and volunteers, delegates to them, and supports them.

6. Reeves, interview.

- Becoming deeply engaged in the struggles for affordable housing, basic health care, improved education, and economic development — while difficult and demanding — is very rewarding in the long run for the growth of both the church and the community.
- Moving from a strategy of charity to a strategy of seeking justice is often the result of an evolutionary process over many years of struggle, education, and engagement.
- Vision for mission frequently arises out of faithful, persistent willingness to do the unglamorous things that build trust, create partnerships, and develop strategic wisdom.
- Strong pastoral leadership, commitment to long-term pastoral tenure, and pastoral openness to doing new things while continuing to affirm older traditions are significant keys to success at Shiloh Church.
- Unexpected losses (the loss of valuable property to the public school system and the loss of a historic sanctuary by fire) can become the occasions for new commitment to mission and service in the community, which ultimately strengthen the church.
- There is a sense of transcendent providence at Shiloh that enables people to see beyond the immediate difficulties and have a faithful confidence in the long-term fulfillment of God's Kingdom. This attitude of faith is one of the dynamic strengths of the congregation and a source for much of its positive accomplishments.

Big Bethel African Methodist Episcopal Church

An exciting new era is underway in the oldest African-American church in Atlanta. What is happening now is the revitalization of an important congregation, the redevelopment of a neighborhood, and the empowerment of a sector of the Auburn Street community both spiritually and economically.

The historic Big Bethel African Methodist Episcopal (A.M.E.) Church celebrated its 150th anniversary in 1997. Founded before the end of slavery, spurred on to great expansion after the Civil War by people freed from slavery, the Big Bethel Church has a long tradition of proclaiming the gospel and serving the community through periods of difficult social struggle.

The church was the spiritual home for many of the first black political leaders who succeeded in being elected to the Georgia state legislature, the first black businessmen to organize successful enterprises, and professional persons serving the African-American community in Atlanta. The church was the site of the first school for black children in the city. It has been a place for great choral music and unique dramatic presentations. The congregation nurtured the founding of a college for black youth. The church has been served by many outstanding preachers. It has nurtured many ministers who eventually were elected by the denomination to serve as bishops. It has hosted visits by President Jimmy Carter and Nelson Mandela, president of South Africa.

This vital church, with over two thousand members in 1997, is gifted with strong lay leadership and a visionary pastor who understands the crucial relationship between the congregation and the neighborhood surrounding the church. "Big Bethel," says the Reverend James Davis, the senior pastor, "is rediscovering its neighborhood and reinvesting its resources in transformation of the community."[1] Auburn Street is a unique and interesting area. Along just four blocks on this street are the following institutions: Big Bethel A.M.E. Church, the branch YMCA, the Wheat Street Baptist Church, the Martin Luther King Jr. Memorial Center, the Ebenezer Baptist Church, and the historic birthplace and home of the Reverend Martin Luther King Jr. In the immediate surrounding neighborhood are a mix of old wood frame houses, newer high-rise apartments, older commercial buildings, and small business buildings. Apart from the Martin Luther King Jr. Center, the area is a declining and deteriorating sector. Most of the people still living in the neighborhood are not church members. There are serious problems of crime, prostitution, drug abuse, homelessness, and human misery.

Challenge Facing the Church

Reverend Davis describes the neighborhood as a declining area squeezed between the encroaching downtown Atlanta commercial center, funded by big business, and the Martin Luther King Jr. Memorial Center, which is maintained by the National Park Service. Big business and the National Park Service want to clear out the neighborhood for their own purposes. The question for the church is, who is responsible for the residents still living in the neighborhood? Many members of Big Bethel Church have moved out to safer, more prosperous residential areas. But they have remained faithful to their church. Now the challenge that is being faced is how to become, once again, faithful to the community around the church.

Big Bethel Church has a history of significant social ministry in the community. In 1967, the congregation made a major contribution to affordable housing by completing a high-rise apartment building, Bethel Towers, immediately adjacent to the church. At that time three-fourths of a city block was cleared for housing and parking. The

1. James Davis, interview with author, Atlanta, 20 September 1997.

project cost $3.5 million and was funded with gifts and long-term financing. In conjunction with Bethel Towers, a significant renovation of the church building was completed. Along with the bricks and mortar there were other people-oriented service ministries launched, including a major Senior Citizen Nutrition Program, the Outreach Social Service Center, Counseling Center, Tutorial Enrichment Program, and the Prison Ministry, which served both women and men. In addition, during the 1970s and 1980s, church members were active in the Christian Council of Metropolitan Atlanta, the Atlanta Mayor's Civilian Review Board, and the Congress of National Black Churches. Big Bethel has always been engaged in leadership roles within the A.M.E. denomination as well as in other ecumenical organizations at city, state, and national levels. Much of its talent and energy was invested in these forms of wider ministry.

During the 1980s, in spite of significant effort by Bethel and other churches, the neighborhood continued to slide downward with drug traffic, unemployment, deteriorating housing, and more church members moving outside of the neighborhood. The Bethel Church sold off some of its adjacent property and was less vigorously involved in the immediate neighborhood even though it continued its ministry of compassion and service. With the coming of a new senior pastor, the Reverend James Davis, things began to change in the early 1990s.

Redevelopment of Congregation and Community

The Reverend James Davis began serving the church as pastor in 1992. He and the congregation together have put the focus of ministry on redevelopment of spiritual life and redevelopment of the community. Davis helped the church become conscious that active ownership of property was vital to community improvement. The church had been working mainly from a "compassion model." There was need for a structural model. Reverend Davis says, "The church has been an oasis in the desert giving food and shelter to people lost in the wilderness. Now the church must become an empowering leader to guide people through the wilderness on a journey toward the New Zion."[2]

Prior to Davis's coming to Bethel, the church had not purchased

2. Davis, interview.

any property for forty years. Now in the past five years the church has purchased thirteen pieces of property that were detrimental to the neighborhood, including a night club (a center of drug traffic), a gambling casino, a grocery store (a hot spot for selling stolen goods), a closed gas station (gathering place for addicts), and several small buildings. The former night club and the former grocery store are being renovated into a Job Training and Employment Center. The former casino will become a sizable new office building. Another building has been transformed into a federally insured credit union operated by the church. The old houses were torn down to create a lovely new open-air theater and park for community groups, and a place for outside worship in the summer. As a result of these initiatives, city agencies and lending institutions now have a positive attitude toward the Big Bethel Church. Instead of the church having to seek help, agencies are now coming to the church offering partnership for community redevelopment. A whole new spirit is breathing through the neighborhood. Good things are happening for people and the best is yet to come. The Sunday of our visit, the mayor of Atlanta was in church for worship, getting in touch with this "new spirit" at Bethel, and courting voters for the upcoming election.

Signs and Symbols of Redevelopment

There are seven significant signs and symbols of community redevelopment that are part of the new life Big Bethel Church is bringing to the community.

- *Purchase of Property.* Reversing the forty-year trend against investing in the neighborhood was not easy. It took several years of thoughtful, prayerful planning and negotiation. Each purchase took special effort, imagination for what it could become, courage to buck the trend of decline, and creative fundraising. After the first significant purchases, the outline for redevelopment is clearer and sellers are now approaching the church. With the purchase of more property there is a growing awareness among the congregation that being part of the neighborhood involves more than Sunday worship and works of mercy.
- *Bethel Credit Union.* A federally insured credit union was cre-

ated in January 1996 with the purpose of providing small business loans and other small personal loans that would enable people to move ahead economically. Its resources are modest — approaching one hundred thousand dollars in assets — but it already has made an impact in stimulating neighborhood redevelopment. The church has put the credit union in its mission budget for a monthly cash contribution to build up the total assets. A board of directors consisting of church members, Atlanta business people, and community members guides the investment of funds, keeps the focus on stimulating development and improving the neighborhood.

- *Professional Office Building and Parking.* The church has purchased a large corner property directly across from the sanctuary, a gasoline station with a large adjacent parking lot, and the large neighboring building that formerly was a gambling casino. This entire area will undergo redevelopment to create a professional office park, which will house multiple office suites and business services and provide secure parking. This enterprise will be an income-producing business that will help to create a cash flow and a positive new climate in the neighborhood. Currently the property provides income from the parking lot and also creates jobs for parking attendants. This is new economic activity for the neighborhood.
- *Bethel Housing Project.* Big Bethel Church has a previous history in the 1960s of constructing affordable housing on its adjacent property. Now the Bethel Housing Board is planning for the construction of new assisted living apartments for senior citizens and handicapped persons. These new units will help both members and non-members stay in the area and have a secure environment and necessary services. Big Bethel is building on the current trend of government financial assistance to partially enable this much needed type of housing. In addition, Big Bethel is cooperating with the local YMCA branch in its neighborhood in a partnership to renovate two sizable, existing, multi-story apartment buildings just one block from the church. Again, this will increase the supply of affordable housing and help to create a more secure environment in the area. Further, these renovated apartments will have supporting social services for residents through the YMCA and the church partnership.

- *The Richard Allen Outreach Center.* The church has operated, since the 1980s, a comprehensive social service center. The new vision now being carried forward is the construction of a three-story building that will be a multi-service center near the church. The church is seeking to do this in partnership with the Fulton County Social Services Agency. The new center will have a wraparound service approach for children, youth, families, elderly, and homeless. The facility will include a cafeteria, a gymnasium, a health care unit, after-school and Saturday programs for youth, counseling, emergency food and clothing, transitional shelter, and social services in cooperation with the county. Dr. Fred Smith, chairman of the project, describes its purpose as a one-stop social service operation that enables the church to meet all the urgent needs of people without sending them all around the city to different agencies. The Social Service Center will provide space for a medical clinic, which will be operated by the local hospital to provide neighborhood health care for uninsured, underserved, unemployed, and working poor people. Services will include prenatal care, pediatric care, primary care for several hundred families, minor surgery, a tuberculosis clinic, mental health screening and referral, connection to a laboratory for testing, a pharmacy, and capability to serve sixty patients per day. The regular, full-time medical staff provided by the hospital will be assisted by volunteer medical professionals and others. A number of the services will be free of charge. Fees will be on a sliding scale according to ability to pay.
- *Homeless Intervention Project (HIP).* The HIP Program is focused on enabling homeless and addicted persons to become drug-free, employed, and self-supporting. It includes drug rehabilitation in cooperation with the Wheat Street Baptist Church, temporary housing for six months (the church operates twenty-three apartment units in nearby buildings), job skill training and placement, a mandated ten-percent-of-income savings plan, and assistance in obtaining independent housing. Of those who make the commitment to the HIP program the success rate is over seventy percent. This program is headquartered in a building two doors down the street from the church in a space formerly occupied by a night club and grocery store. Through this initiative, the drug-free zone around the church has been ex-

panded. The church operates a similar facility for homeless and battered women called My Sister's Place. It is a transitional home serving women and their children. Counseling, support, and life planning are provided in a nurturing atmosphere. Health care and other social services are coordinated to enable women to recover, rebuild, and restart their lives.

It is clear that the church, which has been doing a lot of works of mercy and social service, is now moving to change the structure of the community in ways that will create more permanent improvement. Through creative financing, attracting new businesses, investing in property, creating income-producing enterprise, and securing outside private investment and gifts, the church has enabled systemic change and moved toward greater distributive justice for the people of its parish area.

Worship and Biblical Faith

All of this positive redevelopment is motivated by a deep Christian faith expressed in vital worship on Sundays. Twelve to thirteen hundred people gather for two worship services every Sunday. The liturgy blends the best of classical church music and great gospel hymns, anthems and responses by two choirs, scripture reading and responses, the Creed and Decalogue, a warm and welcoming spirit, biblical preaching for commitment, and invitation to faithful discipleship. A strong sense of the body of Christ, and an extended family of mutual caring, is evident. Those with special needs are affirmed in prayer and action. Congregational stewardship is strong. Sacrificial giving is practiced. A chart showing a range of two percent to twenty percent of income levels is enclosed in the Sunday worship bulletin. Every second Sunday of the month is Nehemiah Sunday (Nehemiah was the Hebrew governor who led in the rebuilding of the city of Jerusalem). Each family unit is asked to give a special offering of thirty dollars or more as a gift to the property acquisition and redevelopment fund. The ninety minutes of worship are filled with reverent, spirited religious feeling and expression. The congregation is nourished and lifted, and then challenged and sent forth into focused and disciplined witness.

Between the early worship service at 7:45 a.m. and the later service at 11:00, there is a large adult education program with classes for couples, singles, young adults, and new members. There is a full church school for children and youth. A church staff of sixteen ordained ministers and numerous lay leaders organize and carry out a full program of study, pastoral care, leadership training, and small group fellowship. During the week there are many Bible study group meetings. The pastor leads a popular Bible study at noon on Wednesdays. It is easy to see how this large, active church with its rich history and complex program has been the place where many bishops have been nurtured and sent forth. But what is really impressive is that in the midst of all this tradition, there is today a vigorous and prophetic engagement in transforming the community, in service that goes beyond compassion toward justice. That is the real story of Big Bethel A.M.E. Church as it moves toward the next century.

What We Can Learn

- Active ownership of significant property adjacent to the church building can be an investment in creating positive human community.
- Being an active participant in the physical and spiritual well-being of the surrounding community is a significant witness to the Incarnation of Christ.
- Systematic giving by a congregation to create a property investment fund for community redevelopment can be creative stewardship.
- Vision comes from imagination, a sense of calling, capacity for seeing possibilities, and commitment to justice. A visionary leader is essential for an urban church to move toward systemic justice.
- Vision and inspiration may come from just a few leaders, but it takes a large body of skilled, persistent, and dedicated workers to turn the vision into reality. Bethel has built up a core group of talented and experienced volunteer and professional workers.
- Partnership with a variety of key institutions is crucial to successful urban community redevelopment. At Bethel, these allies

include the YMCA, Mercy Hospital, local banks, Wheat Street Baptist Church, other churches, and the A.M.E. bishop.

- A large urban church with a long history and significant tradition can move toward systemic change more easily when it is able to see the new agenda as a recommitment to some part of its tradition. At Bethel there was an earlier involvement in the neighborhood social issues and a denominational tradition of black economic development. These reference points helped to strengthen the current movement for socioeconomic redevelopment.

- Continuous pastoral leadership for a significant length of time is essential for successful redevelopment. Large projects take time. Bethel Church, operating within the A.M.E. polity, has a recent history of pastors with relatively short tenure. But many of the congregation's most important accomplishments have occurred during seasons of longer pastorates.

- The rediscovery of local community as the focus of mission also involves the discovery of moving beyond works of mercy toward more systemic works of justice. Bethel has a history of far-flung mission beyond Atlanta. The challenges of the 1990s brought the attention and focus of mission back to their own locale.

- The power to do substantial things for community redevelopment in a neighborhood is greatly enhanced through being a regional church, which draws many members and resources from the larger metropolitan area.

- No matter how strong the stewardship program within the congregation, it is essential to secure significant sources of funding from outside the membership to enable substantial community redevelopment. Big Bethel has been successful in securing funding from government agencies, businesses, entrepreneurial enterprise, institutional allies, and individual benefactors, as well as through special giving by members.

- Engagement in the struggle for community redevelopment has helped Big Bethel Church to grow spiritually and numerically. Commitment to social justice has attracted new members. It has brought a new vitality and excitement into the life of the congregation.

Central Presbyterian Church

Central Presbyterian Church, which stands across from the Georgia State Capitol Building, was established in 1858 and survived the destruction of Atlanta during the Civil War. It became one of the strongest congregations in the region. In the early 1900s, it became a center of the social gospel, founding such programs as the Atlanta Union Mission, the Baby Clinic, and a boarding home for young women, as well as promoting the development of public schools in the city, and helping to reestablish Oglethorpe University.

In the quarter century from 1930 to 1958 when Atlanta was growing rapidly and many congregations were moving out of the city center, the church made clear decisions to stay downtown and become an urban church dedicated to serving people in the city. During the 1960s and 1970s the church provided shelter and encouragement to civil rights workers, trade unionists, anti-war protesters, and farmers who came to present their grievances at the state capitol. The church developed ministries of health care, early childhood education, a night shelter, and outreach to the homeless that became models for other congregations. It has been an active leader in collaborating with other religious bodies to form and coordinate efforts for social service ministries in Atlanta.

The current Mission Statement of Central Presbyterian Church reads in part, "We come to [the church] as a wellspring, bringing our thirst and emptiness, only to discover that our cup is filled by the living Word who sends us to be with those in need, and to call forth

God's justice in a chaotic world." The congregation of over 750 has a rich diversity of professions, talents, skills, and resources among its members. Most of the members do not live in central Atlanta. They are drawn to this historic church by its strong community of caring, its clear commitment to serve people in need, and the excellent preaching and teaching ministry.

Creative Balance Between Prophetic and Pastoral

As one would expect of a church with a long history of social ministry, Central Presbyterian is engaged directly or indirectly in a wide range of service and advocacy projects, using its rich human and financial resources in many creative ways. At the same time, the church has a strong and deep commitment to pastoral, preaching, and teaching ministries to sustain its members. Associate Pastor, the Reverend Kimberly Richter, says, "There is a delicate ecology — a creative balance — in this church between pastoral nurture and prophetic mission."[1] The large majority of members do not live near the church. When they come to the church they tend to come for multiple purposes of worship and service, study and volunteer work, nurture and outreach to the community. Over the decades the church has been known for its strong pulpit and equally strong teaching program. It has always engaged in direct services to people in need, including the homeless, working women, young children, and low-income families. In a sermon early in her tenure as associate pastor, Kim Richter pointed out to the congregation that it was not enough for the church simply to have stayed in downtown Atlanta; staying means a continuous rededication, new initiatives to engage the struggles for justice, and not resting on the good accomplishments of the past.

In recent years Central has moved toward collaborative partnerships and a more systemic approach for its outreach ministry. This can be seen especially in four areas: health care, early childhood education, the outreach center, and in action to bring greater justice for the Atlanta labor pool. These are areas in which Central has long been involved, and where it has built up considerable experience both at the professional and volunteer levels.

1. Kimberly Richter, interview with author, Atlanta, 22 March 1997.

The Ministry of Health Care

Concern for the health of infants and mothers from working families led to the creation in 1922 of the Baby Clinic. With a separate board to guide it, a staff of as many as fifteen doctors giving service, and as many as forty volunteers assisting, the clinic provided free medical care for infants and children. One report indicated that by 1941 the clinic had served nearly twelve thousand patients. The large involvement of church members in this ministry became a contributing factor in the determination by the church to remain at its downtown location.[2] One woman physician, Dr. Leila Denmark, served faithfully in the clinic for over three decades. Gradually, the services of the clinic were expanded. It evolved from being the Baby Clinic to the Central Health Center. This second stage in providing health care still utilized the volunteer services of many doctors and medical professionals. The care was expanded to give primary care to families and special attention to homeless persons. It was still housed in church facilities. The church contributed financially to its operation. There was a regular professional staff of doctors, nurses, and aides providing medical care. Church volunteers continued to play a major role in supportive assistance.

The third stage of the health care ministry began in 1992 when the church entered into a partnership with the St. Joseph Hospital-Mercy Mobil Clinic to provide and operate the medical care and clinic management. Today the Central Health Center offers comprehensive health care to children, adults, and families. There is special focus on providing services for those who are underserved, uninsured, and those who live in the area. The church provides generous space in its newest wing, an ongoing stream of volunteer assistants, and contributes financial support through an annual Christmas offering. This expanded clinic receives support from the Mercy Medical System, local foundations, organizations, and individuals. Special services include care for HIV patients, dental care, mental health referral, and language translators to assist with Hispanic and Vietnamese patients. The Central Health Center has developed into a high-quality, well-managed, and well-funded medical care facility. It makes health care

2. John Robert Smith, *The Church That Stayed* (Atlanta: The Atlanta Historical Society, 1979), 84-85.

very personalized in a time when medical practice has become very technical and specialized.

Child Development Center

Central Presbyterian Church has always had an active program for the spiritual and educational development of children. But in 1972 it took action to create what has become the Central Child Development Center, which embodies a preschool and day-care program for eighty young children. The congregation's awareness of the special needs of preschool aged children from working families in the surrounding downtown area, as well as the children of professional workers commuting into the city center, led to the formation of a high-quality program housed in excellent facilities of a renovated church school building. The Child Development Center was planned with help from Georgia State University, and from its early years has included an early childhood research and training component.

The Child Development Center is intercultural, interracial, and holistic by design. The children enrolled are from ages six weeks through five years. The enrollees come from nine counties in the extended metropolitan region. Participants come from low-income families living in public housing in the area, from business and professional families working at the state capitol and nearby corporate offices (IBM, Georgia Pacific, Coca-Cola), and from workers in adjacent City Hall. Nearly twenty-five percent of the children are on scholarship. The school, which is fully accredited, has a sliding scale of fees according to ability to pay. Further funding comes from an endowment created by the church over the decades, federal block grants, and through partnership with Georgia State University. The center works with the Atlanta Area Technical School to train student teachers. The preschool and day-care programs are a model widely studied by others. The contribution of this program goes beyond the direct educational service to children and families. The benefits include research, training for teachers, and modeling for other centers.

The Mission Statement indicates, "Since children spend forty to fifty hours a week in the Center and are literally 'growing up' here, the center is committed to providing a safe and nurturing environment that allows a child to learn and develop physically, emotionally, socially and intellectually at his or her own, individual pace." The educational program includes careful attention to language development, math and science skills, creative art and music, social skills, and personal self-development. The curriculum includes rich offerings in music, reading readiness, art activities, structured learning experiences, field trips, and use of many outside resource persons. There is a very positive emphasis on warm, loving relationships within the classes and a low teacher-child ratio. The center provides a nutritious breakfast, lunch, and afternoon snack. Parents are encouraged to come in and visit their child during the day, and many do come in during the noon hour. The staff meet regularly with parents, there are personal learning evaluations, and a parent support group. Here, again, is a clear example of the church building upon and expanding its long tradition of ministry to children and families.

The Central Outreach Center and Night Shelter

The church has been providing for the emergency needs of people for more than a century. The church's Outreach Mission Statement affirms that the "Church believes that life and ministry is a response to Jesus Christ. [Over the years] the church has created and joined with others to support diverse ministries of care, hope and compassion. We sustain these ministries with our time, money and vision. In our service to others we proclaim the abundant life we know in Jesus Christ." The outreach center operates in a suite of rooms in the newest church building. Carole Jean Miller, who is an experienced and skilled social worker, coordinates the overall work. On average, help is given to 350 persons a month.

Miller describes the center as "a first-stop emergency outpost" serving a diverse range of persons — the homeless, immigrants, unemployed residents, street people, and low-income families from public housing in the area.[3] The church is close to the downtown bus station. It is often the first stop for persons seeking help after arriving in Atlanta without jobs or family. Services offered include emergency food for families and individuals, employment referral, public transportation assistance, emergency counseling, a computer-

3. Carole Jean Miller, interview with author, 22 March 1997.

ized link for referral services to hundreds of other social service agencies, a night shelter and, above all, a compassionate and caring affirmation of people coming to the center. On a peak day the center may assist as many as fifty persons. The professional staff employed by the church is supported by a large number of church volunteers. They have developed considerable skill in helping persons with employment referral. Often men who are temporarily staying in the Central Church Night Shelter will come into the outreach center for help in finding work.

The church operates a Night Shelter for Men during the winter months from November through March in partnership with its neighbor, Immaculate Conception Catholic Church. The shelter program is directed by a husband and wife team from the Catholic parish and is housed in the facilities of both churches. The combined spaces of the two churches working together can accommodate nearly one hundred persons at night. The men get a hot evening meal, breakfast in the morning, and a sack lunch to take with them. Central Presbyterian Church uses its gym for shelter space. Numerous volunteers support the leadership of the directors.

One unique feature that emerged is the foot clinic, which gives special care to homeless persons with foot problems. Once a week doctors and volunteers gather to wash and treat the feet of homeless people. This service, begun in 1981 and still in operation, continues to soak wounded feet, treat cuts and calluses, and establish communication with homeless people. This healing touch often leads to other links of healing and emergency assistance.

The staff cooperates with numerous allied institutions, foremost of which is the nearby Capitol Area Ministries, which is a social service center supported by many churches and groups. Capitol Ministries operates a Neighborhood Center offering programs for youth, adults, and seniors. Emphasis is on education and improving social and work skills. There is a special Teens Program and a strong summer camp program. There is an outreach to families in the adjacent Capitol Homes public housing and a volunteer tutoring program in the local elementary school.

Systemic Justice: The New Cutting Edge

From long experience with men in the church's Night Shelter and persons coming into the outreach center, members of the staff and congregation have learned firsthand of the unjust treatment of temporary day laborers. In Atlanta there is a tradition, as in many large cities, of homeless and unemployed persons seeking work as day laborers in the construction industry. They come off the street before dawn into a labor pool to be hired at minimum wage for the day. Working conditions are often difficult, especially in the winter. When a person is selected from the line he is transported by the contractor to the work site, provided with a hard hat if required, working gloves if necessary, and set to work doing manual labor. At the end of the day the workers are paid, with deductions made for transportation and equipment. Frequently they are paid with a paper voucher that can be cashed for a fee at liquor stores, taverns, or grocery stores. After a long day, workers end up on the street with only a few dollars.

Men will get up in the middle of the night — at three or four a.m. — in order to walk to the early morning labor pool lineup. In winter this can be an exhausting effort. If they are selected, they go to work, often without breakfast, usually doing outside labor, work hard through the day, and then often end up with only a paper voucher. By making deductions for equipment and transport, the labor pool, in effect, does not pay minimum wage. Working conditions are abusive. The day workers are not protected by labor law, have no bargaining power, no job stability, no benefits, and do not receive fair payment for what they do. It is a highly exploitative situation. There is a growing awareness of the need to make a systematic effort to change these unjust working conditions. With its history of hospitality to striking transit and paper mill workers, protesting farmers, and civil rights demonstrators, the church is well-positioned to advocate for the day laborers.

Strategy for Justice

Even when you allow that there is a legitimate role for temporary day laborers in the construction industry, noted Senior Minister Ted Wardlaw, the labor pool as structured is exploitative and unjust. Persons from Central Church are joining with others from churches and groups in the city to respond to this unjust situation. A new coalition has been formed which calls itself Atlantans Building for Leadership and Empowerment (ABLE), to work for a change in the system.

Changing, through a city ordinance, the working rules that govern temporary day labor is one of the goals of ABLE. The construction industry is the primary employer of temporary day laborers through the labor pool. Construction is a thriving, expanding, multibillion dollar business in the Atlanta region. ABLE identifies the need to secure some basic rights and working conditions for day laborers. The minimum essentials include payment by check to create accountable records; prohibiting deductions from pay for essential working equipment; the elimination of the voucher system with payment by cash or check; and payment of at least the national minimum wage.

Underlying this effort is the realization that there is a growing segment of the American workforce that is unskilled or semiskilled, outside of unionization, living at subsistence level, and not visible to society at large. Their suffering often goes unnoticed. Their voice is not heard. People at Central Church are working through ABLE to bring the voice of marginalized workers to the attention of the public and to city government. They know that the measure of a society is how it treats its weakest members. Empowerment of workers through fair labor rules requires going beyond charity toward justice.

What We Can Learn

- Imagination is essential for justice. Experience reflected upon through Christian faith can stir the imagination and motivate the human conscience toward appropriate action for justice.
- The structures created by a church, such as Central Presbyterian's Health Clinic, Outreach Center, Night Shelter, and Child Development Center, can be the connecting links between the congregation and marginalized people that stir up imaginative action for justice.
- In theological language, we may affirm that the Holy Spirit is at work drawing people into spiritual solidarity to be God's agents of transformation. The world for which Christ gave himself includes the structures of society that need transformation.

- There is no substitute for a church being in a place where one cannot avoid the powers and principalities that influence the shape of everyday life. That is in great part what the urban setting is all about — being in a place where you cannot hide from the human struggle for life, and what God is calling people to do and be.
- An effective downtown church pays careful attention to keeping an appropriate balance between the nurture of members and the empowering of members to serve creatively in the wider society.
- Partnership, communication links, and networking with other urban institutions play a vital role in the effective outreach of an urban church. At Central Presbyterian Church we see this in creative links with universities, hospitals, social agencies, and city government.
- A key factor contributing to creative urban ministry at Central has been long-term, stable pastoral leadership and the ability of pastors to reach out and attract capable, experienced, and deeply committed lay leadership.
- Central Church has over the years fostered strong partnerships with area seminaries and denominational leadership. These links have contributed a stream of ideas and faith resources and have helped nurture a wider perspective.

St. Paul's Christian Methodist Episcopal Church

The St. Paul's Christian Methodist Episcopal Church congregation and its pastor, the Reverend Henry Delaney, are a living demonstration of how a faith-filled vision can become the transforming power of God creating Christian community. Reverend Delaney and his colleagues in ministry are the answer to the key question that runs through this book: how can churches go beyond charity to deal with systemic justice? This story is about how one pastor and a congregation were able to see beyond the plagues of inner-city drugs, crime, unemployment, and poor schools to create a new reality of opportunity, equity, and empowerment through faith, prayer, entrepreneurial spirit, and hard work.

Savannah is a city rich in colonial and Civil War history. It has preserved much of the charm of the old South. There are lovely tree-lined parks, manicured lawns, and well-preserved eighteenth-century homes. In recent decades the area has changed from an agricultural economy into a center for commerce, trade, and banking, and a major port for Atlantic shipping. There is a new civic spirit that affirms ethnic diversity, racial tolerance, and social cooperation. Within the city boundaries the population is approximately fifty-two percent African American. In spite of the fact that there is a new prosperity and a significant black middle class, many of the predominantly black neighborhoods have been bypassed by the economic gains of the new South.

Challenge in the African-American Community

When Reverend Henry Delaney first came to St. Paul's Church in 1989, he came into a neighborhood where drug traffic was thriving, the local elementary school had been closed, unemployment was high, much of the housing was in substandard condition, the church building was in disrepair, and the congregation had dwindled to about two hundred members.

Delaney, a veteran urban pastor who had served in churches in Detroit and other cities for significant periods of time, was not overwhelmed by what he found in Savannah. He has led his congregation in achieving new, dramatic accomplishments without government funding, large foundation grants, or significant financing from the denomination. He has done this by developing local resources.

Delaney and his wife, Ethel, who is a strong partner in the ministry, moved into a house near the church that had been boarded up and used by crack cocaine addicts. This was the first of fifteen houses in the immediate church neighborhood that he led the congregation to renovate. It became a commitment for his staff that they must live in the neighborhood within a few blocks of the church, be visible and active in the area, and make a contribution to redeveloping the community.

He found the church property was about to be foreclosed by the Department of Housing and Urban Development (HUD). He went directly to the head of the HUD office in Savannah and outlined his vision for renewal of the neighborhood, and the deadline was extended. Next, he communicated his vision for community renewal to the president of Savannah's largest black-owned bank. Mortgage loans were negotiated and over the course of the next several years fifteen houses were purchased, drug pushers evicted, and church staff moved in. This dramatically changed the spirit and the reality of the neighborhood. People began to feel safe to walk the streets and to come to the church. The houses were renovated by the volunteer work of church members. As the housing was renewed around the church, the drug-free area was extended. New programming was started and the membership began to grow rapidly. Combined spiritual and community ministry led to dramatic congregational growth.

The transformation in the neighborhood was undergirded by a strong program of worship — three services on Sunday — and a growing program of Bible study and fellowship groups on Tuesday, Thursday, and Saturday. The church building was cleaned up and repaired, and the brick exterior was painted a dignified but lively red, suggesting the new vitality of the congregation. Delaney's conviction is that the key to positive, lasting change in the community is strengthening family life on a spiritual and moral foundation. Numerous initiatives were taken to reach out to families through counseling, emergency assistance, teaching, preaching, and a focus on relating to men. Delaney focuses on men, and his approach is direct. He demands that men live up to their responsibilities and obligations to be husbands, fathers, and economic and spiritual providers for their families. When you talk with Pastor Delaney you sense his deep compassion and his strong character. He is a large, rotund man who communicates with a powerful presence and authority. The men in the neighborhood have come to respect him, seek his counsel, and listen to his guidance. He is the embodiment of a wise and savvy pastoral father figure. The community has responded to his leadership and identified with the church. From 1989 to 1994, St. Paul's Church grew from 216 members to over 2,000 members. By 1997, membership reached 3,800. As membership increased, the church staff also increased and program responsibility has been delegated. In the midst of this rapid growth, it is amazing that Reverend Delaney stays in daily contact with the people of the parish, maintains regular open office hours to give time to people, and remains in close touch with the ebb and flow of the neighborhood.

Focus on Youth

St. Paul's Church is far more than just a neighborhood church. Its pastor and people have been active in Savannah school board politics, helping to bring together a coalition of Black churches to support candidates favoring greater equity and more distributive justice in the city schools. St. Paul's also has participated in the countywide Youth Futures Authority collaborative, which unites many previously competing human service agencies into a coordinated unit to better serve people living at or near poverty level.

The Youth Futures Authority was created by an act of the Georgia State Legislature after strong lobbying by community and church leaders in Savannah. The Authority brings together over fifteen governmental units in a countywide area, including the school system, health and human service agencies, local businesses, area churches, the United Way, and other nonprofit groups. They engage in coordinated planning, joint decision-making, regional communication, mutual support, collaborative evaluation, and accountability. The Authority's vision statement gives clear indication of where its creative efforts are focused: "Every child will be born healthy, grow up healthy, be secure from abuse and neglect, and become a literate, productive, economically self-sustaining citizen."[1] This vision statement is manifested in programs for prenatal care, pediatric health care, parenting education, family counseling, life skills education, and employment training. According to executive director Otis Johnson, the Youth Futures Authority (YFA) has had its greatest success in improving delivery of human services; it has had less success in improving public schools, and very little success in economic development.[2]

Reverend Delaney has supported the Youth Futures Authority, and St. Paul's Church has provided space for YFA programming. The role of churches has been crucial in creating credibility among alienated people in predominantly African-American neighborhoods, where trust in government social work agencies is very low. Delaney believes the secular approach of YFA does not go far enough and cannot get the real job done. He says, "You need to start when children are very young (the teen years are too late), create a spiritually positive environment, establish clear discipline, and require full parent involvement."[3] Further, Delaney believes that the public schools are not doing the necessary things to reach the deep needs of black children and youth in Savannah.

1. Youth Futures Authority, *Mission Statement*, 1996.
2. Otis Johnson, interview with author, Savannah, Georgia, 18 March 1997. The Youth Futures Authority, created in 1988, is a model of political collaboration, widely praised and now being duplicated in other Georgia communities, according to Johnson, who is director of the Authority.
3. Henry Delaney, interview with author, Savannah, Georgia, 18 March 1997.

Creating a New School

In 1993, St. Paul's bought an old public elementary school building, just five blocks from the church, that had been closed by the city of Savannah years earlier. The congregation went to work to renovate the building and opened its own school. By 1997, the school had grades three through eight, served about one hundred children, and had a budget approaching a quarter million dollars. The principal is a former public school principal. All teachers are state certified, some are volunteer, all are dedicated. The school serves boys only. Delaney says the need for strong mentoring of boys in the African-American community and limited resources led to the decision to focus on male students.

The curriculum has a strong emphasis on science, math, and reading. The teaching of Bible, religion, and ethnic history is important in the curriculum. The school has a positive emphasis on creating a Christian identity, and involves parents in reinforcing what children learn in school. Many of the boys are what the public school calls "students at high risk." St. Paul's School takes a firm approach to discipline, establishes clear rules, and expects students to develop a positive attitude about education. Reverend Delaney says, "This is not a reformatory." Very few students are lost because of behavioral problems. The goal is to build up the enrollment so that eventually there will be a graduating class each year of thirty-five young men ready for high school and college. The St. Paul's School is a successful educational alternative in the neighborhood where the public school system had essentially given up and bussed students to schools in other parts of the city.

The financing of the school is a challenge. Tuition is two thousand dollars a year. There are scholarships for those who cannot afford that amount, but every family must pay something according to their ability. Delaney does fundraising throughout Savannah. The school received a substantial gift to create its computer laboratory. Now they are working to create a science laboratory. There is no federal or state money involved in the school. There is lots of creativity in tapping resources around greater Savannah, including businesses, service clubs, churches, and individuals.

Delaney's wife, Ethel, took leadership in organizing the Community Cultural Center for the education of girls and young women.

Ethel, who is a talented musician, knows that the way into the heart of the younger generation is through music. She teaches a group of forty teens and preteens the art of praise dancing, sometimes called liturgical dance. The young women learn rhythmic movement using gospel music. The dances are designed as an act of praise for worship. The energy of young people is engaged in an atmosphere of prayer and self-expression. Along the way discipline, cooperation, and Christian faith are learned. At the conclusion of the year of study and practice there is a dance recital open to the community. It is a rewarding moment of public recognition and affirmation for the young women in the church.

Basic Human Needs

The daily life of the church is deeply engaged with basic human needs. There is a program of food distribution to over five hundred families each month. Breakfast is served to about two hundred homeless persons every Sunday morning. The Kids Kafe serves free meals every Tuesday and Thursday to the children of the community, with much of the food coming through Second Harvest. There is Project Success, which provides after-school tutoring and safe recreation for children. Health Quest, a free health-screening program in cooperation with the Candler Hospital, aims at early identification of potential chronic health problems. The program comes into the church community to be more easily available and user friendly.

A major component of St. Paul's community ministry is the program of drug abuse rehabilitation and recovery. The Hallelujah House is a facility for twenty men who are in recovery and are preparing for reentry into employment. There is a similar facility for women. The residents have already come through the tough detoxification and are drug-free. The church community engages them in Bible study, in community service, and in rebuilding their lives spiritually as well as functionally. The recovery rate is over eighty percent. Most continue their involvement in the life of the church after they leave the halfway house. Delaney emphasizes the need for both the inward change in the attitude of the person recovering and the outward change in the environment to reduce the drug traffic.

The area around the church has become more and more like a

safety zone, a drug-free neighborhod in which the community takes pride. The church purchased a social hall nearby that previously had been a social club, and transformed it into a youth center and safe space for community events. This renewal project is one more addition to reclaiming and taking back the neighborhood for the residents. The fact that the building is within the safe, drug-free zone has enhanced its use and made it an income-producing property.

St. Paul's Church has recognized that improving the economic climate of the community is vital to its people. By 1997, the church had acquired twenty properties, which it maintains and rents to families. The church has also purchased several commercial properties, including an office building, which now houses a community-oriented AM radio station (WIZA), a Community Cultural Center, the St. Paul Teen Drug and Crime Prevention Center, and a commercial bakery. All of these enterprises have improved the livability and safety of the neighborhood. Recently the church purchased and cleared a full city block to significantly increase parking for cars by two hundred spaces. This expansion is a sign that the church — while serving its neighborhood — is also a regional church that attracts worshippers from a much larger area in Savannah.

Worship and Preaching Are Central

Undergirding everything the church does in education, service, and in its quest for justice, is a large and well-attended worship program. Over two thousand persons participate on Sundays in four worship services in the sanctuary — at 8:00 a.m., 11:00 a.m., 2:00 p.m., and 6:00 p.m. The first service brings in the homeless and others who want to join in an early worship followed by a hot breakfast. The eleven o'clock worship is the high point of the week. A large choir accompanied by brass, percussion, and electronic keyboard, as well as piano and organ, fills the large sanctuary with full, rich gospel music and traditional hymn singing that rocks the building with joyful praise. Henry Delaney is a powerful preacher, a large man with a deep bass voice who mixes biblical truth with street-wise savvy to bring people into the presence of God's word. The gospel is proclaimed in a direct manner that makes clear that God expects changed lives, faithful disciples, and transformed community.

Delaney's teaching and preaching ministry is extended through a live radio broadcast from the eleven o'clock worship service and a telecast of the Sunday afternoon service. On Tuesdays he conducts an afternoon and an evening Bible study in the church sanctuary that draws nearly one thousand persons, including many from other churches in Savannah. Intercessory prayer is a strong emphasis that runs through the week from Sunday to Tuesday to Thursday, and again on Saturday as hundreds meet to pray for their families and community. On Saturday mornings there is a prayer breakfast followed by new member training classes that combine fellowship, community building, and education to build up the congregation, which numbered close to four thousand members by 1998.

Delaney teaches that tithing is a means of God's grace for faithful people. "Tithing," he says, "is a spiritual blessing that can provide the material resources for a dedicated ministry that transforms lives and builds Christian community."[4] The undergirding faith is that when the church does God's will in ministry, God shows the way to the necessary financial and human resources. There is a strong entrepreneurial spirit that runs through the many enterprises of the church. This spirit is one of the keys that has helped the church to grow and diversify its ministry. There is a significant commitment to investment in property, community renewal, risk-taking, microenterprise, and self-development. The most basic key is a tough-minded, strong-hearted faith. The final word is persistent prayer. When you meet Delaney you encounter a person who greets you with a word of prayer and, when the conversation is ended, leaves you with a blessing in prayer. Prayer undergirds everything; it is the beginning and the ending of all ministry at St. Paul's Christian Methodist Episcopal Church in Savannah.[5]

4. Delaney, interview.

5. An interesting description of the ministry of the St. Paul's Christian Methodist Episcopal Church and the leadership of the Reverend Henry Delaney can be found in the book by Lamar Alexander, *We Know What to Do* (New York: William Morrow Company, 1995), 69-78.

What We Can Learn

From the story of this church's redevelopment and growth from two hundred members to four thousand members, we can learn a number of important lessons.

- Strong, faithful pastoral leadership is at the center of this amazing congregational renewal.
- Redevelopment is tough, hard work that can succeed when there is tough-minded faith capable of confronting the tendency toward irresponsibility in the community.
- The redevelopment of a congregation must take seriously the redevelopment of the community in which it is located if there is to be permanent change.
- Having a vision big enough to get attention, command resources, and build participation is really the essence of leadership.
- Investment in residential property and its redevelopment can send a strong signal to the larger community of a congregation's commitment to ministry for, by, and with people of the area around the church.
- Redevelopment that is substantial and will have a stable future takes about a decade of dedicated, intelligent work. Continuity in pastoral leadership is crucial.
- Worship, prayer, and study, which builds up faith, is the foundation for all aspects of redevelopment and community ministry.
- Significant redevelopment can be done without government funds.
- Creating a community school in which neighborhood children can receive a high-quality education is an act of evangelism.
- Cleansing the neighborhood of drug traffic created a new and positive spirit in the community.

Olivet Institutional Baptist Church

The Olivet Baptist Church was founded over sixty-seven years ago as an African-American congregation dedicated to the Christian gospel with a strong commitment to self-development of people in the community. It is located in the Fairfax community on the east side of Cleveland in a neighborhood of wood frame houses and duplexes of twenties and thirties vintage.

The roots of the Olivet Baptist Church are planted deeply in the Christian tradition of being a caring community — the body of Christ — in the midst of people struggling to be free as Children of God. The church began in 1931, during the Great Depression. It was a center of hope, compassion, spiritual nurture, and practical assistance to people in a time when thousands were unemployed in Cleveland. The post–World War II era was a better period economically, but racial segregation and institutional prejudice were deeply ingrained in Cleveland. Nevertheless, Olivet Church grew stronger in spirit and in numbers. In the early 1960s the church was challenging institutional racism by taking leadership in the civil rights movement before the movement had widespread support. The church and its pastors were strong voices for racial justice. Dr. Odie Hoover, then Olivet's pastor, opened the church for Dr. Martin Luther King, Jr., to speak and organize for civil rights. This was at a time when churches were reluctant to take that kind of risk. This was the struggle for voting rights, desegregation of public schools, equal access to public facilities, and open housing.[1]

Dr. Hoover worked with the congregation to build a new, larger sanctuary for worship. He led the church to change its name to include the word "Institutional" to indicate its involvement with economic, social, cultural, and political areas of human life. There was a growing commitment to social justice. The concept of the institutional church as a community service institution was symbolized in the theme, "Ministry to the whole person — making our neighborhood a brotherhood." It was expressed through the creation of a Christian Community Center in a separate building. This was a place for many programs of human self-development, music, art, cultural expression, as well as a center of community organization and civil rights action.

In 1974, Dr. Otis Moss, Jr., became the pastor of Olivet Institutional Baptist Church. He enhanced the church's involvement with the Reverend Jesse Jackson and Operation PUSH. This was the time of the struggle to gain equal employment opportunity, promote African-American economic development, and create affordable housing. Dr. Moss served as the chairman of the national Board of Directors for PUSH. The church stood for faith-based leadership in moving toward greater justice for people in the city and nation. Dr. Moss and many Olivet members worked to support the Reverend Jesse Jackson in his presidential campaigns.[2]

In its sixty-seventh year of ministry, the Olivet Institutional Baptist Church is a congregation of over three thousand members. It is a regional church with two-thirds of its members living in Cleveland and one-third in the surrounding suburbs. Through its strong preaching and long record of community service Olivet Church has attracted members from a wide diversity of socioeconomic backgrounds, including many well-educated professional people in business, medicine, law, and higher education. Over a period of several decades, under the leadership of the Reverend Dr. Otis Moss, Jr., the church has used its human and financial resources to accomplish a variety of ministries and large-scale projects. Perhaps the most significant accomplishment is the new medical center.

1. Marna Hale Leaks, ed., *The History of Olivet Institutional Church: Every Round Goes Higher* (Cleveland: Olivet Institutional Baptist Church, 1996), 2-3.

2. Otis Moss, Jr., interview with author, 8 October 1997.

Health, Healing, and Wholeness: Religion and Medicine

The vision for a state-of-the-art medical center that would take a holistic approach to health care emerged in the mind and heart of Dr. Otis Moss. Over the years of his ministry he had seen the great need for good-quality health care in the African-American community. He had felt the pain of people who lacked access to proper health care due to race and economic status. He dreamed of bringing the healing arts of religion and medicine together in partnership. "Quality health care is part of human liberation," says Moss, "It is a basic human right and a moral imperative rooted in our Christian faith." Moss shared this vision with church members, the medical profession, university teachers, and persons in the wider community. Together they began the long and arduous effort of more than a decade of work to realize the dream of the new medical center in the neighborhood of Olivet Institutional Baptist Church. What emerged from this major systemic effort is a model for other cities. There are three key elements in the model:[3]

1. the healing traditions of the church and of the medical arts are affirmed and united;
2. partnership between the church, the hospital, and the university for collaborative practice of the healing arts is established;
3. an integrated approach links lifestyle, education, preventive health care, clinical practice, and a spiritually based positive program for self-care.

As Moss says, the medical center seeks to overcome the divorce between medicine and religion, and reunifies the religious and medical communities into a partnership for health.

The Struggle to Create a New Model for Health Care

How was this new model created? As Moss comments, "Medical practitioners, pastors, and scholars have been interested in the relationship and interaction of their different healing arts for a long time.

3. Moss, interview.

But most of the efforts to work together have taken place in the more affluent areas outside city centers. We knew that creating a new kind of medical center in the city would be more difficult."[4] What were some of the struggles?

- gaining acceptance for the idea of establishing a state-of-the-art medical center, a center of excellence, in the inner city
- overcoming the pressures to make the center simply a clinic for the poor — an outpost of charity — on the margins of the medical community
- persisting through a decade-long struggle to put together a unique partnership
- bringing the different cultures of African-American religion and university hospital medicine together into a working partnership
- assembling the necessary funding for a non-traditional health care project that did not fit into the standard categories expected by foundations, government agencies, and donors.

The obstacles to the creation of the medical center were overcome during a fifteen-year effort. Some of the factors that contributed to the success of the project were:

- strong leadership — pastor and doctors in partnership, united by faith
- efforts of church members in the medical community, including church doctors, worked to convince University Hospital and the congregation of the need for the center
- firm commitment of Olivet Institutional Baptist Church to the vision and long-term effort
- fifteen years of careful planning, hard work, and faithful determination
- allies in the larger Cleveland community, including the Cleveland Foundation
- building support in the neighborhood and surrounding community
- sponsorship from the parent nonprofit corporation, the Olivet

4. Moss, interview.

Housing and Development Corporation, which also obtained land
- experience and perseverance gained from the long struggle for civil rights.

Eyes on the Prize: A Victorious Outcome

On November 15, 1997, the new Otis Moss, Jr.–University Hospitals Medical Center was dedicated. Andrew Young — former U.S. ambassador to the United Nations, former mayor of Atlanta, and civil rights leader — was the dedicatory speaker. The goal to proclaim, teach, and practice health care, healing, and wholeness in a spiritually supportive environment was achieved.[5] The University Hospitals of Cleveland provide the medical staff of six physicians who practice internal medicine, pediatrics, obstetrics/gynecology, and family care in the new center. The Olivet Institutional Baptist Church created the Olivet Health and Education Institute in the medical center. Its professional staff of four gives special attention to health issues that are problematic among African-American people, such as hypertension, diabetes, cardiovascular disease, chemical dependency, and obesity.[6] The centerpiece of the Institute is the preventive health care education program. This program provides individual counsel and group seminars that create a positive approach to behavior and attitudes for good health. The seminars provide instruction in the following areas:[7]

- developing a loving relationship with your mate
- developing positive interpersonal communication skills
- building healthy relationships for parenting
- prayer, faith, belief, and health
- the benefits of fasting for health
- laughter as preventive medicine
- meditation and relaxation skills

5. *The Otis Moss, Jr.–University Hospitals Medical Center Dedication Bulletin*, 15 November 1997.
6. The Olivet Health and Education Institute, "Providing a Spiritual and Educational Dimension to Health Care," November 1997.
7. "Providing a Spiritual and Educational Dimension to Health Care."

- dealing with negative emotions
- learning how to glorify God through the care of our bodies.

A start-up grant from the Cleveland Foundation helped to launch the new preventive health care education program. This entire creative ministry is taking place in the new medical center facility — a 15,000 square-foot building which is a great asset and enhancement to the surrounding inner-city neighborhood. It is a great resource for Cleveland and a model for other cities. The Otis Moss, Jr.–University Hospitals Medical Center and the Olivet Health and Education Institute give embodiment to the church's mission statement, "To practice the unconditional love of Jesus Christ."

Worship at Olivet Church

One of the keys to the active outreach ministry of the Olivet Institutional Baptist Church in the wider community is the vital worship program of the congregation. On Sunday the large sanctuary is filled for two worship services at 7:45 and 10:30 a.m. The sounds of lively and dignified worship rise up as the congregation joins in praise, prayer, scripture, sermon, special mission presentations, tithe offerings, and vigorous singing of hymns. There is strong, positive participation. A mix of classical and spiritual hymns lifts the worshippers, and great choral music from combined choirs (children, youth, young adult, and senior singers) gives voice to faith and thanksgiving to God. Tithing and generous giving are emphasized as acts of serving and worshipping God.

The sermon is an exposition of scripture and application to the challenges of contemporary life. Dr. Moss has emphasized preaching that touches the spirit, inspires commitment, engages the mind, and moves believers into action. His preaching nurtures worshippers intellectually and spiritually. It is faith seeking understanding in order to act constructively. An invitation to follow Christ and to make a faith commitment comes right after the sermon and puts the focus on all worshippers to renew their dedication as disciples of Jesus. In the service there are announcements of and invitations to participate in a wide variety of ministries taking place throughout the week. It is clear that there are many ways to actively worship and serve God beyond the sanctuary.

Olivet members move from worship into the community in programs of prison ministry, the eastside Hunger Center, a tutoring project with youth, work in the Habitat for Humanity housing program, senior citizen ministry, deaf ministry, Boy Scouts, Girl Scouts, staffing the O. M. Hoover Community Education Center, an active young adult group, and a large couples ministry with a marriage enrichment program. The church carries on an active visitation outreach among its senior members, shut-ins, and nursing home residents.

What We Can Learn

- Excellence in holistic health care can be achieved through the intelligent and dedicated effort of a congregation.
- Partnership between a congregation, a hospital, and a university can be a practical vehicle for a holistic approach to health care.
- A congregation with a positive understanding of the role of religion in good health can bring a vital dimension into the healing arts.
- As is often the case, a vision begins with one person — in this case, the pastor — and is transformed into a powerful reality as other leaders become involved and in turn draw a larger community into the process of living out the vision.
- In choosing to focus on a new type of holistic, faith-based health care program, the church went beyond the usual neighborhood clinic model to create a new model of excellence that deserves to be replicated in other cities.
- There is wisdom in limiting what a congregation seeks to do in order to gain a concentration of effort and resources on one central goal. This may be required for a congregation to move beyond low-level works of charity toward a more systematic approach to justice.
- Systemic justice requires engaging the larger institutions of society — in this case the health care industry, the university, and the city of Cleveland — in a process of structural change to gain a more permanent and equitable distribution of social goods and services.
- There is no substitute for a big vision that is compelling enough

to win the support and participation of those who can make it happen.

- Long-term, creative pastoral leadership is one of the keys to success in a large-scale project such as the medical center.
- Faith communities that have struggled to overcome the adversities of racial prejudice often have a special inner strength, which enables them to do great things beyond the ordinary.

Pilgrim Congregational Church

At the turn of the century (1890-1920), the Pilgrim Congregational Church was a wealthy silk-stocking congregation where industrialists, bankers, and business leaders worshipped together with some of their workers. The large stone church building with its beautiful sanctuary and great acoustics was the scene for Cleveland Symphony Orchestra performances. The church was the first building in the region to have electric lights (1893). The congregation viewed itself as progressive. The historic motto of the church was, "An Open Heart, an Open Mind, and an Open Door." The Women's Suffrage Movement found leaders and many participants in the congregation. Cleveland, in the late nineteenth century and early twentieth century, was a center for the steel industry and manufacturing. It attracted large numbers of immigrants from Eastern Europe who came to work in the steel mills and factories. The Pilgrim Church, following its progressive motto, created programs of social service for workers, including English language classes, a visiting nurse for children's health care, a physical fitness program, and a large Sunday school for children and youth.

After World War II, things began to change in Cleveland. The pace of change in the congregation and surrounding community escalated in the 1960s. The wealthy families moved out to newer areas. Many of their large, older homes were divided into multiple dwellings. The residents in the area became more racially diverse. Three major freeways were built in such a way as to carve up the area into a smaller, more restricted neighborhood. Church membership declined. The once proud church fell on difficult times with a reduced staff and congregation, decreased programs, and loss of connection to the community. By the early 1980s, the congregation was without a regular pastor and went through a ten-year period of being served by interim ministers.

By 1990, the surrounding neighborhood was very racially and socioeconomically diverse. The number of Hispanic and African-American families was increasing. There were young families with children concerned about the public schools, senior citizens holding on to their older homes and concerned about safety in the neighborhood, and young adult professionals coming in to remodel some of the homes as an investment in real estate. The upper middle class that had peopled the church for decades was gone.

In addition to Pilgrim Church, there were seven Roman Catholic and three Orthodox churches in the area, serving Greek, Polish, Ukrainian, Slovakian, and Hispanic people. The growing Korean, African-American, and Appalachian communities were largely Protestant, the population most likely to be attracted to Pilgrim Church. By the early 1990s, the Tremont neighborhood was a rich diversity of about 25 percent Hispanic, 20 percent African American, 20 percent East European, 20 percent Appalachian, and 15 percent others.

Recovery and Redevelopment

In 1990, the church was successful in calling the Reverend Dr. Laurinda Hafner to be the pastor of the now greatly diminished congregation. She came to Pilgrim Church from the national staff of the United Church of Christ, which is headquartered in Cleveland. Hafner brought strong leadership, good organizational skills, and lively preaching to the church. She led the congregation in renewing its commitment to a progressive posture and to reopen ministry to the surrounding community. At the same time, her preaching and leadership attracted a wider range of people from the metropolitan Cleveland area.

The congregation, drawing on its love of music and desire to serve the community, launched parallel efforts for recovery and redevelopment. With a capital fund drive and hundreds of hours of volunteer work by many members, the church rebuilt its great organ, redecorated the sanctuary, and opened up the building for a whole series of community programs. In 1992, the rebuilt organ was dedicated. This effort sparked a renewal of the music program, with a new music director and an expansion of choral music. In 1994, the improvement of the sanctuary and chancel was completed. These physical changes enhanced the worship environment and supported the renewal of Sunday worship. Worship attendance increased with more people from the surrounding community coming, as well as others from the larger metropolitan area. Both groups were attracted to the worship and preaching, which affirmed the great themes of the Christian faith with an emphasis on issues of peace, justice, inclusiveness, and social responsibility.

Worship was made more user-friendly for children and families. Many of the neighborhood children came to the church on Sunday without their parents, and often without breakfast. As a welcoming effort, the church provided Sunday breakfast for them before the worship service. Children's bulletins and a Worship Friends Mentoring program, which paired adults with the children for worship guidance, was introduced. The Sunday church school was reorganized, modernized, and integrated with the worship service so that children could participate in both education and worship. Large-print bulletins and hearing aids for senior citizen members, and others in need of such devices, were put in place. Worshippers were invited to pray the Lord's Prayer in the language of their choice. Once a month the Gospel Choir provided the special music. The service now included extended time for welcoming newcomers and personal interaction among worshippers. The young, the old, and those in-between were coming in increasing numbers. All were made to feel welcome.

As the congregation opened its building to the community for weekday programs, it became more diverse and inclusive, which in turn helped strengthen its commitment to social justice. This commitment included voting to be an open and affirming church of the United Church of Christ denomination, welcoming gay and lesbian Christians into every aspect of fellowship. The church mission statement indicates that "Pilgrim Church seeks justice in many areas: racial, social, economic, and ecological. We celebrate the multiracial, multicultural diversity of the human family while maintaining our oneness in Christ."

The Church as a Community Center

The Pilgrim Congregational Church has a large building that includes classrooms, recreational space, a fellowship hall, kitchen, gymnasium, meeting rooms, lounges, and offices. The church is blessed with an endowment accumulated in earlier decades, the income from which now helps maintain the building. Hafner has helped the congregation open up the church's spacious facilities to a number of community-based programs as well as for church-sponsored outreach activity, which brings people into the church building. She is assisted in this effort by the Reverend Craig Schaub, who was called to the church to help give leadership to educational, pastoral, and community ministries. Working together with church members, Hafner and Schaub have initiated or supported many new ventures within the church, including:

- parenting classes
- a preschool support program
- children's reading program
- after-school recreation program
- a tutoring program for elementary school children
- a Youth Ministry Council
- Sunday Breakfast Program for children
- theater performance groups
- jazz trio and art concert series
- a revitalized Sunday school
- children's music program
- Saturday field trips for youth
- youth basketball
- women's exercise class
- parish nurse — community health care
- Senior Citizen Called to Care Program
- Central America Interest Group
- women's and men's study groups
- Habitat for Humanity Project Council.

Once again the Pilgrim Congregational Church building has become a key center for community-creating services and educational activity.

Neighborhood Redevelopment as Ministry

The Pilgrim Church has asserted itself in the redevelopment that is taking place within the surrounding neighborhood. Returning to its long tradition of active social engagement, its members and staff are now involved in more than a dozen ways outside the church in the renewal of the neighborhood. Their involvement includes participation in the following activities:

- Tremont Community Forum on Safety
- Tremont Elementary School Tutoring Program
- Tremont Reads Literacy Campaign
- Habitat for Humanity housing construction
- Senior Citizen Housing Program
- Block Watch Street Safety Program
- Tremont Community Health Fair
- Tremont West Development Corporation
- Art Renaissance Tremont
- Local Hunger Relief Program
- Cooperation with Head Start School
- Merrick House Settlement — Day Nursery
- Annual Gay Pride Parade
- Annual AIDS Education Walk.

These groups and programs are vital strands in the social fabric of the Tremont neighborhood. The church is deeply involved in helping to strengthen these bonds of belonging and meaning. Leadership, promotion, financial support, and active volunteer participation in community redevelopment is understood as Christian ministry. "Pilgrim Church people feel the touch of God's love; blessed by that touch we endeavor to extend it to others,"[1] says Hafner. One of the important contributions to the community redevelopment has been encouraging church members to move back into the neighborhood. So far, a few members have moved back into the community and there will probably be more in the future.

1. Laurinda Hafner, "Pilgrim Church Lighting the Way," 1997.

Two Key Missions: Housing and Education

The decline of the Pilgrim Church in the previous decades was closely associated with the exodus of church families out to newer housing, and the deterioration of the older homes in the church's immediate neighborhood. The leadership at Pilgrim knows that much of its future is now related to the redevelopment of housing. Associate Pastor Craig Schaub indicates there is a tension in the community between the deep need for affordable housing for low-income families and the effort by young professionals to remodel the larger homes.[2] Renovation of older homes is often done as investment for economic gain. The trend toward neighborhood rehabilitation is reinforced by the growing development of restaurants and art galleries, which serve mainly young professionals from outside the community. The community is struggling to find a balance between the needs of lower-income and higher-income residents. Both are important to the future stability and economic development of the neighborhood.

How is the church responding to this key issue? Members and staff are involved in a number of projects that are constructive and which help the effort for more affordable housing. This includes engagement with Habitat for Humanity housing construction. The church is also involved in the Tremont Planning Forum and the Block Watch Safe Streets Program, which are initiatives aimed primarily at the needs and desires of the more affluent residents in the community.

The church supports Habitat for Humanity with financial gifts and volunteer workers. Habitat for Humanity is now starting to construct new low-cost homes with church sponsorship and participation. All of these efforts help to increase the supply of housing affordable to lower-income families, and improve the quality of life in the community. Moving on to the next stage of creating a substantial supply of more affordable housing units is the great challenge now facing the community and the church.

The second major arena in which the church has engaged the community is education. There are four public schools in the parish area — two elementary, one junior high, and one senior high school. The congregation has reached out in partnership with the Tremont

2. Craig Schaub, interview with author, 28 September 1997.

Elementary School. Members are involved with the school in a tutoring program focused on reading, which is a high priority. The Children's Reading Program gives special help to students, gets books into the students' homes for more reading, and helps parents get involved in encouraging their children to read. The emphasis on reading is reinforced in the church, where children from the neighborhood are engaged in the Sunday school, which also promotes reading.

The church is aggressively reaching out to neighborhood families with a children's music program, an after-school recreation program in the church gymnasium, the Sunday morning breakfast program, and the Sunday school. A special outreach effort is the new program of parenting education classes designed to help families with the nurture of elementary school children. The church has created a program for teens which offers an alternative to street life, including a peer support group, tutoring in school studies, after-school recreation, and a youth choir. There is also a scouting program in the church, and a summer softball program for teens.

One of the most creative efforts with teens is the Write Ways Program in writing. A number of young people have been gathered for an eight-week exploration of story writing. The focus is on writing stories about the local community. Field trips to learn about community issues and institutions provide the experiential basis for students to write stories. Volunteer mentors provide guidance in writing. Participants learn about careers in writing. The group meets and works on Saturdays at the church. At the conclusion of the two-month-long program the students select their best stories to be published in a city-wide youth newsletter.

The Pilgrim Church is an illustration of congregational redevelopment by gradual evolution. There is a slow but significant shift of balance. The majority of the present adult members live outside the church neighborhood. But almost all of the children, youth, and incoming families are from the surrounding neighborhood. The staff and lay leaders are building up relationships and creating trust through service to the people of the community. The future of the congregation and the nature of its ministry will be more and more in the hands of the local resident members in partnership with other members from the wider metropolitan area.

What We Can Learn

- Congregational redevelopment can be motivated by the selective and creative use of elements in its history and tradition to be a church that makes a positive stand for justice.
- A good church building with usable space can be a helpful asset for reengaging people from the community and renewing a congregation.
- Building trust, creating supportive community within the congregation, and providing pastoral care help to create the capacity to reach out to the neighborhood community and contribute to positive social change.
- Attracting members from both the immediate community and from the wider metropolitan area brings greater strength and more resources into the redevelopment of a church. The flow of community residents through the church building challenges the congregation to be more engaged in the needs of the neighborhood.
- Lively worship designed to meet the spiritual and cultural needs of diverse groups of people is crucial and is a difficult challenge.
- Strong, skilled, and entrepreneurial pastoral leadership is the key for long-term success in the redevelopment of a congregation.
- A financial endowment can be helpful in giving a congregation the opportunity for new life and a chance to serve the community. An endowment may also defer, or even prevent, fundamental change that is essential for long-term success.
- Moving beyond a service ministry toward systemic change and greater social justice is an ongoing struggle influenced by many factors, including history, tradition, cultural expectations, resources, leadership, and the sense of urgency.
- It is generally easier for churches to deal with personal, aesthetic, and cultural dimensions of life than to deal with socioeconomic and structural dimensions of life. Successful congregational redevelopment must deal positively with both internal church life and external dimensions of community institutions.
- Leadership by both clergy and laity is the key factor for influencing the degree to which a congregation can develop a mature ministry that both nurtures faith and engages the powers and principalities for systemic justice in the city.

Mount Auburn Presbyterian Church

Harold Gordon Porter

The Mount Auburn Presbyterian Church seeks to be a congregational model of diversity and inclusiveness. Just as importantly, it seeks to model theological pluralism within a Christian commitment. At Mount Auburn, to be fully accepted, a person's sexual orientation is irrelevant. It is a congregation neither gay nor straight, but one body in Christ. An egalitarian community beyond gender, it seeks to share the burdens and the blessings of life with no behavior held up for one that is not held up for all.

Since 1991, when it adopted and implemented "The Policy for the Inclusion of Gay and Lesbian Persons," this church has experienced a spiritual depth and richness of the Christian faith not previously known. What was surprising to everyone was that this new birth of the Spirit's embracing way, a revolution in relationships, came about without rancor, division, or significant loss of membership. Instead, love became more real, unity was strengthened, and membership has more than doubled.

The Mount Auburn congregation, one of the eighty-six in the Presbytery of Cincinnati, often felt alone in its journey toward social justice in matters of sexual orientation. Its policy of inclusion was

The Reverend Dr. Harold Gordon Porter is Pastor of Mount Auburn Presbyterian Church in Cincinnati. He is a member of the Executive Board of the Metropolitan Area Religious Coalition of Cincinnati, and a member of the Executive Committee of the More Light Church Network. He is a leader in ecumenical relations in Cincinnati.

overwhelmingly judged contrary to the standards of the Presbyterian denomination regarding gays and lesbians. However, in a denomination that still resists the full acceptance of non-heterosexual persons, Mount Auburn has become one of the denomination's most vital and joyous congregations.

The Historical Context

Mount Auburn had no special gifts to become an inclusive church. Its long history, typical of many Presbyterian churches, was of a healthy conservatism. It was progressive, but not radical in its Christian witness. In 1868, it was one of the first churches built up the hill from Cincinnati's densely populated riverfront basin. Organized in the suburbs (today it would be considered inner city), its first members built a beautiful sanctuary adorned with Tiffany windows, and provided it with a powerful pipe organ. The founders, and those who worshipped in the church on the hill for the first hundred years, were upper middle class.

After World War II, as the city expanded and people moved out to new suburbs, the church began to lose members. In the 1960s, with racial tensions high, "white flight" occurred in the immediate church neighborhood. There was some effort to welcome the incoming African-American people who moved into the neighborhood, and a number who joined at that time remain active today. But the future appeared bleak, and the leadership prepared to turn its large church plant over to the Presbytery for its headquarters, with the remaining members continuing only as a worshipping community. At the last minute this plan was discarded, even though by then only a few of the members lived in the Mount Auburn neighborhood. Over the next ten years from 1972 to 1982, during the ministry of the Reverend Laten Carter, the church was able to stabilize. The congregation decided to stay and create an appropriate ministry.

Other institutions in the area helped to stabilize the church. With the University of Cincinnati a few blocks away and nine major hospitals nearby, there were significant possibilities for ministry.

In 1983, when I was called to the church, there were 224 members on the rolls and far less than half of that number attending worship. The congregation had begun to wrestle with a new mission statement. Mount Auburn had two special assets at that time: (1) its beautiful sanctuary and large education building, and (2) an endowment of $700,000. But if the church was to survive, it was apparent that Mount Auburn needed to become more than a neighborhood church. The nearby Methodist, American Baptist, Episcopal, United Church of Christ, and two Roman Catholic Churches were all in great decline. Still, many in the congregation had the mindset to hold on to the status quo and were reluctant to risk any radical change.

Vision for Change

It is my belief that a pastor must not only have a vision of what a local church could do to foster and enlarge its ministry (given the congregation's gifts and location), but, more importantly, be the primary theologian-in-residence. By this I mean: the pastor is to think about anything and everything from a Christian perspective. Theological renewal was essential, and it became our priority as a way to serve the Realm of God for this world. We decided we must also move beyond the traditional theology that had dominated the church for over a century and had become too outdated to be compelling for people in our time and place.

We realized that the church, when it was most vital, was a countercultural agency with a love for the world. Its mission, as was Jesus', was to enlist itself in shaping the world with the unbounded love of God who is in the world, not out of it. "Being for the world and not against it" would be our agenda.

To accomplish this, a more progressive theology was needed — a theology that is open-ended. Theology needs to be open-ended because it is focused on God who is a living, creative, dynamic being, not captured by the scriptures or our historical creeds. "The Spirit flows free, high surging where it will," and we were ready to move with it.

Theology, Faith, Justice

We began with theology. The first focus was the profession of faith asked of all who joined Mount Auburn. We felt it necessary to move beyond what had become normative in the church, "Do you accept Jesus as your Lord and Savior?" At Mount Auburn we agreed to ask instead, "Will you serve God as revealed in the life and ministry of Jesus?" We wished to acknowledge that above all it is *God* we would serve — a theocentric creed — realizing, as Paul Tillich taught, that God is *more* than the God we worship!

Still, the compelling reference to God for us was the life and ministry of Jesus who differs from us in faithfulness, but not in human experience. We understood Jesus as the breakthrough in history, exemplifying most clearly the pure unbounded love of God for the whole world. He was essential to us, at the center of our faith, but knowing God was even greater than the reality and message of Jesus. God was in all things and all persons.

Two other guidelines were then agreed upon. Both were statements of a process rather than creedal affirmations:

- Faith is to be exposed to reason, and reason enlarged by faith.
- It is not a question for us *if* the church should be involved in the social, political, and economic orders of life, but only a question of *how*.

Thus the world became our parish, including, but not limited to, the neighborhood. We lifted up the two most spiritual concerns of the scripture — justice and love — which faith weds together. It seemed clear to us that Jesus himself judged scripture by the critique of Micah 6:8, that we are required to live achieving justice, applying love to all things, and walking in faith humbly before God.

Community Outreach Through Shared Space

We next applied our theological understanding to our building. Our large properties, with many unused spaces, would be used to serve as justice and well-being centers for our community as well as the world. Groups that needed a location to voice and implement such concerns were invited to be housed here. During the next decade the following groups had their offices at Mount Auburn Church:

- Nuclear FREEZE Campaign
- The League of Women Voters

- Amnesty International
- Center for Peace Education
- The American Civil Liberties Union
- University of Cincinnati Child Care Center
- Woman's City Club (a social justice advocacy group)
- Physicians for Social Responsibility
- Parents and Friends of Lesbians and Gays (P-FLAG)
- Family Care Network (a support group for families with premature babies)
- Cincinnati Youth Group (teenage lesbians and gays)
- Ecumenical Campus Ministries (University of Cincinnati).

By opening our space we attracted new members to our congregation who were justice-oriented. The congregation worked with and alongside community groups as well as developing its own stance, demonstrating openly for justice on many issues in our city and worldwide. When the nearby Planned Parenthood's building was firebombed and destroyed, we hosted the city's response to this tragedy. We continue to be the center in our city that celebrates procreative choice. Many other issues, demanding the attention of justice, drew our involvement.

Acknowledging our building as an integral part of our witness, we next began a building renovation campaign to make our buildings, with their six irregular levels, accessible to all. Beyond the funds raised in our campaign, "That All May Freely Enter," we spent a significant portion of our endowment. A result of making our plant fully handicap-accessible was a far greater use of our sanctuary. A later renovation of the chancel provided opportunity and space for a variety of new activities that the auditorium-type structure did not afford. Our buildings said, "Welcome to all!"

Open Communion and Inclusive Community

The next theological issue of renewal to occupy us was the meaning of Holy Communion. The table, with Jesus as its host, certainly had influenced our membership commitment and the inviting way we would use our facilities, but we needed to be clearer about this sacrament's unique and radical nature.

It became apparent to us that even the Presbyterian Church, with its broad and ecumenical invitation to the communion table, had still placed a "fence" around communion. In the Presbyterian Church, only believers are to be invited, and only "the baptized faithful" at that. It was, for many, a barrier to the grace it afforded. This seemed to us most inhospitable and contrary to Jesus' own table manners. He willingly dined with anyone. For our church to open its doors to all, but in the course of the service declare that we will now partake of this special meal, cautioning those present if they were not a believer to please refrain, seemed not only bad manners but contrary to Jesus' grand invitation. He, after all, is the host for the meal.

After this study, and declaring communion was to be open to all, the session decided in 1989 to send an overture to the Presbytery to amend the denomination's constitution, "to make it clear that all persons who are present when the Lord's Supper is celebrated are welcomed to participate in this meal, baptized or not, Christian or not, child or adult." This overture, which caused considerable debate, was narrowly defeated in the Presbytery of Cincinnati, with a vote of seventy-three in favor, ninety-six opposed. Nevertheless, Mount Auburn continues the practice and is in the process of improving the wording of the overture and resubmitting it to the Presbytery.

Our new policy, "A Table Set for All," became the central focus of our witness, bringing the richest experience of God's unbounded love, focusing clearly the ministry before us. The table at the center of our sanctuary became again what it originally was — the ultimate symbol of the Christian faith, the means to grace, a foretaste of the heavenly banquet. For some who had not previously felt Jesus' invitation was for them, it has led to baptism and church membership. But for all, it has meant they are welcomed, affirmed, and loved. We had come a long way in renewing our theological foundation. We would:

- celebrate open communion
- affirm the biblical witness that all persons are made in the image of God
- lift up Jesus' teaching that all are called, all are chosen
- be about love, but not at the expense of justice
- lift up compassion above the concern for purity
- seek to be an inclusive community.

131

Becoming More Inclusive: Justice and Sexual Orientation

From these understandings, our next policy development — "The Inclusion of Gays and Lesbians" — naturally followed. This policy, formulated in 1991, reads, in part:

> Acknowledging that the reality of prejudice in the church and society gives gay and lesbian persons reason for uncertainty as to their reception, we of the Mount Auburn Presbyterian Church wish to make clear our real and genuine welcome of all persons. We affirm that gay and lesbian persons are part of God's good creation and that they, no less than heterosexual persons, are meant to enjoy God's gifts of love, joy, and intimacy. All who seek and receive God's love are welcomed as full participants in the life and worship of Christ's church without having to deny or hide their sexual orientation. Therefore, we are gratefully open to the service and leadership of gay and lesbian persons including those called to ordained positions in our congregation.
>
> Our loving welcome is unconditional. We further affirm our commitment, along with the General Assembly of our church, to full civil rights and justice for all persons, regardless of sexual orientation, in society and in the church. We will continue to seek *more light* on the ways in which we can offer our support and our love to all the children of God.[1]

I had tears in my eyes as our Church and Society Committee first read these words to our session. I felt a sense of liberation from my own homophobia. It felt more honest to be in the Christian church.

The session approved the policy and went further to state that in contrast to the policy of the Presbyterian denomination, Mount Auburn Church would not abide by any rule in our denomination that abuses or demeans gay and lesbian persons or in any way treats them as less than heterosexual persons. Although our denomination had not made it explicit in its constitution, the "definitive guidance" promulgated in 1978 and affirmed to this day had declared gay and lesbian sexual behavior, regardless if it were mutual, faithful, and loving, to be sinful. The denomination permits homosexual persons to

1. "The Inclusion of Gays and Lesbians," a policy adopted by the session of Mount Auburn Presbyterian Church, Cincinnati, Ohio, on December 19, 1991, and reaffirmed every year thereafter.

132

be received as members in the church, but the denomination excludes them from leadership at any level.

At Mount Auburn we are convinced that this is an offense to the Christian gospel. For us there would be no compromise on this issue. We would identify with those treated as the least in our congregation and as outcasts in our society. We could not serve the unity of the church, even one so democratically constructed as the Presbyterian Church, at the expense of the gospel it is meant to serve. We clearly understood our policy would be perceived by the denomination as ecclesiastical disobedience, but we felt it was the denomination that had the faulty position. Even though we believed strongly in the polity of the Presbyterian Church and had no desire to leave it, we would not become anxious about our future in it. We knew that we must stand uncompromisingly with homosexual persons or they would not feel welcomed at our table. They would know that our invitation to find their place at our "Table Set for All" was only a hollow gesture.

Not surprisingly, we were first motivated to address this issue solely on the simple matter of justice, regardless of how comfortable we were with this minority's sexuality. When the denomination released its second and positive study of this matter, "The Human Sexuality Report of 1990," we did what all churches were asked to do. We studied it. Prior to our study and formulating our policy of inclusion, we were not even aware of any gay or lesbian persons in our congregation! But when we adopted our policy and published it extensively, making it clear that the table in the center of our sanctuary was truly open to all, members unashamedly began to share their family histories, telling of brothers, sisters, children, and other relatives and friends who were homosexual. They were simply overjoyed to feel the full embrace of a Christian congregation for those they truly loved.

We had come to the just and liberating position, so well summarized by the biblical scholar, L. William Countryman, in his book, *Dirt, Greed and Sex:*

> Homosexual orientation has been increasingly recognized in our time as a given of human sexuality. While most people feel some sexual attraction to members of both the same and opposite sex and, in the majority of these, attraction to the opposite sex dominates, there is a sizable minority for whom sexual attraction to persons of the same sex is a decisive shaping factor of their sexual

133

lives. It appears that this orientation is normally inalterable and that there is no strong internal reason for the homosexual person to wish to alter it. To deny an entire class of human beings the right, peaceably and without harming others, to pursue the kind of sexuality that corresponds to their nature is a perversion of the Gospel.[2]

Ecclesiastical Response

What, then, has been the consequence of our policy since it was fully implemented in 1992? Shortly thereafter, the Presbytery of Cincinnati found our policy to be "irregular." They ruled the session had made an erroneous decision. In effect, our policy was not Christian! The Presbytery's vote on November 10, 1992, was 162 to 75 against the policy of Mount Auburn Church. We were ordered to prayerfully reconsider it and to change it. We prayerfully did reconsider it, and unanimously reaffirmed it.

In reaction to our noncompliance, the Presbytery, on May 11, 1993, by a vote of ninety-five to ninety-four, approved an Administrative Commission "to inquire into and resolve" our alleged delinquency. Mount Auburn Church delayed the start of the Commission's study by appealing to the Synod, and then the General Assembly, that such an administrative commission was itself an irregular means of addressing our policy, preferring a judicial review process instead. The Synod and General Assembly sided with the Presbytery, stating that presbyteries have broad latitude as to when and why to establish such a commission to inquire into its churches. However, they stated that neither of these higher bodies decided for or against the substance of our policy, and also warned the Presbytery that any action brought against Mount Auburn might be grounds for Mount Auburn Church to register a complaint against the Presbytery.

The Administrative Commission did come to Mount Auburn, and for nearly a year fully investigated the pastor, session, and congregation. They found Mount Auburn to be a growing and unified congregation, much, I am sure, to the surprise of some members of the Commission and a majority of the Presbytery. The Commission fi-

2. L. William Countryman, *Dirt, Greed and Sex* (Philadelphia: Fortress Press, 1988), 244.

nally decided, "until the constitutional discrepancies [on this issue] are clearly resolved by the General Assembly, no disciplinary action be taken against the Mount Auburn Session and Pastor," and they added, "To take action at this time would destroy the spirit of a vital congregation that will not be moved from its position."[3]

As of this moment, even though the Presbytery still considers Mount Auburn "irregular and delinquent," and has ordered us to re-scind our policy, no ecclesiastical action against the church is presently occurring. Since the Commission's decision, two General Assemblies (1996 and 1997) have come and gone. While the denomination's original antigay policy is still intact and has been hardened, constitutional confusion over this issue remains. While some churches are still facing disciplinary action as to their inclusion policy, Mount Auburn continues even more aggressively to welcome gay and lesbian persons, and to ordain them as deacons and elders when elected by the congregation. We continue to perform same-sex covenant unions which, for us, have the same spiritual meaning as marriage.

An Ever-widening Inclusiveness

Mount Auburn realizes it is not alone in this struggle. In the Presbyterian denomination we are part of a growing number of churches (eighty-six churches at the time of this writing) that have developed similar inclusive policies of "welcoming all." In the Presbyterian denomination we are referred to as "More Light" congregations. There are also inclusive churches in other denominations. Let me list identifying names in other denominations:

"Reconciling Churches"	United Methodist
"Open and Affirming"	United Church of Christ
"Open and Affirming"	Disciples of Christ
"Reconciled in Christ"	Evangelical Lutheran
"Welcoming and Affirming"	American Baptist
"Supportive Churches"	Church of the Brethren
"Supportive Churches"	Mennonite Churches

3. Presbytery Commission, "Report of the Presbytery of Cincinnati Administrative Commission on Mount Auburn Presbyterian Church," 13 January 1996.

| "Affirming Churches" | United Church of Canada |
| "Integrity Churches" | Episcopal Church |

Also, there are groups in the Roman Catholic faith community called "Dignity."

I am sure the members in all of these churches have found, as we have, that it is a joy and a blessing to repent of judgmental exclusion. Such repentance occurs whenever hearts are warmed by the person of Jesus who has enabled love between men and women, women and women, and men and men. Once having become inclusive, these churches are not likely to decide again to become exclusive. They have experienced something similar to the Apostle Peter who repented from his conviction that gentiles were unclean and should be excluded. "God gave them the same gifts God gave us when we believed in the Lord Jesus Christ, who was I that I could hinder God" (Acts 11:17). This story in Acts, Chapter 11, reveals how the church has been struggling to become more inclusive since its earliest years.

What We Have Learned

There are continuing positive consequences from Mount Auburn's repentance and affirmation. *First*, there are healthy differences of opinion in our congregation, but no division. We lost only a few members since declaring that gay and lesbian persons are a part of God's good creation and that they, no less than heterosexual persons, are meant to enjoy God's gifts of love, joy, and intimacy. The congregation remains healthy and united and the rewards, more than we could have imagined, have been remarkable. Most evident has been the evangelistic vitality of this congregation. In the six years since adopting our policy our *average* attendance at worship has doubled, to over two hundred. We have received 223 new members since adopting our policy. Of those persons who have joined, approximately one-third are gay or lesbian. Unfortunately, while they are open to our congregation many still feel they must be closeted to their families and employers.

Second, we have learned that most gay and lesbian persons don't want to be part of a "gay" church. They prefer an inclusive and diverse church such as the Mount Auburn Presbyterian Church has declared itself to be. Simply because most denominations are closed to them, many gay and lesbian persons remain unchurched. Every week at Mount Auburn someone comes to my office to say, "I never thought I had a place in the church, nor have I thought I would seek membership, but here I am."

Third, the great gifts that this marginalized and abused community has brought to our congregation, especially their commitment to the Christian faith, has enriched us beyond measure. We are blessed indeed by those who come with their talents and life experiences from all levels of life's vocations. Several would be clergy, if permitted. Many are outstanding persons in business, university, and professions. Their skills and maturity have made this church much more effective in its community ministry.

I mention the facts regarding growth for one primary purpose. Most churches are simply afraid to openly embrace those of a different sexual orientation because they fear a split in the congregation or a loss of members. But it is a groundless fear. Familiarity with gay and lesbian persons brings the opposite of contempt. It can bring understanding and reconciliation. It is surprising how powerful the gospel of acceptance is when tried and experienced.

In his recent book, *Reclaiming the Church: Where the Mainline Churches Went Wrong and What to Do About It*, John Cobb, one of our country's most eminent Protestant theologians, describes a vital congregation as one that is culturally engaged with the most pressing issues demanding justice today.[4] Certainly one of the most prominent social justice issues before us today, as this twentieth century winds down, is the maltreatment of homosexual persons. For the church of Christ to support this prejudice is the sin. For the church to become truly inclusive is the future in Christ.

---

4. John B. Cobb, Jr., *Reclaiming the Church* (Louisville: Westminster John Knox Press, 1997), 3, 43.

The Episcopal Church
of the Messiah

The Messiah Church parish in northeast Detroit can be pictured in this way:

Neighborhoods declining, decaying, and dying;
Guns, street crime, crack cocaine, addiction;
Gangs, racial conflict, police brutality;
Pain, suffering, sickness, loss, fear;
Anger, rage, fire, violence, death;
People struggling to survive;

And

People opening up to:
Faith, hope, love, peace, justice;
Christian covenant, spirited worship;
Repentance, baptism, beloved community;
Neighborhood redevelopment and cooperation;
Housing Corporation, Harambee Service Corporation;
Indigenous leadership and racial integration;

And

Partnership, neighbors, churches, young and old, black and white together,
standing in solidarity for life and against the powers, principalities,
and forces of death.

This is the story of the resurrection of a small congregation and the redevelopment of a neighborhood on the near eastside of Detroit.[1] The church has a proud history extending back more than one hundred years. At its peak, in the 1920s, there were more than fifteen hundred communicant members. A large stone sanctuary and attached three-story parish education building give witness to the earlier large-scale operation of a once prosperous congregation. The decline of membership began in the late 1940s, and became rapid in the mid-1950s through the 1960s as families moved out to the new suburbs. The incoming population was largely African American.[2] The racial strife of 1967 in Detroit accelerated the trend. When the Reverend Ronald Spann was installed as rector of the Episcopal Church of the Messiah in 1971, it was a very small, struggling group of primarily white members in the midst of a predominantly African-American neighborhood in rapid decline.

Internal Renewal Begins

The early years, 1971 to 1977, according to Spann were absorbed in the recreating of the core group of the congregation as a charismatic community. Leadership roles, including oversight, presiding, administration, preaching, and teaching were understood as functions for which people were gifted by the Holy Spirit in the context of a community of support and accountability. In other words, the pastor shared all these functions with the lay leaders. A number of lay members left jobs to assume full-time and part-time roles at the church. Distinctions between clergy and laity were minimized. The charismatic theology of gifts for leadership given by the Holy Spirit prevailed. Leadership was shared and it developed out of relational, not hierarchical, sources.[3]

1. The author acknowledges helpful interviews with the Reverend Ronald Spann, rector of Church of the Messiah from 1971 to 1996, and with his successor, the Reverend Stephen Bartlett who is the current rector.
2. Vicki McLellan, ed., *Church of the Messiah: A History* (Detroit: Church of the Messiah, 1992), 2. This material is the source for the history that is summarized in this story.
3. Ronald Spann, "Theological Reflections on Priesthood" (unpublished paper, Church of the Messiah, 1992), 5.

Out of this intense spirituality came the formation of a residential covenant community. A number of households, including as many as seven extended family groupings all located close to the church, developed into a "Covenant Community." There was disciplined accountability, common economic life, consensus decision-making, and countercultural lifestyle. The fruit of this charismatic community included extended internal dialogue, theological study and reflection, common prayer, learning to live and work together, and a revitalized congregation. The programmatic expressions of ministry included lively, spirit-filled worship with a diversity of leadership; a new children's ministry of nurture and teaching; a counseling ministry (with training in Gestalt therapy and transactional analysis); the Learning Center (a small, private elementary school, 1973-1986); a day-care center and kindergarten (1969-1986); the Mustard Seed food buying cooperative (1973-1991); a liturgical dance ministry; and the Fisherfolk, a touring drama and music evangelistic team. Most of the energy in this period was focused inward on building up the body of the core community, meeting its needs, and giving expression to its talents and interests. The focus was on internal growth and spiritual life.

An important exception to that trend was the Learning Center School for grades one through six. Creating the school was a vital sign of new life in the community. Most of the students came from nonchurch families, including many single-parent families in the neighborhood. Jackie Spann served as the first principal for the school and, along with others, gave many years of skilled leadership. The Learning Center School met a real need in the neighborhood for good-quality education in a safe and positive environment. It nurtured several generations of young students, helping them get a positive start in their human development and basic skills for learning.

The Church Discovers the Wider World, 1976-1986

In this period there was a growing consciousness in the congregation that God's love manifested in Christ was not just for the church, but for the world — the whole wide world. In the late 1970s and early 1980s the profound issues of world hunger, the global arms race, and especially the growing antinuclear awareness came into focus along with concern for oppression and exploitation in developing nations.

An exploratory meeting at Messiah Church, featuring leadership by Jim Wallis of the Sojourners Community in Washington, D.C., John Perkins from the Voice of Calvary in Jackson, Mississippi, and Graham Pulkingham of the Church of the Redeemer, Houston, Texas, turned the Messiah leadership toward a more politically and socially active model for church life. Members of Messiah began active participation in the peace and antinuclear movements. Social justice concerns became more prominent in worship and community dialogue. Church members participated in protest actions at large companies in Michigan that manufactured parts for nuclear weapons, including the Bendix Corporation, Williams International, and Vought Avionics. They were part of a Memorial Day action at the Selfridge Air Force Base in northern Michigan, protesting against air-launched nuclear weapons.

In the early 1980s there was a growing sense of the linkage between U.S. militarism, the arms race, and oppression in other countries. This led some members to participate in Witness for Peace trips to Nicaragua, Nigeria, and South Africa. The U.S.-backed Contra War in Nicaragua and the struggle for freedom in South Africa became significant issues for study, prayer, and action. These commitments led members to participate in a variety of interfaith coalitions for peace and justice. This was also a time when the issues of gender, race, and class emerged. The prevailing patterns of the leadership oligarchy — mostly white men — were challenged and changed, beginning in the 1970s. Women and African Americans rose up to new positions of leadership and authority in Messiah Church in the 1980s.

In 1977-78, a series of events took place that would, some years later, become a powerful influence for shaping the ministry for justice in the neighborhood. A five-story, twenty-four unit apartment building across the street from the church was a deteriorating property. During the winter a fire seriously damaged the building. The church responded by providing food, clothing, and temporary shelter for residents of the building. These acts of compassion led to further engagement with the need for decent, affordable housing in the area. The congregation decided to buy the apartment building and renovate it. In April of 1978, the Messiah Housing Corporation was formed and chartered by the state of Michigan as a nonprofit organization. The old apartment building was purchased on a land contract, renovated, and reopened for neighborhood people and some church families. The renewed building was named the Mustard Tree. Its renovation involved lots of volunteer work by church members and by the Work Crew, which employed the local neighborhood people. The fifteen-year land contract was paid off in three years — a real victory.

Justice in the Neighborhood

The new housing corporation soon became aware that the trend toward gentrification happening in many major cities could take place in the area around Messiah Church in the previously affluent Island View Neighborhood along Grand Boulevard. The board of the housing corporation decided to take initiatives to develop affordable housing in the neighborhood as a matter of distributive justice. The corporation — a nonprofit 501-C-3 organization — began purchasing a number of large duplex houses, renovating them, and renting them to families at very affordable levels. Beginning in 1981, the housing corporation was able to secure N.O.F. (Neighborhood Opportunity Funds) from the city of Detroit to assist families in repairing and upgrading their homes in the neighborhood.

By the mid-1980s the housing corporation was gaining significant experience in buying, owning, maintaining, operating, and renting real estate. It was managing apartments, duplexes, single-family houses, assisting families in buying and renovating houses, organizing housing cooperatives, and fighting gentrification. All of this housing activity was connected to creating a positive human community in the neighborhood, combating racism, and living out the gospel of loving one's neighbor.

There was a variety of other church-based community ministry engaged in knitting together the socioreligious fabric of the local "hood." A food pantry served more than 150 families, including senior citizens, with food deliveries and home nutrition assistance. A strong youth ministry flourished through the years with many forms and expressions: the Good News Club for teenage males in the neighborhood, Saturday basketball and Bible study, summer employment programs, conferences, retreats, service trips, and summer camp at Bair Lake, Michigan. There were scout troops, drama and dance groups, children's and youth choirs. Significant groups for women included Women's Outreach, for relationship building and communication; Women's Bible Study; and Wednesday night prayer meetings. A major commitment at Messiah Church over many years has been to deal constructively with racism. Conferences, study groups, dialogues, sermons, covenant group partnerships, shared community living arrangements, and African-American and Caucasian leaders/teachers in residence have helped with this ongoing struggle in the church and in the surrounding community. The personal lives of hundreds of people have been significantly touched by the racial dynamics at Messiah Church.

Messiah Housing Corporation

Perhaps the most visible and tangible accomplishment of the church during the last twenty years is in the area of creating affordable housing. The Mission Statement of the Church of the Messiah Housing Corporation (CMHC) says clearly what, in fact, has actually been done: "To purchase, rehabilitate, construct and manage housing for low-income families as part of a strategy to improve the overall quality of life in the community."[4] The CMHC was incorporated in 1978 to help address the serious problem of housing deterioration and the trend toward demolition, gentrification, and exploitation in the Island View neighborhood around Grand Boulevard on the lower eastside of Detroit. For a small church of fewer than two hundred members, the record is amazing.

- Over two hundred units of affordable housing have been created.
- Over four hundred families have been served during a twenty-year period.
- Repair of over six hundred family dwellings has been facilitated.
- In 1978 the Mustard Tree apartment building, with twenty-four units, was purchased and rehabilitated into a low-rent, self-managed cooperative. The cooperative has owned the building since 1984.

4. Church of the Messiah Housing Corporation, *A Progress Report*, November 1992, p. 1.

- In 1987 the St. Paul Manor apartment building, with thirty-six units, was purchased and remodeled into a low-rent cooperative for families with children.
- In 1991 the Kingston Arms apartment building was rehabilitated into twenty-four units of low-rent housing.
- In 1993 the renovation of the El Tovar apartment building (purchased in 1988) was completed, with seventy-two units of moderate-rent family housing.
- The Field Street Housing Development, newly constructed townhouses, provides forty-three units of rental housing for low-income families.
- Field Street Homes — seven older, family homes — have been rehabilitated.

In addition, much earlier — in the 1970s — the church renewed a number of duplex homes and single-family houses for the church members involved in the covenant community. These were all within several blocks of the church. The evolution has been from servicing the housing needs of middle-income, white, church families toward renovating existing apartments for low-income neighborhood residents, to new construction of affordable homes and townhouses for African-American families in the wider community.

The Housing Corporation has matured into a wide-ranging nonprofit organization that:

- owns property
- maintains property
- manages rental property
- trains and prepares families for home ownership
- trains and assists residents in forming cooperatives for self-management
- promotes, plans, and organizes collaborative, ecumenically-sponsored new housing
- shares its wide experience and expertise gained from two decades of development work with other housing projects.

The Housing Corporation is a major professional enterprise with a staff of twenty-two people. It has facilitated directly or indirectly over $20 million in housing development. In recent years it has reached out to other faith-based partners, including such groups as the St. Charles Catholic Church, Genesis Lutheran Church, and Trinity Deliverance Church to form collaborative ecumenical sponsorship for affordable housing. It has supervised funds from the city of Detroit for the repair of over six hundred homes in the wider community.

The Housing Corporation's Home Buyers Club helps aspiring homeowners to work out credit problems, prequalify them for mortgage loans, help connect them with lending institutions, and train them in home maintenance. All of this activity has contributed to making life in the neighborhood more humane and stable. The Housing Corporation was a charter member in creating the Christian Community Development Association in 1989. Its mission is to bring people together, from all across the nation, who are engaged in community redevelopment, to share experience and encourage the work of the Christian Community Development movement. Its focus is "the whole church applying the whole gospel of Jesus Christ to the whole person in communities of need."

One of the most important learnings modeled by the Housing Corporation is the strategy of finding and securing a wide variety of funding and technical resources in support of housing projects. This is the key to how a small church can do big things. Small amounts of original capital can leverage much larger loans and capital investments needed to produce good-quality housing at affordable levels. Some of these key resource partners include:

- the Enterprise Foundation, for technical assistance, seed money, and planning grants
- the National Congress for Community Economic Development, a network for sharing expertise and technical assistance
- the U.S. Housing and Urban Development Department, which provides grants for affordable housing efforts
- banks, large and small — the federal Community Reinvestment Act puts banks into active efforts to educate community groups about development of housing
- World Vision International, which provides grants for church-based, collaborative community planning networks
- the Michigan Neighborhood Development Association, which provides planning consultation, technical assistance, and resource information.

Of course, the housing and redevelopment program is all about much more than bricks and mortar. It is all about empowering disenfranchised people, building community spirit, and creating the conditions in which the human spirit can thrive. It is about transformation.

These major accomplishments in creating good housing and community redevelopment came about at a human price. There was struggle. There was resistance, anger, and conflict. There was racial tension and trouble. There were differing views of development and competition for leadership and control. There was even the murder of a deeply committed leader in the cooperative movement. These are things that can happen in the struggle for distributive justice. It is not a Sunday school picnic. It is life in its fullest complexity.

Reflecting back over the past twenty years, Becki Bishop wrote, "In many ways Church of the Messiah is a completely different parish than it was twenty years ago. Our faces have changed, our living situations have changed, even our language has changed. . . . What is present now has grown out of our past and is very much a part of the early vision (1970s) of living out the gospel and being reconciled to one another. What was once a largely white middle-class congregation of 'imported' suburbanites has now become a racially mixed church whose members mostly live in the surrounding Island View neighborhood."[5]

Now, ninety percent of the church members live within walking distance of the church. About eighty percent are African American and so is the leadership in the congregation. Ron Spann ended his long pastorate at Messiah in 1996. He had written these words earlier: "We are called to become an indigenous church and we must produce a new complement of indigenous leaders who will continue the journey."[6] The journey has come full circle. The people of the neighborhood are now the people of the church. And the church is everywhere present in the neighborhood. The journey goes on.

5. McLellan, *Church of the Messiah*, 30.
6. Spann, "Theological Reflections," 8.

What We Can Learn

- Moving outside itself to engage the public sector can be a source of stimulation for inner strength in a congregation. Such public engagement brings both pain and purposeful action.
- Creating affordable housing in communities of great need is evangelism. It is doing the work of living the gospel.
- Worship can be greatly enriched by reports from members of the ongoing struggle to be faithful in the public sector. It can make prayer, preaching, and giving go beyond generalities to specifics.
- Engaging people of different racial, ethnic, and socioeconomic backgrounds, listening to and learning from them can help a congregation move beyond preoccupation with private life and parochial concerns.
- Action that begins as a compassionate response to an urgent human need can mature into a sustained, systemic effort to root out the causes and change the conditions which give rise to human suffering and injustice.
- A congregation that becomes involved in substantial creation of affordable housing will encounter resistance from government agencies, vested real estate interests, and community power brokers. Affordable housing always comes at a human cost. Conflict, struggle, and sacrifice are involved.
- Developing property, securing financing, and serving a diverse public sector demands long-term commitment, professional skill, patience, tolerance, and a profound understanding of human nature.
- Creating racial justice in a congregation and a community is a difficult, painful, and intense struggle and is rarely achieved, although the commitment and effort are necessary and worthwhile.
- Renewing a congregation and redeveloping a community always extracts a human price. People burn out. People divide in anger. People leave. Sometimes people die. Wherever profound challenge occurs, conflict and struggle will be part of the process.
- Christian faith and worship in a community can provide the resources and support that enable people to deal with, live through, and emerge triumphant from the stresses and strains of deep change.

- In fact, the faith of Christians and the strength of the church probably are at their best only when challenged by the pain, suffering, and struggle of life.
- After Good Friday comes Easter Sunday. Thanks be to God who gives us the victory.

St. Andrew–Redeemer Lutheran Church

St. Michael and All Angels' Day, September 29, 1982, Pastor Bill Hopper had just finished a morning prayer service. He went out the front door of the church, slammed it shut to make sure it locked — and the forty-foot-high domed ceiling of the seventy-five-year-old building collapsed! In seconds the entire first floor was reduced to a pile of rubble. The old dome, weakened by years of water damage, fell in and pulled the remaining cement plaster corners with it, smashing everything below. The Detroit Fire Department, the City Building Department, and the Lutheran bishop came, and all proclaimed, "The building is a total loss." Death had occurred. The miracle of resurrection was about to begin, but at that moment no one knew it.

The St. Andrew–Redeemer Lutheran Church is the result of a merger of two congregations in the mid-1960s, one an ethnic German congregation and the other a more racially mixed congregation of both Germans and African Americans. By 1982, St. Andrew–Redeemer was a predominantly African-American church. Located in an older residential neighborhood on the west side of Detroit, the small church of about 125 adult members was struggling to create a ministry within an area that changed greatly after the 1967 riots in Detroit. The collapse of the church building seemed to bring a death blow. But there were strong and determined spirits within this congregation that, when challenged by overwhelming adversity, would rise up to meet the challenge.

At the time the old sanctuary collapsed, the young pastor had served for only about one year. "We were creating a youth program, ministering to about 150 children in the summer, and operating a soup kitchen for the neighborhood where unemployment was very high."[1] The building crisis was a wake-up call for the congregation. They wanted to rebuild, but they did not know if they could do it. There were only four families in the congregation who had regular, full-time employment and a stable income. The company that had insured the old building did not want to pay. The insurance company claimed the collapse was due to time and deterioration of the old building. The national church had no funds available for construction.

Victory Out of Disaster

There was some "good news." When the insurance company refused to pay the claim, the congregation got angry. There was a resolve to respond. People said, "We are not going to let this big insurance company take our life away." An Episcopal lawyer, Tim Whittlinger, came to the aid of the congregation and a lawsuit was filed in federal court, contesting the insurance company's decision. The process dragged on more than a year.

Meanwhile, a number of other, larger city and suburban Lutheran churches began to review their insurance and to reconsider whether to continue their building insurance with the company refusing to pay this claim. Finally the insurance company decided to make a settlement, which consisted of a substantial cash payment plus a large tent that the congregation would use in the warmer months of the year for worship and program. It was a major victory widely celebrated in the neighborhood and among allied churches that had supported the claim against the insurance company.

After nearly three years of interim arrangements in a community center building and in the summer tent, the congregation's "pilgrimage in the wilderness" came to an end. A new building was dedicated on the second Sunday of the Easter season, 1985. There were over 350 people in attendance. The stone had been rolled away from the tomb and resurrection was taking place. The new church building

1. William Hopper, interview with author, 9 April 1997.

was designed as a rectangular structure of three thousand square feet. About half of the space was designed to be a worship area and the other half as a multipurpose community center facility.

The congregation had learned a lot through its immersion in the challenge of real estate, building construction, financing, and creating credibility. With good management of the financial resources from the insurance settlement and with careful planning of a functional new building, the congregation opened its new facility without debt.

Before the campaign to rebuild, the congregation was planning to get involved in redeveloping residential housing in the neighborhood. After the rebuilding campaign the congregation shifted its attention to a more urgent problem, which was unemployment of more than seventy-five percent in the neighborhood. The new vision was a sense of calling to engage in economic development to create jobs. Without some form of stable employment there could be little hope for renewal of the community or the congregation. An advisory board was created with membership from the church and from partner churches who were owners and leaders of businesses. The need for job creation was identified as the number one priority. A search for ways to develop new jobs was launched. Then a funny thing happened on the way to economic development — a long but profitable detour — that helped to create the foundation for eventual employment opportunity.

Refugee Resettlement

During the struggle to construct the new church building, a number of partnerships were formed with suburban Lutheran congregations. One of those suburban churches "suggested" that St. Andrew–Redeemer Lutheran Church adopt a Laotian refugee family. (Lutheran Immigration and Refugee Services was encouraging churches to sponsor Laotian refugee families.) That church indicated that they could provide financial and technical support, but they thought the refugee family would be more comfortable among the African-American people of the city rather than living in the suburb. The process of creating hospitality began. At first it did not go well. Some members of the congregation wondered how they were going to provide for a refugee family when they already had severe economic problems of their own. To its credit, the church did agree to welcome the family and work out necessary arrangements. So the first Laotian family arrived.

Other Laotian Christians began attending St. Andrew–Redeemer. It was not long before one of the new members asked if the church would sponsor another group of family members who were still in a refugee camp and were facing the prospect of forced return to Vietnamese-controlled Laos and probably death. The St. Andrew–Redeemer Church accepted this new challenge. The second sponsored Laotian family came, and other Lutheran congregations joined in financially supporting the whole group. This pattern worked so well that a third wave of refugees were sponsored and relocated. From this experience emerged a Laotian person of leadership ability, Khamnoy Chanthavong. She was hired as a lay minister and began teaching the pastor to speak the Lao language. The Laotian refugee project involved the pastor and lay minister traveling to refugee camps in Southeast Asia to assist in reuniting families. In Laos and Thailand the pastor sharpened his language skills. In all, seven extended families were eventually sponsored. This was a major victory and accomplishment for a small church.

The pastor and lay minister translated the Lutheran liturgy into the Lao language. The pattern of worship changed to reflect the changing makeup of the congregation. This Lutheran congregation had already adapted itself to the spirituality of its African-American members. Sunday morning worship included a gospel choir, hymns, and spirituals from the African-American community, and a time for testimony. The new church building was furnished with a baptismal pool as well as the traditional Lutheran font. Now, hymns were sung in both English and Laotian languages. A new, rich worship life emerged.

Economic Creativity

As the congregation grew in numbers and strength, the sense of urgency to create jobs greatly increased. The Laotian people brought a strong work ethic into the community. An Economic Development Corporation called ST.A.R. (acronym for St. Andrew–Redeemer) was formed as a "for-profit" venture.[2] In 1990, with help from several Lutheran partners, an abandoned commercial building just a block away from the church was purchased. The building had been sitting idle for nearly thirty years. Two people from outside the community gave crucial support through a financial gift to the newly formed development corporation. The commercial building was in a very bad state of repair, so the first challenge was to renovate it extensively.

Working with very little capital, ST.A.R. organized a volunteer effort based upon the "sweat equity" principle to repair the building. Persons who volunteered to work on the building renovation were given points. Records of hours worked were systematically kept. Those persons with the highest level of consistent work were given the first priority for the new jobs that were to be created in the building when it was finished. For more than two years the volunteers worked, installing a new roof, new plumbing, wiring, windows, doors, and heating.

A new business opportunity emerged with a company that manufactured cleaning supplies. The renovated facility would be used as a center for bottling cleaning fluids. Large drums, holding 275 gallons of cleaning fluid, were trucked in. A fluid filling machine was installed. Five people were put to work transferring cleaning fluids into gallon and quart containers. These containers were then packaged and shipped out. The Aid Association for Lutherans provided enough cash to purchase the fill machine and start up the packaging process. The new job-creating venture was launched in early 1993, and has continued.

The people who had put in the most work on renovating the commercial building got the first jobs. Khamnoy, the lay minister, was hired as the plant supervisor. Many partnerships with individuals, churches, and other organizations helped to give life to ST.A.R. The new economic activity proved to be a "star" in the neighborhood as it brought excitement, jobs, and income into an area where all were greatly needed.

ST.A.R. expanded its business when it began filling larger drums and totes (jugs with a handle) for its customers. Additional jobs became available when ST.A.R. began manufacturing ventilation filters

2. ST.A.R. Development Corporation, "Leading the Way in a Competitive Market Place," 1993.

for use in automobile factories. The corporation's annual gross income grew from $65,000 to $150,000 and then to $350,000. During the course of four years, over twenty-five people got jobs and earned much-needed income. All previously had no stable work. After getting a start at ST.A.R., most workers were able to move on to other, better-paying jobs.

Through the ST.A.R. enterprise much has been learned about operating a small business. Confidence and pride have been created. A working knowledge of business management, day-to-day operation, technical skills, and a sense of ownership have been developed. Above all, where there was no work, now there is real work. Where there was very little hope, now there is confidence. Where there was no economic activity, now there is actual economic development. Where there once were only four families in the entire congregation at St. Andrew–Redeemer who had jobs, now there is a growing number who have substantial and stable work.

Congregational Growth Through Struggle

The redevelopment of the St. Andrew–Redeemer Church has not been a quick or easy phenomenon. It has been going on for more than fifteen years. It is still going on today. There have been victories, and there have been defeats. A human price, as well as other costs, has been paid for this transformation.

The two major struggles — to rebuild the church sanctuary and to create jobs through ST.A.R. — have contributed to the inner strength of the congregation. There are other significant ministries of this church that have been motivated, initiated, and carried out with positive impact because the vision of the people was stretched through struggle.

The youth ministry is an ongoing collaborative effort of the pastor and people. It encourages and supports young men and women to get an education, to learn valuable skills, to experience the wider world beyond the neighborhood. Young people have taken leadership in helping the church set up and operate a computer system. They have been part of the outreach of the congregation to partner churches. They have helped to build bridges across racial divides, with people in the suburbs and in other Detroit churches.

The Community Center Ministry in the new church building has expanded. It is a significant source for social service help to people in the neighborhood. There is health screening and testing. There is counseling for HIV concerns. There is guidance in dealing with city and federal agencies. There is a Community Meals program which provides well-balanced meals three days per week to hundreds of people each month. More significantly, the church's Community Center is the meeting place for people to come together around a variety of personal and social concerns. It is a place of genuine hospitality in an area where that is in short supply.

The people of St. Andrew–Redeemer Church have given graciously of their friendship and spiritual partnership with numerous groups from many Lutheran and other churches in the region. Programs of shared worship and dialogue have created the way for interracial understanding and development of more mature Christian community among people of diverse backgrounds. These are valuable gifts which the congregation gives. The congregation has grown numerically and spiritually, but especially in confidence and leadership.

What We Can Learn

The process that began with the collapse of the old church building — a symbol of death — has brought resurrection and new life. The redeveloped congregation has created many substantial signs of new life:

- The congregation has grown numerically and spiritually.
- A rich worship life now includes elements from three cultures — African American, Laotian, and German.
- Church members have become financial givers and good stewards for the life and work of the congregation.
- The African-American, Laotian, and Caucasian members have come to accept their cultural differences and have developed a working partnership with each other in the congregation and the community.
- The pastor, who is Caucasian, has been accepted as a friend, coworker, and leader by the congregation, which is predominantly African American and Laotian.
- Twenty-five persons gained jobs and significant work experience

at ST.A.R., with many able to move on to even better-paying jobs.

- Many people learned how to enter the economic life of the city and become self-supporting.
- Seven extended Laotian families, who were resettled in Detroit, learned to survive and thrive in the urban culture.
- The congregation as a whole was able to move beyond being a welfare church through self-sustaining economic enterprise, and gain a new sense of identity.
- New leadership emerged. Some older leaders of a different mind-set stepped aside. New lay leadership has taken hold in every aspect of the life of the congregation.
- The focus is now on people maturing in the church and society. Inward spiritual life and outward economic development are understood to be inseparable and interdependent.
- The great value of long pastoral tenure is illustrated in the ministry of Bill Hopper (twenty years) at St. Andrew–Redeemer Church.
- At St. Andrew–Redeemer Lutheran Church there now is a pervasive realization that life together can become the community through which God's spirit works to transform both persons and institutions. In the words of Bill Hopper, "Life is a transforming journey. Different streams of people come together, flowing for a time in one direction, then diverging and going separate ways so that others may enter the stream to continue the common effort."[3]

3. Hopper, interview.

The Church of St. Edmund (Episcopal)

African-American community redevelopment does not begin with an analysis of problems and pathology; it begins with the positive, prophetic imperative, "Let justice roll down like a mighty river and righteousness like a neverending stream." This is the belief and working faith of the Reverend Dr. Richard Tolliver, the rector of St. Edmund's Church since 1989. He has led the congregation in a nonstop campaign of church renewal and community redevelopment which some call the "miracle in Washington Park." Since 1990 church membership has doubled from four hundred to over eight hundred; a church-sponsored community school — St. Edmund's Academy — has been opened; a new community development corporation has been created to rehab and/or construct 193 units of affordable housing (a $20 million project) with 207 more units in the planning stages; a safe-streets community organization and a Community Alternative Policing Strategy (CAPS) program have been launched to draw families back into the neighborhood.[1]

The spark that ignites all of this positive progress comes from fifty-two-year-old Richard Tolliver, Episcopal priest, former Peace Corps director in Africa, and former professor at Howard University in Washington, D.C. He served in Episcopal parishes in Boston, New York City, and Washington, D.C., before coming to Chicago. The

---

1. Ron Stodgill, "Bringing Hope Back to the 'Hood'," *Business Week* (19 August 1996): 70-73.

Washington Park neighborhood, located southwest of the well-known Hyde Park (University of Chicago) area on Chicago's South Side is a devastated war zone. It has lost more than two-thirds of its population since the 1970s (down from ninety thousand in 1970 to nineteen thousand in 1990), has five of the lowest achieving public schools in the city, and nearly half the housing is boarded up, burned out, or demolished. Over sixty percent of the population live at or below the poverty line. In the midst of this decay, decline, and devastation the St. Edmund's Episcopal Church has come back strong from its own low ebb to be the catalyst for the redevelopment of the surrounding community in the 1990s.

"It begins with a faith-based community and the church's commitment to invest its human and financial resources," says Tolliver. He outlines the faith that comes from within the African-American church tradition and provides the bedrock for renewal and redevelopment:[2]

- the Judeo-Christian prophetic call for justice
- the cooperative self-help economics of African culture
- the liberation of human spirit, mind, and body from oppression.

From this faith comes a sense of calling to engage in the systemic struggles of Christian community development which, according to Tolliver, include:

- affordable housing
- quality education
- economic opportunity
- safe and secure community.

The African-American church, because of its unique history, has the vision and vitality to minister to the mind, body, and spirit in a holistic approach. This approach is now especially needed in an era of government budget cutting and pullbacks of funding for public services.

In the 1950s, this historic African-American congregation had over two thousand members. It was the elite church for upper-

2. Richard L. Tolliver, Rector of St. Edmund's Episcopal Church, interview with author, Chicago, 5 March 1998.

middle-class black business and professional people, drawing members from all over Chicago and the suburbs. The social turbulence of the 1960s changed all that, and put the church into decline as the neighborhood fell victim to population flight. When Tolliver arrived, the church was only a few years away from closing. There had been discussion of selling the building, which was in disrepair, the congregation was aging, and the school was closed. The community was in deep decline.

Father Tolliver led the congregation in cleaning up the church building, repairing and refurbishing the sanctuary, and restoring the historic structure. A wonderful set of thirty-three new stained glass windows was installed. They show the great leaders in African-American religion and culture, including such notables as Crispus Attucks, Harriet Tubman, Sojourner Truth, Thurgood Marshall, and Nelson Mandela, along with black religious figures St. Augustine, St. Cyprian, Archbishop Desmond Tutu, Martin Luther King, Jr., and Bishop Barbara Harris. The sunlight showing through these thirty-three colorful windows in the upper walls of the sanctuary fills the worship space with the warm and powerful spirit of a great crowd of witnesses, heroes, and martyrs from black history. Their spirit is alive in this congregation.

Community Begins in Worship

Two Sunday masses, at 8:00 a.m. and 10:30 a.m., engage the congregation in the high Anglican tradition of Eucharistic liturgy. A well-rehearsed choir with top-flight, professional direction leads the congregation in singing the prayers and responses. The *Episcopal Book of Common Prayer* is used. The prelude and postlude are Bach. The spirited congregational singing combines hymns from the African-American hymnal, *Lift Every Voice and Sing*, and from the 1982 Episcopal hymnal (both hymnals are produced by the Episcopal Church). The anthem is gospel music, e.g., *Every Time I Feel the Spirit*. Preaching is skillfully crafted and polished to engage the mind and the spirit. It applies the meaning of biblical text to the particular challenges facing the congregation in their setting. There is a positive dignity in the worship. The best of the rich Episcopal tradition is present and celebrated. The best of African-American religious culture is integrated into the liturgy. There is Bach and there is gospel music. There is Episcopal order and African-American spirit.

The Sanctus and Benedictus are sung and the Nicene Creed is affirmed. Following the Prayers of the People there is the passing of the Peace of Christ with person-to-person interaction. There is also the *Agenda for Action*, which brings the struggle for justice and the life of the community into the worship of the congregation. The action agenda is followed by the offering, which is a vital expression of members' commitment. Beyond supporting a growing operating budget, the congregation has given nearly a million dollars to repair and refurbish the church and to reopen the St. Edmund's Academy school building. Worship concludes with the celebration of the Eucharist. It brings people together in the sacrament of communion, and then sends them forth with a charge and blessing. Worship is clearly the spiritually energizing center of the congregation's ministry. It is the dynamic that bonds the people and empowers the program for community redevelopment. Most of the worship participants come from outside the local community. This is beginning to change as local families are drawn into the support of the new church-sponsored school and neighborhood programs. New members are received every month in a special, incorporating communion service. The church is growing. It does many of the things you would expect a congregation of eight hundred to do, including: a positive program of adult Christian education, children and youth programs, special choirs, a men's club, women's guilds, a thrift shop, mission study projects, Boy and Girl Scout troops, Advent and Lenten speakers, special fundraising events, and more.

Rebuilding Community

The church does a lot of things that most churches do *not* do, and that is the focus of our story. There are political candidate forums for city council elections. There are meetings in the church with the Chicago Commissioner of Housing. Father Tolliver is a recent appointee to a new City Housing Advisory Task Force that will make recommendations for a five-year affordable housing plan for Chicago. The church has helped to promote and organize block clubs in the neighborhood, and they meet in the church. The local Community Alternative Policing Strategy (CAPS) group meets in the church. They collaborate with the police to improve safety in the neighborhood and reduce street crime, which is down by fifteen percent since 1993. The heart of the neighborhood renewal is the St. Edmund's Redevelopment Corporation (SERC) which operates out of an office in the church parish house with a staff of four, and a hands-on, policy-making board of directors of eight. SERC is where the "miracle in Washington Park" neighborhood comes together. Here is where the St. Edmund's Church story is different from most other church redevelopment stories. The pastor is president of the board of SERC and the chief executive officer. He is a hands-on leader with the following guiding principles:

- The inner city must be saved block by block.
- There is no quick fix. Redevelopment takes a long-term commitment.
- Successful redevelopment needs a mix of working-class and middle-class families, which bring to the community a strong work ethic, stable incomes, and role models for youth.
- The church as the only remaining stable institution in the neighborhood must lead in recreating the social fabric necessary for community.
- Partnerships with public and private sector organizations must be formed to gain the human and financial resources needed for redevelopment.
- The federal Low Income Housing Tax Credit Program is one key financial resource that can help to leverage larger funding needed for rebuilding.

This approach has enabled the St. Edmund's Redevelopment Corporation to create an extraordinary amount of affordable housing in just eight years.[3]

1. Sixty-seven units in five older apartment buildings, all within three blocks of the church, were renovated for affordable housing at a cost of $6.2 million, using low-income housing tax cred-

---

3. Richard L. Tolliver, "The African American Parish and Economic Development," *Anglican Theological Review* (1996): 1-3.

its. The developments are called St. Edmund's Place, St. Edmund's Square, and St. Edmund's Corners. This was the first large-scale rehabilitation of buildings in the area, and it stimulated several other independent owners to do rehabbing of their buildings.

2. A new 61-unit senior citizen apartment building, located one block from the church, was constructed for $5 million. St. Edmund's Tower is the first new apartment building in the Washington Park neighborhood in two decades. The $4.6 million in Section 202 funding came from HUD (U.S. Housing and Urban Development).

3. Six more apartment buildings in the neighborhood were purchased for renovation at an estimated total cost of $8 million, which will create sixty-five more units of affordable housing. The rehabilitation project, currently underway, is called St. Edmund's Plaza, and includes the renovation of a much-needed grocery store. This redevelopment illustrates the creative financial partnerships necessary to do large-scale rehab, including the National Equity Fund, the Local Initiatives Support Corporation (LISC), and the City of Chicago Empowerment Zone program.

4. Current negotiation is underway with the Chicago Housing Authority to purchase fifty-six townhouse, four-bedroom, family units owned by the city. SERC proposes to rehab the townhouses which are located directly across from the church, then lease twenty-five percent back to the city for low-income families, rent sixty percent to poor but working families, and rent twenty percent to middle-income families. Chicago Housing Authority Director Joseph Shuldiner has indicated, "This is the kind of new thing we want to do . . . we get better housing, an income mix, and we help to revitalize the community."

5. Two abandoned three-story apartment buildings with six units were purchased. Working with the city, a number of senior high school youth are employed to do the work of rehabilitation, under supervision, through the schools' skilled trade program. Called the Youth Build Initiative, youth learn on the job as paid workers, and help to rebuild the community.

6. The church purchased a thirty-unit building and applied for low-income housing tax credits for gutting and rehabilitating the entire apartment building.

7. Several vacant lots are currently being arranged for purchase to construct fifty-two new townhouses that will be rental homes.

The St. Edmund's Redevelopment Corporation Board of Directors insists that the general contractors it employs hire minority subcontractors and also hire neighborhood residents to work on the rehab projects. A constant stream of new jobs is generated in the community and a multimillion dollar cash flow comes into the neighborhood. The renewal of housing is the most important economic enterprise in Washington Park today. It is putting people to work, generating new economic assets, and improving the quality of life all at the same time. One of the positive values which comes from the church being the developer for housing is that the church is in this effort for the long-term. Tolliver indicates that the community is gradually coming to see that long-term commitment, after eight years, and as a result trust and hope are increasing. These are the precious intangible gains that are so necessary for successful community redevelopment. The church has taken another initiative to help heal the community and create confidence for the future. It has reopened its school.

Creating Educational Excellence

The new St. Edmund's Academy opened in 1994. Tolliver states emphatically that it is *not* a parochial school. The school is a day school separately incorporated, but sponsored by St. Edmund's Church. It teaches character values based on the Judeo-Christian tradition, including honesty, cooperation, responsibility, respect for others, hard work, self-discipline, and the pursuit of excellence. The children are invited to attend the church's Youth Service on each third Sunday of the month. There is a chaplain for the school who relates to the students. Now in its fourth full year, the academy has forty-five students enrolled in kindergarten through fourth grade. The plan is to add one class each year through the eighth grade. The headmistress of the academy is Gladys J. Ray, a former public school principal. The academy meets the school standards of the state of Illinois, and goes beyond in its pursuit of excellence. Classes are small and teaching is personalized. The staff is committed to creating a positive learning environment characterized by love, empathy, encouragement, and sensitivity to individual needs of students. The curriculum is enriched with instruction in Spanish language, a computer technology project, a new media center, and a strong emphasis on language arts, math, and science. In addition, the academy provides an after-school enrichment program. The students come from the neighborhood. Tuition is charged on a sliding scale, according to income. There are scholarships for all students. Actual cost per student is $6,500 per year; tuition is $3,200 in 1998. Every family pays something. The minimum tuition on the sliding scale is $1,100, but children who live in the neighborhood surrounding the church receive an automatic $500 tuition remission, which means they pay only $600 per year. The Redevelopment Corporation staff fundraiser invests part-time in seeking outside grants and gifts. The St. Edmund's Church has given over $400,000 to upgrade the academy building.[4]

The academy classrooms are light and bright. The walls and shelves have an abundance of visually stimulating materials. The school serves a hot, well-balanced noon meal. The nearby YMCA provides instruction in gymnastics and swimming. The Parents Association organizes volunteers to assist in the classrooms, help with lunch, and guide student field trips. Parent participation in the educational process is part of the academy philosophy. Parents are learning how to help their children learn at home and assist in creating a climate for educational excellence. Raising necessary funds is the academy's biggest challenge.

Is it appropriate to invest the money and human resources necessary to educate forty-five children when there are seven public elementary schools in the Washington Park area? Tolliver, the Redevelopment Corporation, and St. Edmund's Church all give a loud and clear "yes" response to the question for the following reasons:[5]

- Five of the seven public elementary schools are among the poorest performing schools in Chicago.
- The public school environment is negative, with drugs and surrounded by crime and violence.
- The St. Edmund's Academy students have high achievement,

4. Flynn Roberts, "After Seven Years St. Edmund's School Reopens," *Chicago Tribune*, 6 November 1995, section 2, p. 1.
5. Tolliver, interview.

receive individualized instruction, and are encouraged toward excellence.

- The St. Edmund's Academy students are learning positive social attitudes and a sense of responsibility to the community. Their school experience is part of the positive redevelopment of the neighborhood.
- The community is proud of the academy school and understands that it is part of their effort to rebuild the neighborhood.
- The academy has attracted many outside visitors, including Mayor Daley, the archbishop of Canterbury, South African Archbishop Desmond Tutu, U.S. Senator Carol Braun, and Martin Luther King III. These and other friends of the academy have helped to bring a stream of financial and human resources into the school and the neighborhood. Without the Academy none of these people or resources would be in the neighborhood.
- Without the academy, families with young children will not move back into the new and renovated housing in the neighborhood. They want a good school. To achieve a socioeconomic mix in the 193 units of rebuilt family housing there must be at least one very good elementary school. The St. Edmund's Academy is that school of excellence.

As Tolliver says, "It is a holistic approach that must include all the essential elements to make redevelopment a lasting accomplishment." Those elements include affordable housing, quality education, economic opportunity, and safe streets. In some of our urban neighborhoods only the church can make this happen.

What We Can Learn

- The church as a community developer brings certain advantages such as credibility, visibility, long-term commitment, and pastoral leadership.
- Redevelopment can be strengthened with mixed-income housing which helps to bring middle-class families back into the community. Their work ethic and social norms help create a stable neighborhood.
- Creating profitable long-term business relationships builds sus-

tainable economic enterprise, which is the material basis for re-development. In contrast charitable, do-good projects, such as soup kitchens, fail to create a lasting economic base necessary for redevelopment.

- It may be easier to create a nonprofit 501-C-3 redevelopment corporation when it is sponsored by a church in contrast to more complex community organizations which may operate more slowly. Having a clear value consensus among the core leadership may help speed up action and make for a more flexible posture.

- Forming the public-private sector partnerships necessary to secure capital funding for housing renovation may be easier when a church is at the center of the venture. Lending institutions and larger donors may prefer to deal with a redevelopment entity that is supported by a church in contrast to more complex organizations composed of competing interest groups.

- Redevelopment projects can produce income that can be put back into the community as investment capital to generate even more goods and services in the neighborhood. Rental income and management fees paid to the Redevelopment Corporation not only pay off mortgages but also can eventually become seed money for new development.

- One of the most important products generated by the church-based nonprofit redevelopment corporation is hope. Church-led redevelopment is in a strong position to create positive attitudes, build trust, bring credibility, and generate staying power. All of these intangibles can become the living substance of hope that is essential for lasting redevelopment.

- It takes lots of cash to do substantial housing redevelopment. A wide variety of sources are necessary. The use of low-income housing tax credits as made available through a syndicator such as the National Equity Fund corporation, an affiliate of the Local Initiatives Support Corporation, is one important source.

- Successful redevelopment projects use a variety of financial sources including tax credits, section 8 funding, section 202 senior housing funds, Enterprise Zone grants, bond issues, small business loans, foundation grants, denominational grants, celebrity donors, and local capital campaigns.

- Entrepreneurial ability, visionary leadership, and long-term pastoral commitment have all come together in the work of St. Edmund's Episcopal Church, St. Edmund's Redevelopment Corporation, and St. Edmund's Academy. The "miracle in Washington Park" is not a mystery. It is the result of long, persistent, skillful, hard work and the partnership of local people with key financial investors. The future is far from certain. There is, however, solid, creative accomplishment and real hope for a positive future in Washington Park.

St. Pius V Roman Catholic Church and the Pilsen Area Resurrection Project

Charles W. Dahm, O.P., with Nile Harper

Seven Roman Catholic parishes have been involved in community organizing in the Pilsen area of westside Chicago for many years. In 1994, they established the Resurrection Project, which together with the seven parishes has become a powerful force for redevelopment of the community. In this chapter, due to space limitations, we have focused on the community-organizing efforts of St. Pius V Church — the largest parish and one of the most active. The other six parishes have played important roles, provided leadership, community meeting space, and member participation in the Resurrection Project.

St. Pius V Roman Catholic Church

In 1874, Jesuit priests organized a new mission congregation on the western outskirts of Chicago to serve Irish immigrants. Many had left their homeland, pushed by the potato famines and pulled into what is now called the Pilsen area of Chicago by jobs opening up on the railroad, the Chicago Canal, and in local factories. The mission eventu-

The Reverend Dr. Charles W. Dahm, O.P. is the Pastor of St. Pius V Roman Catholic Church in Chicago. He has served as a pastor and teacher in Bolivia, South America. He is an author, teacher, and a member of the Board of Directors of The Resurrection Project, Inc. in the Pilsen area of Chicago. He served for a number of years on the staff of the Eight Day Center for Peace and Justice, located in Chicago.

ally became St. Pius V Roman Catholic Church, a territorial parish serving the Pilsen neighborhood. As other European immigrant groups arrived in the area, including German, Czech, Slovenian, Lithuanian, and Italian, additional ethnic churches were formed. Another wave of immigration swept into the area after World War II, bringing large numbers of Polish people. Thus, the Pilsen district has long been a port of entry. Although many of its residents remained in the neighborhood for long periods, others moved on to more affluent areas, making room for the latest newcomers.

In the late 1950s, the construction of new freeways through the area adjacent to Pilsen displaced many Mexican families who spilled into Pilsen to find new housing. In the early 1960s, the establishment of the University of Illinois's Chicago campus just north of Pilsen forced Mexican families to relocate. Hundreds of Mexican families poured into Pilsen. Many of the displaced Mexican people moved into the homes and apartments in the Pilsen area that were being vacated by other ethnic groups. The membership of churches in the area began to change. In 1963 the first Spanish-language Mass in the neighborhood was celebrated at St. Pius V Church. By 1974 the majority of its parishioners were Spanish-speaking, and the first Spanish-speaking pastor was appointed to the church.

When the Reverend Charles Dahm, O.P., the current pastor, began in 1986, over ninety percent of the members of St. Pius V Church were Hispanic. A new and different era of ethnic community was underway, bringing all the challenges that accompany a new group seeking to establish itself and its culture in the neighborhood institutions.

New Pastor Brings New Focus

Father Dahm brought a unique set of experiences to his service as pastor at St. Pius V Church. He is a native Chicagoan and a priest of the Dominican Order who served for five years in Bolivia, South America, where he became fluent in the Spanish language. There he gained experience in community organizing, creating Christian Base Communities, and developing programs for adult education. All these experiences occurred during the period of new openness following Vatican II. It was a time when liberation theology was developing and creating new ways of doing pastoral ministry among Catholics. The experience in Latin America motivated Dahm to pursue graduate studies in political science and earn a doctorate in that field at the University of Wisconsin. After his studies, which helped him understand the relationships of Christian theology and public policy in relation to oppressed people, Dahm cofounded and served for twelve years on the staff of the Eighth Day Center for Justice in Chicago. With this background he came to St. Pius V Church in the Pilsen neighborhood in 1986, at a time when the existing efforts in community organization were in need of new inspiration.

St. Pius V Church is a large congregation of more than 3,500 families. It operates a parochial school known for its excellence and community involvement. Approximately ninety percent of its members are of Mexican-American origin, and over fifty percent of the members are recent immigrants with great needs but limited expectations. Many Mexican people coming into the United States bring a number of religious and social norms that tend to prevent them from engaging in organized community action for justice.[1] These attitudes and beliefs include the following:

- *Suffering is good.* Suffering is an essential part of the Christian life by which the believer "pays" for sin and gains a higher place in heaven. Because Jesus suffered, we must also suffer.
- *The kingdom of God is in heaven.* Life on earth is a time of trial to prepare for the next life in heaven after death.
- *Politics is evil.* The organized use of power results in corruption, deception, and manipulation. Power is negative. It is used for oppression, not for justice.
- *We have no power to make a difference.* Centuries of oppression have created a consciousness of servitude, inferiority, and alienation from the processes of social change.
- *Life in the United States is far better than in Mexico.* Most immigrants achieve a higher standard of living in the United States than they had in their homeland. Even though they live in substandard housing, work at low-paying jobs, send children to overcrowded public schools, and are neglected by city government, their improved condition generates a certain level of satisfaction.

1. Charles Dahm, O.P., "Transforming the Neighborhood," in *A History of St. Pius V Roman Catholic Church* (unpublished MS., 1998), 2.

In contrast, Father Dahm taught an incarnational theology, which sees in Jesus an affirmation of human dignity, transformation, and struggle for justice. Jesus is understood as rejecting inequality between rich and poor; challenging unjust power; denouncing discrimination against women, foreigners, and outcasts; repudiating abusive treatment of the sick, the elderly, and the weak. The church, as the body of Christ, is the continuation of Christ's prophetic mission. Part of its calling is to expand in the world God's justice, peace, and love. Consequently, the church must challenge injustice, affirm human rights and responsibilities, and work to establish in society an order that builds up life in accord with God's creation. Pope Paul VI, in *Populorum Progressio*, called on Roman Catholics to take the initiative freely to infuse a Christian spirit into the mentality, customs, laws, and structures of the community in which they live.[2]

Organizing for Justice and Community

In the Pilsen area there is a long history of community organizing. In the 1960s the Pilsen Neighbors Community Council (PNCC) was formed to obtain greater accountability from government and business institutions for the common good of the community. During several decades this structure worked in connection with churches and other existing organizations to identify and train local leaders, gather local people to define common issues of concern, and organize groups to gain sufficient social and political power to accomplish selected goals. Several Pilsen area Catholic churches supported this movement in different degrees with membership dues, church member leaders, and meeting space for training and organizational assemblies. St. Pius V Church was the backbone of institutional support for this organizing effort. Some of the improvements secured through PNCC organizing were:[3]

- *A new, public high school.* Benito Juarez High School was constructed in Pilsen to serve with special sensitivity the needs of

2. Pope Paul VI, *Populorum Progressio*, cited by Dahm, "Transforming the Neighborhood," 2.
3. Dahm, "Transforming the Neighborhood," 8-9.

Hispanic students. The PNCC led the struggle to obtain land in the community and to garner city and state funding for the school.

- *A credit union.* Using some significant church-related political connections, the PNCC secured a federal grant of $280,000 to initiate a new community credit union to help local people buy and improve homes in the Pilsen area.
- *A Catholic Youth Center.* Working closely with the pastor and people of St. Pius V Church, the PNCC collaborated in the creation of a new Catholic youth center located immediately adjacent to the Benito Juarez High School.
- *A new city technical school.* A long effort of community education and political mobilization contributed to the decision of the city of Chicago to locate a new multimillion dollar technical training school on the west side of the Pilsen community. This new facility has enabled many people to develop skills needed in the Chicago job market.

These were great victories. It is impossible in this brief account to give adequate description of the great effort, energy, persistence, and resources that went into these struggles. A lot of conflict and pain was endured. A lot of sweat, blood, and tears was invested. As always is true, a human price was paid for these social gains. Part of the gain from these several decades of PNCC effort were valuable lessons learned by the churches about the limits of traditional organizing. The learning may be summarized in this way:

- A creative balance must be struck between organizing around self-interests and organizing to create a vibrant community that will last beyond the mobilization of the moment. Building a cohesive and informed community is ultimately more valuable than rebuilding physical structures.
- The churches need to assure that community leaders understand the way in which their faith must guide their leadership (the model of Jesus and justice). The ultimate goal is not power to accomplish social change, but a strong, ethical, Christian community that lives the values of God's kingdom.
- A theology of a Christian-based community must undergird and guide efforts to organize broad-based, representative democracy

as well as the sociopolitical understanding of how power can be developed and used to obtain social good.

- Local issues, such as the need for housing, education, employ-ment, and health care, although important and even urgent, must be viewed within a larger transcendent frame of reference that provides an ethical standard for guiding the process. This view puts checks and balances on power and limits the tendency to make the end (common good) justify unethical means.

- Churches that want to participate in doing substantial commu-nity organizing need to accept responsibility for educating their people to be prepared for the rough and tumble politics of social struggle, provide ongoing support, and be in close communica-tion with organizing leadership.

- Churches must become players in the action, not spectators on the sidelines; otherwise, they will lose their members because of burnout from intense community action, or because of unethi-cal conduct.

- Churches need to avoid creating a new political elite among those members active in community organizing. Christian for-mation for a healthy community means more than training a handful of strong leaders who can direct the community from on high. Rather, churches must develop a strategy for con-scientizing and involving the base, or grassroots.

A New Pattern Emerges

Discontent with the PNCC grew among pastors of the seven partici-pating Catholic parishes. Pastors observed that: (1) the paid profes-sional staff set direction for organizing; (2) the core leadership lost meaningful contact with the institutional base in the churches; (3) the mass membership was neglected and uninvolved; and (4) be-cause the organization developed independent sources of funding, it became less responsive to the interests and guidance of member churches.[4]

Pastors became increasingly convinced that the churches needed

4. Material in this section is summarized from the more comprehensive ac-count given by Dahm, "Transforming the Neighborhood," 11-15.

to be more directly engaged in community organizing, and in a manner that would be more reflective of their faith. In 1988, six Catholic parishes in Pilsen hired Mike Loftin, a professional organizer who had briefly worked for the PNCC. In consultation with pastors, church members, and community leaders, Loftin formed a new organization called the Catholic Community of Pilsen (CCP). Each pastor identified two church members to serve on the CCP Board of Directors to begin organizing work around the issues of housing, youth gangs, and community cleanup. A later attempt to broaden the membership of the organization to include some small Protestant churches and numerous Pentecostal churches was unsuccessful.

The new organization worked closely with the churches and pastors to build an informed, broad participant base. For example, in the Lenten season of 1990 it organized sixty small neighborhood groups that met in homes of residents once a week for four weeks. They focused on their experience with youth gang violence in light of biblical teachings about compassion and justice, and discussed possible solutions. At the conclusion of this effort a community assembly of over four hundred persons gathered at St. Pius V Church to meet with Chicago city officials from the Police Department, Departments of Housing and Buildings, and the Office of the State's Attorney General. A number of working, citizen committees formed to follow up with the city. There were specific results:

1. *Regular city garbage and trash pick-up was increased,* and periodic street sweeping was established.
2. *A comprehensive housing strategy* led to the construction of new homes and the purchase and rehab of older buildings to provide affordable rental units.
3. *Communication with police* led to the assignment of six additional police officers to the area to work with the community in order to crack down on drug traffic and street crime. This was a major victory.

The new movement was grounded in Christian faith. A series of training classes were developed and offered to a wide range of church participants. Father Dahm played a major role in the design of the new classes. The classes, taught in English and Spanish, focused on the prophetic teaching of Jesus, the role of the church in seeking justice, and the importance of building people power for justice. The training was given to all the lay members of the growing Christian Base Communities, not merely the leaders. The teaching methodology, based upon the empowerment model of Paulo Freire, described in his book, *Pedagogy of the Oppressed*, focuses on the people's experience and concerns instead of abstract ideas. It helps people identify, value, and analyze their own experience of oppression and learn how to develop solutions.[5] Further, it emphasizes that all the people are both learners and teachers. People learn from one another, not merely from authority figures. The focus is on building positive relationships of community and solidarity for power to challenge and change unjust conditions. With this spiritual nurture that produced indigenous leadership and a more informed base of community participation, the movement began to grow.

The Resurrection Project

In 1994, the leadership of the parishes decided to merge their relatively new community organization with their Pilsen Resurrection Development Corporation, which had existed for two years as a nonprofit entity for economic housing development. The new corporation was named The Resurrection Project (TRP). A local Pilsen resident and member of the St. Pius V Church, Raul Raymundo, was hired as the executive director. The Board of Directors for the new, combined organization reflected the base of support in the six local Catholic parishes in Pilsen, with representation from St. Adalbert, St. Procopius, St. Pius V, Holy Trinity, Providence of God, and St. Vitus Catholic churches. Later, St. Ann's Church joined the group. The support of the churches was crucial because they provided the constituency and base of power for the new organization. TRP has accomplished an outstanding series of community improvements in the decade of the 1990s.

5. Dahm, "Transforming the Neighborhood," 18-19.

A Decade of Community Redevelopment

The Resurrection Project's accomplishments are many and include projects in affordable housing, small business development, community education, child care, cultural programs, housing for seniors, a shelter for homeless women, community block clubs, and the development of sufficient political power to obtain needed resources for the community from city, state, and federal government entities. TRP has generated over $18 million in investment in Pilsen and currently is managing $25 million in construction, rental renovation, and facility development.[6]

Affordable Housing. Ninety-four new homes have been constructed. Over 150 apartments have been rehabilitated and rented at affordable rates. A three-story warehouse was converted into a twenty-five unit, rental apartment building — Casa Guerrero. One hundred nine families have been assisted in purchasing their own homes in the area. Over the last seven years TRP has made 187 loans for new homes, home repair, and conventional mortgages, and there have been no defaults. "We don't just build buildings, we create community," said Salvador Cervantes, a project organizer.

Construction Cooperative. Construction is now a growth industry in Pilsen. TRP has helped twenty-five local, minority contractors to form and develop their own businesses, as well as to organize the Resurrection Construction Cooperative. The Cooperative helps these local Hispanic contractors find jobs, access financial capital, estimate bids, establish accounting procedures, and work on larger jobs together. For example, several Co-op contractors recently remodeled a convent at Our Lady of Tepeyac Church into a clinic for St. Anthony Hospital. Hundreds of new construction jobs have been generated in Pilsen, with the number of businesses increasing each year.[7]

New community center. The centerpiece of The Resurrection Project is the successful conversion of the shuttered St. Vitus Catholic Church, rectory, and school into the Centro Familiar Guadalupano (a $1.2 million project), honoring the patron saint of Mexico — Our Lady

6. Susana Vasquez, Director of Resource Development, The Resurrection Project, interview with author, Chicago, 4 March 1998.

7. Dahm, "Resurrection Celebrates Construction Co-op," in *The Messenger of St. Pius V* 4:1 (Winter 1998): 3.

of Guadalupe. After the Chicago Archdiocese closed St. Vitus parish, and after the parishes negotiated two years with archdiocesan authorities, Joseph Cardinal Bernardin decided to sell the whole complex of buildings to TRP for a symbolic ten dollars. The school was renovated into a facility for a day-care and after-school program, serving over two hundred children. The former rectory was remodeled into office space for the growing staff of TRP. The former sanctuary has been turned into a community arts center with resident Latino theater, music, and dance companies performing and conducting classes for the community. The plaza in front of the community center is decorated with colorful murals depicting Mexican community culture.

Senior Housing. After years of poor maintenance, declining conditions, and rising crime, the senior residents of the 210-unit Las Americas apartment building (owned by the City of Chicago Housing Authority) were mobilized by TRP to seek change. TRP helped residents to study other senior housing and discover what was possible through better management. In just over one year of work, the seniors convinced the city to privatize the building management and maintenance, and then selected the management company, Habitat Uno, to clean up, repair, and manage the apartment complex. This was a major victory for the residents and TRP.

Supportive Housing for Battered Women (Casa Maria). TRP acquired a three-flat apartment building and completely renovated it into six living units, plus offices for staff, for a new transitional shelter for homeless women and children. Casa Maria established agreements with twenty-two local agencies to provide medical, legal, counseling, and job training services. This collaborative arrangement means that Casa Maria does not duplicate services. Women and their children are housed and assisted to become self-supporting and independent on their road to recovery and reentry into society. Currently, TRP is rehabbing a building three times the size of Casa Maria to create a new transitional shelter for women and children, Sor Juana, in the adjacent neighborhood of Little Village.

Community Block Clubs. TRP is committed to creating a healthy community. One of the key ingredients of this commitment is to facilitate associations of residents in block clubs. Over the past two years, eleven block clubs have been formed to strengthen the social fabric of the neighborhoods, sponsor cooperation with community policing, gather neighbors for social and cultural events, and unite residents for worship at mass on the street during the summer. These clubs are the building blocks of representative democracy and the underlying fabric of a better community. They help to instill in families a pride of ownership and property maintenance, and promote constant socialization, which encourages people to remain in the neighborhood.

Family Hope Project. A program of family education and development, based on the successful model developed at the St. Pius V parish, was adopted by TRP as a new project called Family Hope. The program provides a variety of faith-based, culturally sensitive courses to help families improve their communication and parenting skills. In the spring of 1998 these courses were offered in two more parishes and in a public school. The Jane Addams College of Social Work at the University of Illinois at Chicago supports the project with three graduate interns each semester to conduct research in the community and do outreach for the project. Family Hope casts rays of hope into the darkness of family disintegration.

New Opportunity on the Horizon

The University of Illinois is currently planning a major expansion of its west side Chicago campus into the area immediately adjacent to Pilsen. TRP is organizing local residents to respond to this development as a new opportunity for healthy growth rather than as a threat of displacement and gentrification. TRP has helped Pilsen residents become involved in the planning processes of the University in order to advocate for construction of more affordable housing, small business development for area merchants, educational and recreational programs for youth, and jobs for local workers and contractors. TRP has brought the Pilsen community to the point of confidence, skill, and experience in dealing with major government institutions. Now there is a well-trained and very knowledgeable cadre of leadership in the community that can engage the University of Illinois as a powerful partner to shape the planned expansion in such a way that the community, the university, and the city will all be winners. This emerging new engagement reflects TRP's mission of developing people to act from their faith and exercise their social power to bring new life into an older community.

TRP has developed a solid pattern for success. It gathers people through institutional memberships of the seven Catholic parishes and motivates them through their positive commitments of faith. It facilitates many local block clubs to build up the community social fabric, and reaches out to banks, businesses, foundations, and governmental agencies to form working partnerships. It creates affordable housing units and helps families to buy them. It strengthens local culture and family life by providing day care for children and education for the family; by working with abused and abandoned women; and by developing music, art, theater, and dance programs. And, finally, it prepares citizens who are proud of their community to deal effectively with the large institutions that shape urban life.

The Resurrection Project as an effective organization is an amazing story. In less than a decade it has grown into a broad-based entity which in 1998 has a paid staff of twenty-five persons and an operating budget of $1.3 million.[8] Fifty-one percent of its budget comes from fundraising gifts and grants from foundations, corporations, and individual donors who are favorably impressed by TRP's solid accomplishments. Twenty-five percent of the budget comes from various government grants from city, state, and federal agencies to create affordable housing. Twenty-two percent comes from earned income from property rents, management fees, and fees for services rendered. During the past decade talented, capable people have been identified within the community, trained, and lifted up to become the executive leadership of the organization. TRP has created, directly or indirectly, more than one hundred significant jobs in the neighborhoods and stimulated numerous new businesses. Above all, it has given effective voice to local people and stayed close to its base of support in the Catholic parishes of Pilsen. The organization has won many awards from national and local groups in recognition of its effective work. Raul Hernandez, TRP Board Member, summarizes much of what the people of Pilsen have learned about social responsibility: "There are many problems in Pilsen, but we cannot run away from them. Instead of moving to a better community, we must build on what we have. We know we are responsible for each other. I want to teach my children to accept their responsibility in the community,

8. The Resurrection Project, *The Annual Report, 1997*.

not run from it." Clearly there is a new commitment to life in the community and a new sense of pride in accomplishment. Dreams have become reality in Pilsen.

What We Can Learn

- Continuity of pastoral leadership over a long term is a crucial factor in the church's successful mission in the wider community.
- Understanding the life situation and cultural heritage of the Mexican-American residents of the community has contributed greatly to the effectiveness of the church's ministry.
- Church-based community organizing can help to create a more positive, informed, and spiritually motivated community redevelopment movement.
- Faith-based community organizing can create a movement for justice rooted in the commitment of many individuals to struggle for the common good. Motivated by faith, people more readily find their own self-interest fulfilled in the material and spiritual well-being of the whole.
- Churches can utilize their teaching resources and ethical tradition to help people understand the need for mobilizing political power for justice within the Judeo-Christian heritage.
- Often in the city center, churches are the only remaining voluntary institutions through which people can find their collective voice for self-development and renewal.
- Community organizing that is built upon institutional membership, i.e., seven churches, helps to create a larger membership base with more human and financial resources, and, consequently, greater power.
- Church judicatories, such as a diocese, can greatly enhance faith-based community redevelopment through appropriate gifts of property and money. Church buildings no longer needed for worship can be renovated into centers for much-needed community services. The Catholic Archdiocese's gift of the St. Vitus church buildings (Vitus means life) to TRP, facilitated great accomplishments by the people in the neighborhood.
- The Resurrection Project dramatically demonstrates the holistic

approach to community redevelopment that brings together co-ordinated efforts for affordable housing, economic development, improved education, safe streets, the formation of Christian leaders, and the strengthening of the social fabric of both the churches and the broader community.

Grace United Church

Waves of change have swept over Kansas City in the decades from 1960 to 1990. The 1960s was a time of white flight from the central city. The 1970s was a period of rapid increase in the African-American population. The eighties brought a large increase of Hispanic and Asian peoples into the city. Multiple social pathologies were on the increase including deteriorating housing, declining public schools, increased unemployment, rising school dropouts, increasing teen pregnancy, AIDS, and other health problems.

These and other causes contributed to the decline of neighborhood churches in northeast Kansas City. During this extended period, both the Grace Presbyterian Church and the Independence Avenue Methodist Church were on the verge of closing. Instead, a decision was made to form a cooperative union that would enable the two churches to work together as one congregation. Grace United Church on the northeast side of Kansas City, Missouri, is thus a union of two congregations — Presbyterian and United Methodist — that began cooperating for urban ministry twenty-five years ago. In January of 1997, the two churches became one, as a plan of union was put into effect under the leadership of the Reverend Sharon Garfield, after a unanimous vote by both congregations.[1] The mission statement of the new church reflects its focus on ministry for, with, and by the

---

1. "The Plan of Union: Grace Presbyterian Church and Independence Avenue United Methodist Church," adopted 16 June 1996.

people of the larger community: "The mission of the Grace United Church of Kansas City is to be an inclusive, caring, healing, community of disciples in Jesus Christ. We are seeking to live out the gospel in worship, nurture, and service to God."[2]

Sharon Garfield first came to Kansas City as a teenager participating in a summer service project with other Methodist youth. Beginning with that experience, continuing in service through college, maturing during theological study at the St. Paul School of Theology, and coming to a focus in years of developing a shelter program for battered women, her calling to Christian ministry in the city led her to become the senior pastor of Grace Church in 1990.

Garfield had significant experience in Kansas City before coming to Grace United Church. She had served a number of years as a street worker with troubled youth, as a community organizer in public housing, and as a crisis counselor with the delinquency prevention program of the Boys Club of Kansas City. The most powerful, formative experience was her engagement in the 1970s in organizing the first shelter program for battered women, New House, which opened in 1979. These were pioneering years of bringing community resources into cooperation to create the support necessary for the shelter and getting it into operation. She served as director for nine years, helping to lead the struggle to get Kansas City to enact a fee on all marriage licenses to provide funding for the shelter. She prevailed upon her Methodist bishop to ordain her to "ministry with women having special needs." After long years of service in Kansas City, she was called to serve the United Methodist Church national agency, Peace with Justice Program, in Washington, D.C. She served in that agency four years.[3]

Church Redevelopment

In 1990, Sharon Garfield returned to Kansas City to begin the redevelopment of Grace United Church. She began with a handful of people — about twenty-three persons — to bring new life into the congregation. The church neighborhood is an area with high unemployment,

2. Grace United Church, "The Mission Statement," January 1997.
3. Sharon Garfield, interview with author, Kansas City, 2 July 1997.

high crime, and high violence, where people have multiple needs. The church had very few resources and a very old building in disrepair. But Sharon Garfield made the decision to look for the positive resources. She saw good people with talent, people with a desire for change, a city full of potential resources, the skills to mobilize them for the transformation, and some encouragement from Methodist and Presbyterian Church judicatories. She developed a perspective of asset-based renewal.

Redevelopment began with responses to basic human need. Garfield organized people from the neighborhood to create the Food Pantry Program to provide better nutrition in the community. Instead of bringing in volunteers from outside the area, she inspired persons in the immediate neighborhood to do the work themselves. The food pantry became a program in local leadership development. Currently the program serves over 450 families per month with basic food staples and fresh vegetables. Beyond supplying food, there is guidance in nutrition, family-menu planning, and related health education.

Response to Violence

As the Food Pantry Program grew and other initiatives were envisioned, Garfield led the congregation to create a new Church Council that includes members, staff, and community people who are not members but are active participants. The emphasis is upon getting the community people involved in planning, and moving from passive recipients to active leadership. The people at the highest level of risk in the community are the children, youth, and young adults. With this clearly in mind, Grace United Church has created a very successful Peacemaking Academy. The goals of the Academy include these special emphases:[4]

- teaching nonviolent survival skills to provide powerful alternatives to the violence of gangs, abusive homes, and bad schools
- providing a safe day-care program for young children, many of whom have no parent or guardian at home during the daytime

4. Grace United Church Peacemaking Academy, "Mission Statement and Goals," 1996, p. 3.

- teaching the cultural heritage of diverse ethnic/racial groups participating in the church and surrounding community
- teaching a spiritual viewpoint as a basis for self-worth and an understanding of life and the creation of positive opportunities
- building community to create a network of safety, caring, and support in contrast to school busing which fragments the neighborhood
- providing children and youth with direct experiences of how violence destroys life, through visits to prisons, rehabilitation centers, and local jails
- teaching children and youth to give through community service projects and to see hopeful possibilities for their lives.

Currently there are 232 children and youth enrolled in the Peacemaking Academy. Daily attendance is high, averaging 120. The academy functions as a full-time summer program for eight weeks in the months of June, July, and August. Then it continues as an after-school program during the regular academic months of September through May. The summer weekday schedule includes five units of activity focusing on: (1) *Bible Study* — Jesus as peacemaker; finding peace within; peace and justice in the family, school, neighborhood, city, nation, and world; (2) *Cultural Awareness* — African American, Native American, Hispanic American, and Asian American; (3) *Conflict Resolution* — anger control, self-esteem, mediation skills; (4) *Service* — projects in church and community; (5) *Creative Expression* — art, music, dance, drama, writing, and gymnastics as alternatives to gang activity. On Friday each week during the summer there is a field trip into the city to experience the consequences of violence and the alternative opportunities available in the Kansas City region.

Biweekly events bring parents and family members into the academy and into close cooperation and participation with the students and staff. Staff come primarily from the community. They are trained, supervised, and paid. Garfield indicates that experience over the years has taught that it is usually more helpful to utilize local people instead of outside volunteers. They have the advantage of understanding the students, belong to the congregation, and have an awareness of the neighborhood culture. Teaching becomes a process of local leadership development, which strengthens the community and congregation.

Alternative Education

The aim of the Peace Academy goes beyond service to individuals toward laying a foundation for institutional change. This is done in partnership with the public school system, city government, and the denominational agencies of the United Methodist Church and the Presbyterian Church. The goal is to change the institutions that have major impact on the people of the northeast neighborhoods. Already there are publicly supported classes for English as a second language, family nutrition, high school tutoring with city-supplied tutors, and a program of legal advocacy.

Grace United Church is laying the groundwork for an alternative school to be created in the church education facilities. Planning is going forward to have a public school for children with significant behavioral problems that keep them out of regular schools. The tendency for the school system is to suspend or expel children with repeated behavioral difficulties. Many of these children have language problems, lack parental guidance, or come from dysfunctional homes. With initiative from the church, strong support in the community, and cooperation from key officials in the public school system, a new alternative school may soon be developed at Grace United Church.

One program that has helped to bring together youth of diverse ethnic and cultural backgrounds is Tomorrow's Leaders and Community, a summer youth employment project that uses city funding to help develop jobs. The city Full Employment Council is a partner with Grace United Church in providing some funding. There is a crisis intervention program, which helps young men and women to come out of street gangs. The program offers opportunity to make a break from gang life and get training in peace and reconciliation skills and job skills. At the time of this writing, thirty-two young men and women were enrolled through Grace United Church. The program helps to break the cycle of poverty and violence. It gives opportunity for a number of young adults to make a new start and experience the reality of transformation.

Hispanic Ministry

Beyond the Peace Academy, alternative school, and the food pantry, another major initiative in the Grace United Church redevelopment is the new Hispanic Ministry. This began with a street evangelism outreach of neighborhood calling and family counseling, and has matured into a lively worshipping congregation, English language program, and a resident Hispanic pastor who nurtures leadership. Now fully one-third of the Grace United Church constituency is from the Hispanic community. Many Hispanic people come to Kansas City as migrant agricultural workers, especially people from Mexico. Others have come as refugees from Guatemala and El Salvador.

A breakthrough in engaging this sector of the community came with the decision to fund a Director of Hispanic Outreach Ministry, Ana Velasquez-Stone. Her good work built up the connections between many Hispanic people and the Grace United Church. As the critical mass grew larger, a second strategic decision was to secure a Hispanic pastor. The first was the Reverend Juan Carlos Ramon, followed by Juan Ordonez, the current Hispanic pastor. Juan Ordonez and his family live in the Grace United Church apartment and give leadership to the Hispanic segment of the church. A part-time staff member, Vincente Sanchez, also gives leadership for street evangelism in the neighborhood. In the early stages of developing Hispanic ministry it was decided by the church council to offer a Spanish language worship service. This has helped to knit the Spanish-speaking segment of the congregation together. There is Bible study and pastoral work that is done in Spanish.

Significant numbers of Hispanic people participate in and help to give leadership to other areas of ministry that are English language programs, including the Peace Academy, day care, youth ministry, food pantry, and the Urban Training Center. As in all multicultural and bilingual situations, there are challenges and problems to be resolved. These include questions of leadership, authority, funding, and policy. But these are the necessary issues, which are viewed as opportunities to learn to work together across barriers of culture. Creative struggle with these questions is helping Grace United Church to mature, develop, and grow.

The Urban Training Center

An outstanding example of the creative entrepreneurial spirit of the church and its senior pastor is the Urban Training Center. This center combines mission, service, and fundraising into one enterprise. The church has a rich, ongoing life that involves almost every aspect of inner-city culture, human need, institutional challenge, and creative initiatives by the faith community. As a result of many requests from churches, seminaries, colleges, mission committees, and judicatory agencies for mission study visits, the Grace United Church created the Urban Training Center. A church member was employed to be the director. The center arranges custom-designed mission study experiences for various groups. Study periods range from a weekend to several weeks. The Urban Training Center is a life experience learning laboratory for persons and groups who want to gain a deeper understanding of the dynamic of city life, multicultural community, urban politics, and the creative spirituality that arises from the diverse mix of peoples in the city center.[5]

Linda Franklin is the center director. Together with Sharon Garfield, the Hispanic pastor, the Hispanic outreach director, the youth ministry leadership, church members, and numerous volunteers, Franklin has arranged and coordinated a set of urban experiences and leadership training that can be adapted to fit the needs of seminary students, lay leaders, urban pastors, and a variety of others. The center has a busy schedule during the spring, summer, and fall seasons. It shares the wide-ranging experience, skills, and expertise developed within the church community. The center has become a revenue-producing enterprise for the Church as well as a service to the larger church and community. Students at the St. Paul's United Methodist Seminary, local colleges and universities, as well as many lay leaders and pastors have benefited from the training program. The church provides sleeping accommodations, meals, and hospitality as well as significant educational experiences. Grace United Church has become a teaching church for the wider faith community.

5. Linda Franklin, "We Need You for the Grace United Church Urban Training Center," 1997, p. 6.

Economic Development

The experience of generating income from the Urban Training Center, as well as the constant demands for program funding in the church, has set the congregation to thinking and planning for new ways of economic development. The church has recently acquired adjacent property with a view toward expanding some of its revenue-generating programs. "This is a beginning," says Pastor Garfield, "but we need to do much more." The message is clear that for urban churches to thrive they need to find new ways of creating essential income that go well beyond the usual assumptions about member giving and judicatory support. At Grace United Church, the total budget for all ministries is over $600,000 a year and about ten percent comes from member giving and member income-producing activity. Funding from many church partners, "Angels of Grace," foundation and government grants, community agencies, as well as denominational support, makes the full mission possible. The senior pastor invests a very significant percentage of her time in fundraising and public interpretation activity. Her creative leadership in assembling the necessary funding is a remarkable accomplishment. However, she sees the clear need for increasing the ability of church members to earn better income, give more, and for creating new businesses in the community that will generate income.[6]

Garfield indicated that the best-paying jobs for her people are now in the suburbs, so there is a concerted effort to arrange for transportation to get workers out to those better-paying jobs. Beyond this important step, the church in cooperation with the Kansas City Full Employment Council trains, prepares, and places young adults in stable jobs in the city. New initiatives are being planned to create two small businesses to be owned and operated in the neighborhood. One proposed enterprise will produce specialized T-shirts with customized logos and art designs for sale to companies, organizations, churches, and other groups. A second small business in the planning stages is a furniture-making shop that will both teach the craftsmanship of furniture-making and create wood furniture products for sale.

An interesting and significant innovation in the planning stage is the creation of a series of support services to help parents be away

6. Garfield, interview.

from home and child-care responsibility. This program will include transportation, expanded day care, and nighttime child care. The new nighttime child care is a response to the fact that many available jobs are in the evening or night shifts in the metropolitan area. To take these jobs parents need safe and good-quality child care at times other than the traditional day-care programs. So Grace United Church is seeking to step up to the challenge.

A Rich Worship Life

All of the diverse programmatic activity and expressions of ministry are unified in the gatherings for congregational worship. Recent renovations and improvements to the church buildings have included an expansion of and opening up of the chancel area in the sanctuary. A wide platform or stage area has been created in the front of the sanctuary. The new open chancel area is suitable for dramatic presentations, big enough for an orchestra, and helps to create an open and participatory atmosphere for worship.

Worship is definitely a celebration of the good news of Jesus Christ and of the resurrection community, which He gathers to praise God and go forth to serve the world. The liturgy brings together contributions from African-American, Hispanic, and traditional Protestant streams of experience. Music and singing play an important role. There is variety in the music and the hymns. The music includes electronic instruments and has a lively tempo. The spirit is one of praise and joyful expression. The music also has a message oriented to life and service in the city. An extended time for congregational joys, concerns, testimonies, and requests for prayer is an important part of worship. Preaching is lively, biblical, relevant, and challenging. There is a clear invitation to faith and membership in the church. The focus of worship includes praise to God, nurture and teaching of members, and inspiration and call to service in the church and world.

Special seasons, holidays, and events play an important role as occasions for celebration, special liturgy, and preaching. One example is the Christmas season, which highlights the cultural diversity in the church. The celebration of the Mexican Posada includes procession, dancing, storytelling, drumming, and special music, all coming to focus on the nativity. The African-American tradition of the Kwanzaa celebration is also carried out, reflecting the special history and cultural experience of the African tradition. A Gospel Choir is part of the worship leadership. There is also a Hispanic Choir. All ages are involved in worship leadership and participation. A unique part of the service is the use of the Church Mission Statement, which is read in unison by the congregation, as a part of the call to worship. This helps to focus worship around mission. This is important in a congregation where change is constant, membership for many is transient, and life is an ever-moving stream.

What We Can Learn

- Consolidation of two congregations and the combining of facilities and resources can create a base for a more viable redevelopment of ministry in a transitional neighborhood. This can be done successfully across denominational lines.
- The selection of a mature pastor with prior, substantial experience and tested skills is crucial to the redevelopment process.
- Commitment of resources and support by denominational judicatories is an important factor in redevelopment. It is a worthwhile investment to encourage creative ministries among oppressed people.
- A useful way of serving youth and children in violence-prone communities is to create an academy that engages them in an alternative community that demonstrates nonviolent ways of conflict resolution.
- Affirming leadership capabilities and educating neighborhood people to take charge of church and community programs for self-development is one key to success in the redevelopment process. This is asset-based congregational development.
- Creating training, job opportunities, and leadership roles for women of culturally oppressed minorities opens up a new source of strength for redevelopment.
- Culturally appropriate worship that engages the mind, heart, and soul of people is crucial for redevelopment. Music plays a key role. Opening up the sanctuary for a diversity of cultural expressions in worship is helpful.

- Securing Hispanic leadership for improving ministry to the Spanish-speaking community can greatly increase participation and effectiveness in ministry.
- The creation of an Urban Training Center utilizes the skills of the church community, expands its range of witness, produces income for the church, and serves the wider church. It is important for the congregation to experience giving something of value to the wider society.

Palestine Missionary Baptist Church

Racial segregation in housing and public institutions was the firm reality of life in Kansas City in the 1950s. But there was a growing desire for change in the African-American community, and a quiet courage was at work to bring about a more just and equitable society. In 1955, Earl Abel and his family moved into a racially changing neighborhood. They were the third African-American family to come into the block. It took courage and determination to be among the first to integrate a neighborhood. The closest African-American church was nearly two miles away, so a few families began to meet in homes for worship and mutual support. By 1959 they decided to organize a new church in their neighborhood. The Palestine Missionary Baptist Church was born, with about eleven people, on January 2, 1959.[1]

The small congregation secured a place to worship in the nearby YMCA building. The YMCA board of directors, staff, and all of its members were white, so "renting space in the YMCA was a giant step forward for the young church," says Pastor Abel. The YMCA Board was very cooperative; the new congregation could not have developed as quickly as it did without the support of the board. The congregation grew rapidly, and within a year they purchased land in the neighborhood, at 35th and Monroe streets, as the site for a church building. Three years later the congregation of 175 members built a new sanctuary that would seat twice that number. They had growth in

1. Earl Abel, interview with author, Kansas City, Missouri, 5 October 1997.

mind and planned for it. The new building also included classrooms and assembly space for a growing Sunday school. Within two years the church had doubled in size and a second worship service was added. A few years later a third Sunday service was needed.[2]

The great needs of the community were (1) children's day care and preschool education, and (2) youth ministry as an alternative to street gangs. This motivated the growing congregation to build a new educational facility in 1971. The new building, joined to the sanctuary, provided fifteen new classrooms, a gymnasium/multipurpose room, and a large kitchen. The church was a beehive of activity with many families in which both parents were working. Consequently, there was great need for good-quality day care for children.

The day-care program was opened with a staff of three people. A decade later it had grown into two centers for day care in separate locations with a staff of ten full-time and a number of part-time employees. More families were attracted to the church by its ever-expanding array of positive programs for children, youth, and parents. In 1981, a new sanctuary was constructed adjacent to the two older buildings. The new worship space seated twelve hundred people. The three Sunday worship services were continued. The physical facilities were now in place for large-scale programming to serve the wider community.

Meeting Community Needs

The central theme that runs through all the variety of ministries at Palestine Missionary Baptist Church is meeting community needs, according to Pastor Abel. "Our church began by meeting the need of African-American families for worship. It grew as we served the needs of children, youth, and adults for spiritual guidance and educational development. We have matured as the church has engaged the challenges of racial justice, youth education, affordable housing, economic enterprise, and service to seniors."[3] All of these social justice themes are illustrated in two areas of the Palestine Church commu-

2. Earl Abel, "A Historical Summary," contained in a letter to author, 8 October 1997.

3. Abel, interview.

nity ministry: constructing housing, and creating the Outreach Center.

In 1990, when the church began to construct apartment housing, it had grown from its beginning with eleven people to over three thousand members. The church secured a U.S. Department of Housing and Urban Development (HUD) 202 loan to construct fifty-eight units of apartment housing for senior citizens. It was a need-based project. As more and more of the church members and others in the community reached retirement years, there was a need to provide affordable housing to help people stay in the community. Meeting the challenge of creating good-quality senior housing at a reasonable rent was a dream that had emerged over a number of years. Constructing the first apartment building of fifty-eight units was the outcome of that dream. It required the church to sponsor a separate housing corporation and learn how to work with the federal government.

While researching, preparing, and planning for the construction of the senior apartment housing, the building committee saw the need for a program and facility to provide education, health care, nutrition, and stimulating social activity for senior citizens. It was not enough just to create housing. A program to promote a better quality of life was needed. The church launched a campaign and built a $2.4 million senior activity center. It is a special place for senior adults where they can gather in a safe, secure environment; engage in programs of spiritual life, exercise, study, and recreation; and enjoy friendship. There is a dining room where seniors can enjoy a well-balanced, midday meal for $1.50. There is a chapel for worship and a Bible study for those who want it. There are outreach programs for transportation, shopping, health care, and cultural trips. The center creates a positive influence in the lives of hundreds of people.

The senior housing and related activity center have been so successful that a second HUD 202 development is now being constructed to create sixty-eight additional units of senior apartment housing. This housing project is scheduled for occupancy in the spring of 1998. With the completion of the new apartments, the church-sponsored Housing Corporation will have constructed a total of 126 units of affordable housing. It has created a positive living environment and stable community for hundreds of people during a decade of housing ministry. It has enabled retired people to stay in the community and in the church.

"But we don't stop with this accomplishment," says Pastor Abel, "because the needs keep emerging. Our future plans are to build units of congregate housing where people can live independently while having their meals and medication prepared professionally."[4] Congregate housing is a step beyond senior housing for people who need professional assistance, but can still manage most of their own daily routines. Developing this supportive approach for senior care is another step in the program of ministry at Palestine Church, where every major project has evolved around meeting a need in the community.

The Need for Education in the Community

The second major arena in which the Palestine Missionary Baptist Church has served the extended community is education. Three education projects illustrate how the Palestine Church has developed education in the community. The earliest major effort was the development of the day-care program in 1971. Using its new education building as an attractive setting, the church established a day-care center. The new center served many families in which both parents were working. The program included many elements of early childhood education in a loving environment. For many families the connection with the day care center became the avenue for entry into the church. This often developed as families were attracted to family life workshops and parenting classes. As the popularity of the day care center grew, the church expanded the size and scope of the program.

In 1992, Palestine Church bought an existing building one mile away and turned it into an outreach center for educational programming. Along with other programs, a second day-care center was created in this space, doubling capacity to serve families. The new outreach center also provided the space for a greatly expanded summer day camp program for children and youth between the ages of six and fifteen. During the nine months of the school year, a program of tutoring and mentoring is operated. The church has established a special working relationship with the Rogers Middle School for tutoring.

4. Abel, interview.

In addition, special tutoring is provided for high school students in math, including algebra, geometry, trigonometry, and calculus. The aim is to help students prepare for college.

The most recent new educational development is the extension of the mentoring program beyond the high school level to the college level of education. Over seventy church members have become mentors, providing a support network for college students. Students are matched with mentors who give encouragement, share their own career and Christian experience, and help the church keep in touch with students during college years. The church further supports its college students through a scholarship program to assist them in meeting their educational costs.

For several decades the educational ministry of the Palestine Church has had major programs during the summer months, reaching out to all age groups. Coming out of this ministry was the dream that some day the church could develop a camp and conference facility outside Kansas City. That dream was fulfilled in 1997. After a decade of planning, hard work, and fundraising, the Palestine Camp and Conference Center, located about sixty miles outside the city, was opened. This $5.2 million camp is situated on 140 acres of gently rolling land that includes a seven-acre lake for recreational use. The facilities include sixteen sleeping cabins that can accommodate 250 children, a conference lodge that can accommodate 128 adults, a large cafeteria and dining hall, a recreational building, meeting space, a worship chapel, a swimming pool, a maintenance workshop, and a residence for the permanent caretaker. This large, new facility makes it possible each year for several thousand people to experience the beautiful Missouri countryside, find rest, spiritual renewal, and be strengthened in the bonds of Christian community.

Worship Motivates Ministry

With the tremendous emphasis on meeting human needs in the community one must ask, from where does the motivation, the commitment, and the energy come to inspire such a large program of ministry? The answer is clear — motivation for ministry comes from the rich worship life of the church. The 1200-seat sanctuary is filled three times on Sunday — at 6:45 and 10:45 a.m., and again at 7:00 p.m.

The early worship service of prayer and praise is broadcast on local radio station KPRT. It is followed by a fellowship breakfast. This gathering starts the Sunday program at a high energy level. The Sunday church school brings hundreds more people into the church between 9:30 and 10:30 a.m. At 10:45 the main morning worship service moves into high gear. The music program is powerful, with several choirs — the senior choir, the men's chorus, the women's chorus, inspirational choir, youth choir — and strong support from the organ, piano, and instruments. Congregational singing led by the choir, prayers, welcoming of visitors, receiving the tithes and offerings, and special mission emphases all give opportunity for active participation by worshippers. Then the moment comes for preaching, which is the centerpiece of worship. The pastor presents the scriptural text and applies it to life, with great energy and power. The congregation listens actively, joins in reinforcing and affirming key points, and moves with the preacher toward an enthusiastic response at the conclusion. There is an invitation to faith in Christ, a call to come forward for commitment, and a closing prayer and benediction.

The evening worship again has a strong musical program with choirs and vigorous congregational singing. This service is sometimes led by a group — such as the Board of Deacons, the Men's Group or the Senior High Youth — in addition to the ministers. The evening worship may include a special presentation by the Drama Guild, Men's or Women's Chorus, or the Gospelair Choir. Worship is the motivating center that brings people together and energizes their going out in ministry. The network of communication moves out from the worship center. Various groups and planning committees frequently meet prior to or just after the evening worship. There are many great strengths in the worship services. One that deserves special mention is the emphasis on tithing. There is a deep commitment to giving as an expression of Christian grace and thanksgiving to God. What the congregation has accomplished through mission giving and in creating ministry programming and facilities is a vigorous testimony to tithing.

There is a midweek prayer meeting on Wednesday evening, and numerous Bible study groups that bring people together through the week and give spiritual direction to the lives and ministry of members. Saturday also is a day of great activity, with meetings of the Church Brotherhood, and many choral groups in rehearsal. The Palestine Missionary Baptist Church is clearly a community of faith for all times and seasons, seeking to be the body of Jesus Christ in the community of need.

What We Can Learn

- Generous response to community needs can build up a congregation in strength and size.
- Long-term pastoral leadership can bring stability and continuity to the life and development of the congregation.
- Lively worship in a participatory style can energize and empower a congregation for a wider mission.
- Serving particular needs of families through education, pastoral care, and in worship can help a congregation grow.
- The congregation is more likely to give generously when it can see the results of giving in human needs being met and people being served in the local community.
- Appropriate music is a vitally important medium through which people are attracted to worship and drawn into a sense of belonging and joyful celebration.
- Constructing a larger sanctuary sends a positive signal of vitality and readiness for growth to the community.
- Using a variety of financing vehicles, including interest-bearing bonds, tithing, capital pledges, special gifts, as well as bank loans, helps a congregation to be more in control of its own financial development.
- There is no substitute for faithful people who remain persistently engaged through the decades in building up the body of Christ.
- The long pastorate (forty years) and strong leadership of Earl Abel have contributed greatly to the growth of the Palestine Church and its creation of three church buildings, the outreach center, the church camp, and the senior housing and activity center.

Our Savior's Lutheran Church

For over one hundred years Our Savior's Lutheran Church has been a congregation for the people of the Capitol Hill neighborhood in Denver. The sanctuary, built in the 1920s, is located just six blocks southeast of the Colorado State Capitol Building in Denver's city center. The church is a gathering of faithful people dedicated to serving the community. In the 1950s, the church made a conscious decision to stay in the central Capitol Hill area. In the early 1960s, the church renovated the sanctuary and expanded the education and community space in order to serve the changing neighborhood. It is a community of just over two hundred persons focused on faith and justice in the ever-changing Capitol Hill neighborhood. The church doors are painted red to signify vitality, energy, and welcome. The mission statement symbolizes the current ministry: "It is our intention that the faith we profess be translated into caring, responsible, and joyful participation in the neighborhood and in the city."

The biblical faith of the congregation is expressed in worship and in many cooperative action-oriented programs of service, advocacy, and systemic justice. The biblical roots of Our Savior's congregation are suggested by two great texts. From the Old Testament:

> What is acceptable to the Lord? Is it not . . . to loose the bonds of injustice, to undo the bindings of slavery, to let the oppressed go free, and to break every yoke? Is it not to share your bread with the hungry, bring the homeless poor into your house, clothing the na-

ked when you see them, and not turning away from your own people? Then you shall call, and the Lord will answer; you shall cry for help, and God will say, Here I am (Isaiah 58:6-9).

From the New Testament in the Gospel of Luke, Jesus' affirmation of the connection between loving God and loving one's neighbor is symbolic for the congregation: "You shall love your God with all your heart, soul, strength and mind; and your neighbor as yourself" (Luke 10:27). These texts of biblical faith are frequently found in bulletins, newsletters, and interpretive program statements of the congregation. They suggest the faith foundation upon which the ministry of the church rests and by which it is empowered to act.

A Redemptive Community

Our Savior's congregation is a very diverse body of people. There is an older group of long-time members, some neighborhood families, many single adults, some families from the suburbs, and a number of senior citizen members. There are young adults from the Urban Service Corps, residents from adjacent senior apartments, and people from the wider metro area. It is a mix of people from the neighborhood and from the city at large. Sunday worship is the integrating center that brings the diverse array of people together and creates the bonds of a faith community. The plurality of backgrounds of the members is served in the diversity of worship styles. At the 8:00 a.m. service there is quiet, contemplative spirit of prayer, communion, homily, reflection, and response. This service is attended by some of the core leaders, neighborhood members, some single adults, and others. It is followed by the Sunday Church School and Adult Christian Education program, which brings more energy into the building and gathers a wider, more diverse collectivity of people.

At 10:00 a.m., the main worship service of word, prayer, and sacrament takes place. According to Pastor Bruce Johnson, this is a wonderful mix of classical music and contemporary songs. There is the great organ music of Bach and Mozart, along with lively, lyrical rhythms of the Sing a New Song band, using guitar, piano, mandolin, and drums. Worship follows a pattern of rotation between three basic liturgies — based in the Lutheran Book of Worship — for worship in traditional, contemporary, and blended expressions. Other contemporary worship books are used, such as *With One Voice*, and *Borning Cry Book*. Four to five hymns and/or contemporary songs are sung. Choral anthems and liturgical responses are sung with vitality. Congregational singing is spirited. Music is a central carrier of the spirit of worship. There is a gathering time before the liturgy for singing a number of hymns and songs as a prelude to worship. The announcements before the service, the prayers of the people, sharing the peace of Christ, and the offering all provide points in which the congregation makes connections between prayer and current human and social needs in worship.

Scripture and preaching are central in the services of worship. It is customary to have at least three scripture readings, including selections based on the lectionary from the Old Testament, the New Testament gospels, and the epistles. However, it is not unusual to have four or five scripture readings, including Psalms and additional New Testament texts. Pastor Johnson describes his preaching style as conversational. He moves away from the pulpit, gets closer to the congregation, and speaks personally to the gathered people. The preaching is biblical interpretation and application to current-day realities of personal and social life. There is the celebration of the Eucharist every Sunday at each service. The communion is a central community-creating and empowering act of worship. There is a relaxed approach to worship, a spirit of mystical presence and redemptive community. The main worship service proceeds for about an hour and a quarter. There is good communication and interaction among the congregation following the service. Lots of informal meetings, sharing of information, networking connections, and nurturing fellowship take place before, during, and following the worship. The signs of a caring, nurturing, redemptive community are very visible.[1]

The Church as a Neighborhood Center

The Capitol Hill area around Our Savior's Church is a densely populated, multiracial, ethnically mixed territory. The area houses significant populations of young single adults, professional people, African

1. Bruce Johnson, interview with author, 27 March 1998.

Americans, Hispanics, families, and elderly persons. There is a significant community of gay and lesbian people in the area. A mix of well-maintained older homes, large houses have been converted into condominiums and apartment buildings. Some of the older houses are being renovated, refurbished, and redeveloped as homes and as investments. The value of property is increasing, rents are going up, renovated houses may double in value in just a few years, and there is high demand for city-center dwellings that are close to offices and the downtown hub. This is the environment around the church that creates many of the challenges and opportunities for ministry. It produces challenges of affordable housing, gentrification, displacement of low-income persons, and the special needs of families, the elderly, and the gay community. There are the opportunities for service by young professionals, talented seniors, college youth, and urban volunteers.[2]

The church has developed the concept of being a center for ministry in the neighborhood over a period of several decades. The previous pastor, the Reverend Luther Johnson, who served Our Savior's Church from 1982 to 1996, played a major part in leading the church into community service. The current pastor, the Reverend Bruce Johnson, continues that commitment. The church building, and many of the members, are engaged in serving the community through a number of initiatives headquartered in the church facilities and staffed by church volunteers. Here are five illustrations of community center outreach by the church.[3]

A new senior citizen residence. A number of years ago the congregation sponsored the construction of Emerson Gardens. It is a HUD 202 housing project under section 8 guidelines for seniors of low income. Emerson Gardens, located next to the church, is a thirty-unit apartment complex offering safe, quality residential accommodation and supportive services. The church ministers to the residents by providing a senior activity center in the church building. The senior center provides a friendly environment and gathering place for seniors and their friends. A hot meal is provided every Thursday at noon. Health information, transportation, and entertainment are also part of the program. The housing and the senior center help to make it

2. Peter Kjeseth, church member, interview with author, 23 March 1998.
3. Johnson, interview, and church program documents.

possible for older people to stay in the neighborhood even as housing becomes more expensive in the area. The board of directors for Emerson Gardens is composed largely of church members who take responsibility for maintaining the building in good condition and providing high-quality service to residents. This senior housing project was one of the early developments in Denver that was sponsored by a church. It has been a model for projects that followed.

Project Angel Heart. This is a food distribution and nutrition program that was organized by the congregation. It now operates as an independent 501-C-3 nonprofit corporation. It has a staff of seven persons who prepare and deliver meals six days a week to over two hundred people. Special attention is given to homebound persons, and particularly to HIV-AIDS persons with limited mobility. The Angel Heart Project recruits and utilizes many volunteers. The professional staff provide counseling for HIV-AIDS persons, many of whom live in apartments in the Capitol Hill area within a three-mile radius of the church. The church provides a commercial kitchen used for the food preparation, as well as office space for the headquarters of the project. Many church members serve as part of the volunteer staff that provide the food delivery service.

CHARG Resource Center. This is an innovative program of care for mentally ill persons in the area. At the church, professional staff operate a drop-in center. This is a place where persons who are living with mental illness can find a community of support, counseling, self-help programs, and education activity aimed to help them become more self-sustaining and able to manage their illness. CHARG is supported primarily by grants and some gifts from many churches and friends of the center. The focus of the resource center is on recovery, self-management, and reentry into society. The church provides space, volunteer workers, and helps to promote a network of support for the center and its program. Church members have played a key role in the creation of this highly successful mental health ministry.

Needs of the People project. This social service project provides emergency food and clothing to low-income families. Although the program was temporarily closed in 1997, it has long standing in the church and is being reactivated, a new director is being hired, and planning for its redevelopment is proceeding. The Needs of the People operates a food distribution center at the church, which in a typical year serves over one thousand families with food secured through donations and from the U.S. Department of Agriculture surplus food program. A supply of used clothing is made available to persons in need. The church provides space for the operation and many of the volunteer workers serving under the leadership of a professional director.

Gay and Lesbian Welcoming Community. The church, by action of the Church Council, declared the congregation to be a "Reconciled In Christ Lutheran Welcoming Community" for gay and lesbian persons. The church is perceived as an accepting community and a safe place for gay and lesbian people to find friendship and participation in the life of the church. A significant number of gay and lesbian persons have joined the church and participate in the worship and mission of the congregation. The position of the church is that all believers have been redeemed in Christ and all are thereby reconciled to God and to one another. All members are called to seek to demonstrate the love of God to the world in human relationships. There are no intentional barriers to membership or leadership in the church.

Urban Network for Justice

The members and clergy at Our Savior's Lutheran Church are active participants in a number of networks in Denver that engage in advocacy and action for justice. The church has a long history of creating partnerships with other churches and service agencies to develop a larger base for social action in a wider arena. Three illustrations of urban networking at Our Savior's Church are the Urban Servant Corps, the Capitol Hill United Ministries, and the Lutheran Office of Governmental Ministry in Denver.

The Urban Servant Corps is a regional program that recruits, trains, and places young adult volunteers in one-year service positions in the Capitol Hill area of Denver. Servant Corps volunteers work in Denver social service agencies, area feeding programs, hospice programs, the Women's Resource Center, health clinics, Habitat for Humanity, and in school tutoring programs. The Servant Corps is a 501-C-3 nonprofit entity. It is an independent body sponsored by Lutheran churches and closely associated with Our Savior's Church, which housed its headquarters in its early years. The Urban Servant Corps now uses space at the church for some of its training events.

The current director previously served as a volunteer in the community ministry of Our Savior's Church. The Corps brings college students into Denver for an Alternative Spring Break Program, which gives students an urban plunge and an introduction to possible service careers. The Spring Break Program is based in Our Savior's Church facilities. The Corps sponsors an annual Palm Sunday Walk-a-thon for area Lutheran churches to participate in fundraising for support of the volunteer service program. Over the years, several thousands of young adults and college students have given valuable services, learned important skills, and gained understanding of urban life and possible careers in the city. A central emphasis is on learning what it takes to create and maintain positive community life in a city. Learning to care for one another is an expression of Christian faith. Volunteers relate to area churches during their yearlong program.[4]

The Capitol Hill United Ministries (CHUM) began in the early 1980s and it includes nineteen churches in the area. They have joined together to more effectively work cooperatively with the human needs of hunger, homelessness, chronic mental illness, HIV-AIDS support, and youth. CHUM seeks to provide collegial support to the clergy of area churches, communication, coordination of effort in social ministry, and provides hospitality, advocacy, and community for people in need. The organization supports six specific area programs with grants, referrals, and public interpretation. Two of these programs are based in Our Savior's Lutheran Church — Project Angel Heart and CHARG Resource Center. The Reverend Luther Johnson, the previous pastor, was a leader in forming the Capitol Hill United Ministries, and Our Savior's Church is a strong supporter of this network organization in central Denver. Its focus is on welcoming all people, in a community of diversity, with justice.[5]

The Lutheran Office of Governmental Ministry is a network of Colorado Lutheran congregations. It is headquartered in Denver, and focuses on communication, education, and advocacy on state legislation. The ministry operates an office in Capitol Hill. It is staffed with a lobbyist to inform the churches of significant legislation pending, alerts churches of specific issues of interest to the faith community,

4. Bonita Bock, "Urban Servant Corps Mission Statement," and "Service Progam Bulletin," 1998. Bock is director of the Urban Servant Corps.
5. Capitol Hill United Ministries, "Program Bulletin," 1998.

and creates study committees to consider theological and ethical perspectives on legislation. The office is a clearinghouse for information. It aids churches in speaking effectively in relation to legislation. The Governmental Ministry conducts an annual Lutheran Day at the Legislature, which promotes communication with legislators, focuses on key issues, and helps to create an informed participation in the democratic process. Our Savior's Church is a strong supporter of this network of advocacy for social justice in legislation. Recent key issues have been the civil rights of gay and lesbian people, welfare reform, and regional planning guidelines in the Denver metropolitan area.

Other network programs in which the members of Our Savior's Church participate include the Denver area Habitat for Humanity housing projects, partnerships for tutoring in the public schools, and a new and emerging alliance in support of the Denver Institute of Urban Studies. Our Savior's Church has been a key supporter and promoter of the formation of the Institute, which will bring together resources from several area theological seminaries, universities, and urban churches into a program of education and skill training for clergy and laity. Dr. Peter Kjeseth, a member of Our Savior's Church and a Lutheran theological professor, is one of the early promoters of the Institute.

How Personal and Social Realms Connect

In urban churches, one often finds that the experiences of individuals in their personal life lead them to interact with the realm of social, economic, and political issues. Persons are living in both an individual personal world and the social, economic, and political world at the same time, but often it takes some unusual experience to make people aware of that reality. Churches can be the communicative context within which persons are helped to make creative connections between their individual life experience and the larger social, economic, and political structures. Several stories will help to illustrate this important connection and how the church can nurture it.

Karen May is an active member of Our Savior's Lutheran Church. More than twenty-five years ago, she and her husband moved to Denver to start a small construction business. They intentionally moved into inner-city Denver to live, and became active members of the church. Karen is a nurse and worked in that profession while also helping her husband with the growing construction business. Quite unexpectedly, her husband was killed in an accident. Suddenly she was confronted with the choice of whether or not to continue the contracting business. Friends and church members urged her to take over the business. She decided to do so, and with help from other family members and friends, she made a success of it. Prior to the loss of her husband, she had been a volunteer and then assistant director of the church's senior center program for older persons in the Capitol Hill neighborhood. During her grief she found comfort and support from a number of the older women who came to the senior center. They understood the feelings of losing a husband, the shock of a sudden and unexpected death, and the need for personal sharing and listening. Out of this mutual listening and learning came encouragement for a project that people had been talking about for some time — a new senior apartment housing development to be sponsored by the church. The struggle of older, widowed women to find adequate and affordable housing in Denver was a challenge that church members and neighborhood residents could join if there was leadership. Karen decided, along with others, to make a commitment to provide that leadership. As an experienced contractor she understood construction. As a friend of many older women and men, she understood their urgent need. As a Christian and member of Our Savior's Lutheran Church, she sensed this was a challenge that called for her positive response. With encouragement from Pastor Luther Johnson and other church members, she served as a key leader in the construction of a new, three-story apartment building — Emerson Gardens — with thirty units of affordable housing for senior citizens. Sponsored by the church, built on church-owned land next to the sanctuary, and related to the senior center program conducted in the church, this new housing facility became the hub of a strong community of older citizens in the Capitol Hill neighborhood. Out of personal experience through the church community can come significant action for social justice. Leadership can come from unexpected sources when people are affirmed, encouraged, and supported to use their skills in a faithful commitment.[6]

Karen May would be the first to insist that this successful senior

6. Karen May, interview with author, 2 April 1998.

housing ministry is the result of the commitment of the whole congregation and the hard work of many people, including Pastor Luther
Johnson. Of course, that is correct. However, in the midst of every
significant, organized, long-term effort for community improvement
there are usually one or two persons who are the persistent leaders
and movers who inspire others. The faith community is energized by
them and enabled to make the extra effort it takes to accomplish substantial progress.

A second story helps to illuminate this reality. Ted Gleichman
was attracted to Our Savior's Lutheran Church through the anti-war
movement. He was a young, ardent peace activist looking for connection with others who had a deep commitment to peace. Through several years of shared peace activism, demonstrations, campaigns,
study groups, and many conversations with friends in the peace
movement who were also members of Our Savior's Church, he was
attracted to the church. As many serious peace activists do, he was
searching for deeper understanding of the forces that make for war
and the forces that make for peace. He found greater understanding
and depth of commitment among peacemaking friends who were
thinking theologically about what contributes to lasting peace. That
meaningful encounter brought him into the church. In the context of
Christian worship, theological study, and faith community nurture,
he gradually became involved in other areas of the church's urban
ministry. Beyond this, Gleichman continues his commitment to
peacemaking with others through a variety of activities, including the
Amnesty International Chapter in Denver (headquartered in Our
Savior's Church) and the Friends of Namibia, Africa — a Lutheran
network for justice in southern Africa.[7]

Experience in one area of personal life can lead to connections
with other arenas of social justice through the nurture of the church.
Real peace persons do not quit, they move on to new arenas of action
for justice, with the understanding that peace is both an inner spiritual reality and an external social/political movement. Our Savior's
Lutheran Church nurtures that creative connection between the inner spirit and positive social expression. The church is a positive witness that big things can come from smaller-sized congregations that
have vision, courage, and long-term persistence.

7. Solveg Kjeseth, church member, interview with author, 2 April 1998.

What We Can Learn

- It is possible for a congregation of modest size to have a big vision and accomplish substantial outcomes for community improvement.
- A long and focused pastoral tenure can foster significant contributions by a small congregation to the surrounding community in a large city. Luther Johnson's focus on peace, service, and justice has made a lasting contribution.
- A smaller congregation can sometimes meet community needs more easily than a large church, with less layers of decision-making, greater flexibility, and a smaller circle of communication.
- Leadership that is mature and skilled is important, but perhaps even more important are commitment, persistence, courage, and knowing how to get help. These qualities of leadership are very important for small churches to succeed in creating stable, long-lasting ministries of justice and community development.
- Worship that is culturally appropriate can provide the unifying center within a diverse congregation, as well as the spiritual nurture for socially relevant ministry.
- A clear biblical theology that is consistently related to individual and social circumstances can become the seedbed for imaginative ministries of justice.
- History is important. In the 1950s and 1960s, a number of central Denver churches were deciding to move out of the city. Our Savior's Lutheran Church decided to stay in the Capitol Hill area, expand its facilities, and minister to the changing neighborhood around it. In that process it was transformed and its ministry redirected. Congregations that anticipate change, plan for it, and make a commitment to a new future have a much better outcome than those who deny change, delay responding, and change reactively.
- Welcoming a variety of local, national, and international organizations to use church facilities can bring the leavening into the loaf that causes the bread to rise. In other words, new partners can bring positive influences that help a church become more responsible and proactive in the community.
- Creating a healthy balance between the inner spiritual life of the

congregation and the outward community engagement is an on-going challenge. The worship and faith-nurturing ministry of the church and the social justice and community service ministry are inseparable. One cannot thrive for long without the other.

Montview Boulevard Presbyterian Church

One of the great challenges of the decade for mainline Protestant churches is seeking to engage, involve, and minister to the "baby boomer" generation. The adult population now between the ages of thirty-five and fifty-five has stayed away from traditional, mainline churches in large numbers. They have often found the church uninteresting, unhelpful, and unnecessary in their lives. The boomers' preference for individual autonomy, personal choice, social freedom, and primacy of expressive experience over traditional forms of authority has challenged conventional mainline churches.[1] In the decade of the 1990s, some urban churches have changed and learned ways of being more effective in relation to the boomers. The boomer population has also changed somewhat, and discovered positive value in church participation. The story of the Montview Boulevard Presbyterian Church in Denver is, in part, a story of the significant reengagement of a generation of upwardly mobile, professional families.

In the 1950s, the Montview Church was a large, thriving congregation with over three thousand members, lots of young families, youth, and children. It was the very symbol of successful, Presbyterian, middle- and upper-class prosperity. The church is situated in the Park Hill community, a fine residential area of large, spacious homes. The congregation has always attracted members from all over the city

---

1. Wade Clark Roof and William McKinney, *American Mainline Religion* (New Brunswick, NJ: Rutgers University Press, 1992), 60-63.

of Denver. In the late 1960s, change began. The first challenge was how the neighborhood would respond as African-American families began buying homes and moving into the community. There was a crucial point when pastors from a number of the Protestant churches in the Park Hill neighborhood preached on inclusiveness, welcoming black families, and affirming the responsibility of local churches to serve all people. Montview Church, along with other churches, helped to prevent white flight, stabilize the neighborhood, and welcome new neighbors. The motto over the door of the sanctuary, "A House of Prayer for All People," became more of a living reality. The neighborhood became racially integrated. The Montview Church received some new black members. The area remained a strong, middle- and upper-middle-class community.

Nevertheless, during the decades of the 1970s and 1980s, the Denver suburbs expanded greatly. Newer housing, larger schools, more spacious shopping malls did attract families out of the city into the growing suburbs. The church continued to be a strong congregation. There is a significant group of older members who have been in the church through the decades. They remain strong supporters and faithful participants. As changes came, the church became more intentional about ministry to particular segments of its membership. In 1963, the church sponsored the construction of Montview Manor, a twelve-story apartment residence for seniors. In 1964, the Montview Preschool for young children was established in the church building. These initiatives helped to connect the church more directly to the city.

There is a growing body of younger families — the boomers — who are now at the center of church program and leadership. There are a significant number of single adults in the membership and in the constituency served by church programs. The current church is a lively, vital, and creative congregation of 1,340 members. A number of interesting and significant factors have contributed over the years to the continuing vigor and witness of Montview Church. We will describe several of these factors, including worship, collegial ministry, community center concept, partnerships in mission, and the pursuit of excellence in Christian education.[2]

2. Cynthia Cearley (co-pastor), interview with author, 23 March 1998.

Worship is Central

In an era when many urban congregations were adapting to the electronic culture, contemporary music, and more praise-oriented worship, the Montview Church has affirmed, strengthened, and continued its reformed tradition of classical worship. The liturgy is organized in three parts: gathering in God's name; listening for God's Word; and responding to God's grace. The acts of worship are the traditional Reformed elements, including prayers of praise, confession/pardon, thanksgiving, intercession, and petition; congregational hymn singing and choral music; scripture reading; sermon; sacraments of baptism and communion; and offerings of money and service. There is little that is different from many other mainline churches. What marks this worship as special is the excellence of content, style, and leadership. There is careful attention to language; it is inclusive and sensitive. The preaching is biblical, faith-affirming and related to daily life. The classical choral music is offered by well-rehearsed choirs (adult, youth, children). Children are welcomed and come to the chancel for stories of biblical faith, well told. Prayers of the people are supportive, but not intrusive. Commitment to justice is promoted and mission is celebrated. There is confession of sin, as well as assurance of pardon and redirection toward transformation. The affirmation of mission is connected to prayer. There is an atmosphere of quiet reverence and mystical spirituality. Worship leadership by the three co-pastors is strong and articulate. Worship is clearly the unifying and empowering center for the congregation.

Collegial Ministry

Most large congregations that have multiple clergy on the staff have developed a hierarchical pattern with a senior minister as the head of staff, and other ministers as associates and assistants. Since 1975, Montview Church has developed a very different approach to pastoral leadership. The Montview model is a co-pastor team in which the pastors are equals serving the congregation, each with full pastoral status, duties, rights, responsibilities, and leadership functions. In the past several decades, Montview Church has had a team of three co-pastors, all of whom brought experienced, skilled, and mature leadership to the ministry. There is full sharing in the principal public roles of preaching, worship leadership, pastoral work, and moderating the church governing body. The concept emphasizes that ministry belongs to the whole church. Pastors are equals among the people in sharing leadership for ministry.[3] The Montview co-pastor model visibly shows that talented, skilled, professional people can relate, cooperate, strengthen one another, and create a climate within which other talented persons can find a spiritual home. This culture of colleagues in ministry has helped to produce an environment that is attractive to younger couples and families seeking to practice equality in their partnerships. A large number of younger professionals and boomer generation families with school-age children have been attracted into church worship and membership.

Implicit in the collegial working model are certain values highly prized by members at Montview. Some of these values are competence, creativity, responsibility, partnership, expressive talent, teamwork, and excellence. The interpersonal skills for cooperation, collaboration, and contribution to congregational ministry internally and in the community are gifts that many members bring to the church. Montview may be characterized as a caring congregation with a gracious spirit, a progressive theology, and a capacity for generous giving. It has always had a strong commitment to supporting the wider mission of the church in Denver and beyond. It has participated in the work of schools, hospitals, and churches in Alaska, Bolivia, Bangladesh, Haiti, India, Kenya, Nepal, Nicaragua, Mexico, and Senegal. The collegial, co-pastoral model of ministry leadership is a positive and powerful symbol of a church that gives itself freely for the city and the world.

The Church as a Community Center

The Mission Statement of the Montview Presbyterian Church, which appears in the Sunday worship bulletin, puts the emphasis on nurturing the spirit of Christ in the community of faith:

> We believe God is the redeemer of all. The mission of Montview Presbyterian Church is to nurture the spirit of Christ that is within

3. Cearley, "The Co-Pastor Model" (Doctoral diss., Princeton Theological Seminary, 1995).

each of us. Together we create a supportive community of faith through worship, education, evangelism, fellowship, Bible study, prayer and social justice.

Since its earliest years, the congregation has affirmed and worked to make the church a center of service to the wider community. Its faith that God's redemption is a gift of grace for all people has compelled it toward mission in the community and the wider world.

There are many community groups that feel at home in the Montview Church building as a place for their regular meetings and activity. There is an excellent preschool for young children. There is a counseling service for the community. The Denver area Habitat for Humanity involves a number of Montview members, and the church has supported the construction of a number of houses built in Denver by Habitat. There is an active Justice-Love Committee working on the issues involving sexual orientation in Denver. A gay men's musical chorus rehearses in the church. Montview Church makes financial grants in support of a number of community groups in the Park Hill area and in the Denver metropolitan area.[4]

Of special interest is the strong support and active participation by members of the Tutoring Program in the public schools. A long-standing partnership with the Park Hill Elementary School engages members on Tuesday afternoons and with Ashley Elementary School on Wednesday afternoons. Tutoring is also done at the Denver Manual High School on weekdays and after school. A special part of this partnership is focused on career assessment counseling with senior high school students. Perhaps the most challenging and rewarding community service through Montview Church is members' involvement with the People's Learning Center. Here they serve in tutoring adults who are completing their high school equivalency program to receive the GED certificate. This adult education program is linked to employment.

Montview members are key leaders in organizing the annual CROP Hunger Walk in the Park Hill area. Church members are active in the local Bread for the World hunger education and legislative advocacy program. The Peace and Justice Task Force relates to a number of local programs in the area. There is strong support for the work of

4. "Habitat for Humanity Dedicates Presbyterian House," *The Montview Messenger* 56:6 (9 March 1998): 15.

Church World Service and its global outreach for refugees, victims of war, famine relief, and agricultural mission. The congregation enjoys a special partnership with a number of churches and other religious traditions in the community. There are several fellowship events with the nearby Macedonia Baptist Church, an African-American congregation. There is a Palm Sunday breakfast and worship event with the nearby Blessed Sacrament Catholic Church. There is an annual Interfaith Thanksgiving Service shared with Buddhist, Jewish, Muslim, and Unitarian congregations of the area, and a World Religions Seminar is held each fall.

There is a strong commitment to serious study of Christian faith and current political, social, and justice issues in the Adult Christian Education Program of the church. Study is organized into a series of six-week program units. Beyond the usual units of Bible study and theological issues, there are justice issues with experts in each field doing the teaching on such topics as: The Struggle for Affirmative Action; How is Welfare Reform Working; The U.S. Tax System in Relation to Housing; The Challenge of Affordable Housing in Denver; Confronting Racism; The Church and Homosexuality; Colorado Election Issues; Sharing Ways to Balance Family, Work, Love. It is not an overstatement to say that there is a constant, creative give-and-take between the faith of the church and the ongoing struggles in the wider community.[5]

Partnerships for Global Mission

The Montview Church is anticipating and planning for its centennial celebration in the year 2002. One of the most important commitments in preparation for the 100th birthday is a Centennial Fund Campaign to raise at least one million dollars. This fund is to be equally divided, with half of the funds used for renewal of the church building and organ, and half for ten major mission projects outside the United States as well as four mission projects in and around Denver. The concept of equal sharing of mission resources puts the church into substantial involvement with partners in Nepal, Bolivia,

5. "The Church Education Bulletin," *The Montview Messenger* (Fall, Winter, Spring issues, 1997-1998).

and China. In the mountains of Nepal, near Kathmandu, the Montview Church will be in partnership with the Patan Hospital to finance the construction of a new sixty-bed pediatric unit to provide medical care to children. The present Patan Hospital is operating at 150 percent occupancy, so the new unit is desperately needed. Also in Nepal, the Montview Church partnership will help finance and build two new elementary schools and five new community health clinics. A husband and wife medical missionary team, members of Montview Church, has been engaged for years in remote areas of Nepal creating schools and clinics. They will enable the church project to have expert guidance in collaborating with the people of Nepal. An adult work trip to Nepal to participate in these construction projects is planned for the year 2000.

In the city of Hangzhou, China, the Montview partnership will be with the theological seminary. Funding from the church will enable additional building construction to serve a rapidly growing student body. It will also help provide scholarships for lay persons who are being trained for leadership. The Christian churches are growing in China at the rate of ten new congregations per week, or over five thousand new churches a year. Montview's minister for pastoral care was a former Presbyterian mission teacher at the seminary in Hangzhou. So there are direct personal links to the seminary. The churches in China may be growing faster than in any other place in the world today.

In Bolivia, the Montview partnership is with the women's movement that is developing community banks in rural areas. The church's investment, together with that of other partners, will help to create ten new community banks. These rural lending institutions make small loans to families that enable them to increase production of saleable crops, obtain small machines for agriculture, and develop their marketing. It is estimated that the new banks will benefit over two hundred families with about twelve hundred people. Women are at the head of most of these working family groups, and until recently they could not obtain loans at all. The rural banks are opening up significant new opportunities for life improvement and greater socioeconomic justice. A Montview Church member who is a veterinarian has served the rural people of Bolivia for a decade.[6] It

6. "Remember — Renew," *The Centennial Campaign*, January 1998, pp. 2, 4-5.

is the hope of the church that contact with these projects will continue for several generations. All of this helps to strengthen what co-pastor Cynthia Cearley calls the faith and vocation connection. Members are commissioned as people in mission for service in places around the world.

Partnership for Local Mission

After a process of consultation within the congregation to determine what the members of the church wanted to do in local mission, four local partnerships were chosen — two local social service agencies, the Denver Habitat for Humanity, and a regional Presbyterian Conference Center. In Denver, $50,000 will be divided between two social work agencies — the Metro Care Ring, and the Home of Neighborly Service. Metro Care Ring provides emergency food, clothing, and counseling to people in need. The gift will enable the agency to create a new program of assisting families to find affordable housing in Denver. This is an urgent need citywide. The Neighborly Service provides a variety of emergency care and resources to people throughout the metropolitan area. The church has a long history of partnership and support of these social work agencies. Montview Church will invest $100,000 in the construction of two new houses, through Habitat for Humanity, for low-income families in the Park Hill area. Church members will be involved in the construction in partnership with the families whose homes the houses will become.

The other local project that will benefit is the Highlands Presbyterian Camp and Conference Center near Allenspark, Colorado, with $100,000 invested in new buildings. This regional facility is used by many churches and serves thousands of youth and adults, including many from Montview Church.

The special Centennial Fund Campaign continues and strengthens a number of significant working relationships with community organizations. It will reinforce avenues of member involvement in service and justice efforts that will extend into the next century. There is a strong emphasis on the laity using their professional skills and personal talents for service in Christ's name in the community and around the world. The hands-on mission projects with direct action involvement and tangible results are an authentic expression of the congregation's mission tradition.[7] It is also a clear statement of the boomer generation with its preference for experientially-oriented religious life, interest in achieving positive results, and trust in locally determined initiatives. These are some of the values that Montview enables its members to carry out in mission.

User-Friendly Christian Education

The key to much of the vitality and growth at Montview is described by Co-Pastor Cearley, when she says, "We seek to unite families." The church's Christian education program has a strong element of nurture that helps families. Everything from the weekday preschool to the pattern of short-term six-week classes is planned to help unite families and make the church a place where families can come together in worship and learning. The Sunday church school strives for excellence. One pattern that helps is the six-week terms. It is easier to recruit top teachers for short terms. Talented artists, musicians, gifted teachers, skilled storytellers, or experienced computer wizards will make the commitment to teach children and youth for limited terms. So there is a rich variety and rapid rotation in the faculty of the school. The Sunday church school is thriving. It has an enrollment of over five hundred, which is outstanding in this era of decline in most Sunday church schools. Altogether, over one thousand adults, youth, and children are involved in the education program. Integrated into the Montview program is a series of choirs for children and youth in which students learn the classical tradition of church music and hymns. Children are welcomed in church worship and there is a focused time in the liturgy following scripture reading for special words to children. They come to the chancel area numbering forty to fifty in a group. There is a very positive environment for children at Montview. They are valued, nurtured, affirmed, and drawn into the community of faith with adults.

The Adult Education Program is a multi-faceted diamond through which the light of learning comes to persons from many different angles. There are the series of six-week classes in four tracks: (1) Knowing the Word, (2) Living the Word, (3) Sharing the Word, and

7. Glendora Taylor (co-pastor), interview with author, 31 March 1998.

(4) Exploring the Word. There are a large number of small Bible study groups meeting throughout the week and on Sundays. There is a conscious effort to teach the Bible at a sophisticated level, using the best scholarly texts as well as recruiting visiting teachers from local seminaries and university faculties. Groups and classes are specially designed for women and for men to focus on the issues and concerns unique to each gender. All age groups can find gatherings planned for them. A number of groups integrate fellowship, study, and mission. There is balance and inclusiveness with study of scripture, world religion, men's and women's issues, ethical and justice concerns, and spirituality. This wide variety of Christian education opportunities encourages persons to connect with study when and where their schedule and lifestyle allows. Always there is choice. Members can sample or go more deeply into serious study. The liturgical seasons, great worship events, holidays, and musical performances help to knit it all together.

Life in Denver, in comparison to many other larger American cities, feels a bit more relaxed, more comprehensible, more enjoyable, and more manageable. There is a full range of urban challenges, but perhaps they are not so deep nor out of control as they seem to be in some other metropolitan areas. So, also, one might say of the Montview Presbyterian Church that its worship, spiritual life, and community mission have a high level of comfort and great stability. Relationships are warm, supportive, and stimulating. Program planning is well done within a comfortable timeframe that encourages good things to develop and mature. There is good quality in all the major areas of church life. There is a strong and significant commitment to service within the church and in the public sector. The church is on the threshold of moving beyond service toward engagement in the struggle for justice. It is definitely a congregation with a plan for moving positively ahead into the next century.

What We Can Learn

- Ministry that successfully involves professional families needs to be user friendly and develop ways to bring families together in church.
- A collegial co-pastor model of ministry is helpful in attracting a younger generation of members into the church.

- Worship services that combine christocentric faith, excellent music, and insightful preaching in a traditional Reformed approach can be very appealing to a generation of worshippers seeking meaning and spiritual guidance.
- A tradition of global mission involvement and public service helps to keep a congregation's life vital, energized, and constantly moving beyond self-preoccupation.
- Forming partnerships with other faith-based agencies of community service enables a congregation to move beyond charity toward efforts for justice. Commitment to social justice is not just having the right ideas; it is also corporate action that seeks greater justice in society.
- Good, long-term, advance planning greatly increases the opportunities for members' engagement in meaningful projects that express the faith of a church. The five-year advance plan for the Montview Centennial is a model for maximizing participation of members, producing new mission, and building partnerships that will last long into the next century.
- The Montview Church should be saluted for its wisdom in having three mature co-pastors providing leadership for its ministry. Their creative leadership also shows the benefit of long-term pastoral tenure.
- Montview demonstrates that it is possible to be a regional church and also serve a local neighborhood. Its emphasis on excellence attracts members from the metropolitan region. Its community-based programs engage the neighborhood. Together they make a strong congregation.

Windsor Village
United Methodist Church

"They shall repair the ruined cities and restore what has long been desolate" (Isaiah 61:4). This is the central vision of transformation that guides the Windsor Village United Methodist Church in Houston. The ministry of the Reverend Kirbyjon Caldwell, since 1982, has provided creative leadership for the rebirth and redevelopment of the Windsor congregation from twenty-five members to over ten thousand members in 1998. The key to the transformation, according to Caldwell, is understanding the Kingdom of God as a comprehensive vision that includes all aspects of human life. Biblical spirituality is not limited to the inner spiritual world. True spirituality is inclusive of people's everyday social, physical, material, and religious well-being.[1]

From a theological point of view, says Caldwell, "We believe God is just as concerned about the salvation of the whole community as about the salvation of the individual. Anyone who seeks to separate the two has failed to understand the ethos of the Old Testament and the teaching of Jesus Christ as seen in the New Testament."[2] Members of the Windsor Church are nurtured in a community that embodies the expectation that they can and will make a positive difference in the larger society. The church believes that it is called to be a living incarnation of the gospel active in the world.

1. Kirbyjon Caldwell, interview with author, 13 October 1997.
2. Robbie Morganfield, "Power Center: Model for Urban Life," *Houston Chronicle*, 10 September 1995.

This kind of dynamic faith has empowered the church during the past seventeen years to create a ministry that includes, but is not limited to, the following areas of ministry.[3]

- *Worship.* Four Sunday services and one Saturday service pulsate with power for ninety minutes of lively singing, multicultural music, dynamic preaching, practical spirituality, affirmative praying, and witness to the power of Christ through whom all things can be done. Over six thousand people come to worship on Saturday and Sunday.
- *Education.* The church operates a large Sunday school plus a weekday IMANI School for children from age three through twelve. (*Imani* is Swahili for "to believe the power of God.") In addition, there is a large program of adult education, including the College of Business Technology. The Kingdom Builders Prayer Institute, founded by the pastor in 1995, is a major effort to foster intercessory prayer, train people in the art and discipline of prayer, and create active expression of prayer power for the city, the nation, and the world. A state-of-the-art telecommunication prayer center operates continuously. It was assisted by a financial gift from world boxing champion, Evander Holyfield.
- *Economy.* The church organized the Pyramid Community Development Corporation to improve the quality of life in southwest Houston. Pyramid became the vehicle for purchasing an entire K-Mart Shopping Plaza in the area and renovating it into the Power Center for economic and community-building activity. The Power Center includes a major commercial office building, a conference center, business services, a branch of the Texas Commerce Bank, health care center, educational facilities, and a chapel. It is an income generator, a job creator, and has sparked renewal in the area.
- *Health.* The church has created a health center — a large health clinic located in the neighborhood Power Center building, owned by the Pyramid Development Corporation. The medical program is operated by the University of Texas Herman Hospital and provides primary care for hundreds of families. The health ministry also includes a strong Aids Pre-

3. Caldwell, interview.

vention and Care Program and outreach into public housing projects.

- *Social.* The church has attracted and organized a number of social service and self-help programs, including an art gallery, children's theater, comprehensive job training, Women-Infant-Children (WIC) assistance, career planning, education for home owners, financial planning, and entrepreneurial training. There are many support groups with emphasis on empowerment and self-development. For example, UJIMA Incorporated provides tutoring, job training, and spiritual support to over 350 families and 500 young adults in four Houston apartment complexes. WAM, the Windsor AIDS Ministry, provides health education, HIV screening, and support counseling through a network of eight programs. Emphasis is on both helping individuals and connecting families with the church and community agencies.

- *Housing.* The church strongly encourages home ownership. It helps families plan and prepare for ownership responsibilities and promotes the discipline of earning, saving, and investing. It has created a spin-off corporation to plan and construct a new subdivision of moderate-cost family housing. In partnership with the Texas Housing Authority, the U.S. Department of Housing and Urban Redevelopment, and local banks, a development of 436 single-family homes is being constructed. Market research showed a strong interest among one thousand families in the church and surrounding neighborhood for such housing. Purchase prices range from $65,000 to $125,000 depending on size and floor plan. The vision of creating affordable housing and stable community reflects the wisdom of Jeremiah, "Seek the welfare of the city where I have sent you. Work for its welfare. Pray to the Lord on its behalf. For in seeking its welfare you will find your own welfare" (Jeremiah 29:7).

The creation of healthy, growing, strong community is the transforming dynamic that has helped the Windsor Church develop from twenty-five members in 1982 to over ten thousand members in 1998. Although the congregation comes from the metropolitan region, it has a majority core of members in the surrounding neighborhoods. Over eighty percent of the members are within fifteen minutes of the church. Over sixty percent are involved every week in church worship and programming.

The Struggle of a Black Church in a White Denomination

When Caldwell was appointed by the United Methodist bishop to be pastor of the Windsor United Methodist Church it had only twenty-five members, its property was for sale, and it was struggling to survive. The surrounding neighborhood was shifting from white to black. A friend told him, "There will be plenty of room for the church to grow because those few members who are there are going to leave when you get there." When Caldwell's high-energy leadership, spirited preaching, and commitment to the community began to be known, the church began to grow. It grew rapidly in the 1980s, becoming the fastest-growing congregation in the United Methodist denomination. The congregation was transformed from a small, dying gathering into a church that attracted eight hundred to one thousand new members a year by the late 1980s. Caldwell's unique education (Carleton College BA in Economics, University of Pennsylvania MBA in finance, theological education at the Perkins School of Theology in Dallas) and his experience in business with the Wall Street firm of First Boston and the Houston investment company of Hibbard, O'Connell and Weeks, contributed to his skills and confidence in organization and leadership for growing the church. It helped him envision creative financing for church ministry projects. It also helped in attracting middle-class black families from the Houston metropolitan region.

While Caldwell found ready acceptance in the business community, the denomination seemed reluctant to believe in his success. With a rapidly growing congregation it became evident that Windsor Church needed a larger sanctuary. Caldwell took the congregation's plans for building expansion to the Methodist Board of Missions for approval, and the board rejected the plan. Caldwell proposed a plan to finance the new building by selling interest-bearing bonds instead of the more conventional method of borrowing from banks. The mission board raised many questions and objections. Three times Caldwell presented the plan, each time supplying more information, dealing with objections, answering questions, and providing documentation. One member of the mission board who supported the bond financing plan reported that at the fourth request for approval it was asked, "Why are we being so critical of this plan? If this was a white church we would have approved the plan six months ago." That day the vote to approve the project plan was taken and it was unanimously approved.[4] The new sanctuary was constructed, the bond finance plan worked, the congregation continued to grow, and the plan for sale of bonds worked well. "The church needs new ideas, some imagination and the willingness to risk. If you always do what you have always done, then you will always get what you've already got," says Caldwell.[5]

In 1992, the Methodist hierarchy asked Caldwell to accept pastoral responsibility for St. John's United Methodist Church in downtown Houston. This was another small, dying congregation in a large old building, trying to serve homeless street people. His response is a creative symbol of what is needed in numerous struggling downtown, mainline churches. Caldwell indicated he would not move to the St. John's Church, but would accept responsibility for pastoral oversight if given a free hand to be creative. The bishop agreed and Caldwell installed a husband and wife team as lay pastors. Rudy and Juanita Rasmus do not have formal theological education, but they bring a deep Christian faith and many professional skills to the leadership at St. John's Church. He is an experienced real estate professional and she is an experienced financial planner. Their positive leadership has helped the church become renewed and do amazing things in urban ministry. Their story is told later in this book.

Working for Systemic Justice

From his experience in the business world, Caldwell understands the importance of corporate systems and how they shape and influence the lives of people. As an example, he has reported:

> It takes, on average, thirty thousand tax dollars a year to keep an African American in prison, but only five thousand dollars a year to

4. Mimi Swartz, "Race, Religion, and Economic Opportunity," *The Texas Monthly* (September 1996): 138.
5. Caldwell, interview.

keep the same person in school. A disproportionate percentage of the prison population is Black and poor. So the issue is how to change the systems, structures, and processes of society so as to constructively engage their collective gifts and talents. Without economic power there is no hope for positive and long lasting change.[6]

Caldwell engages this issue of economic development personally and directly as well as within the program of the Windsor Church.

He personally lobbied Houston's Herman Hospital to increase the number of minority contractors in its many multimillion-dollar construction projects. He helped the Texas Commerce Bank become a major lender to minority-owned businesses. He was an effective leader in recruiting well-qualified minority candidates for election to the Houston School Board, with a view toward improving public education for minority children. As a result of his nonconfrontational style of negotiation he was elected to serve on a number of significant boards of directors, including the board of the Houston Commerce Bank, the Herman Hospital Board Investment Committee, and the board of governors of the Houston Forum Club. He carries the message in these circles that investing in minority-owned businesses is good business, and permitting a widening gap between the haves and have-nots is bad business. He works to support affirmative action hiring and active minority group political participation.

The Windsor Church is the embodiment of positive economic action. It starts with Caldwell's preaching. He frequently affirms that the Old Testament has a strong stream of economic justice running through it and that over half of the parables of Jesus have economic themes and deal with money. He preaches, and the church teaches, the discipline of systematic saving, investment, and sacrificial giving. The congregation's commitment to developing the Power Center — a complex of business facilities in the church neighborhood in a former K-Mart Shopping Center — has created an economic input of over $25 million into the local minority economy over a three-year period. Beyond this economic impact in a transitional neighborhood, it models black economic enterprise, stimulates entrepreneurial vision, and promotes community confidence. The current development of a major new housing subdivision of 436 units is an economic investment to produce affordable homes, the construction of which will create hun-

6. Swartz, "Race, Religion, and Economic Opportunity," 138.

dreds of good-paying jobs and help minority contractors. The church emphasizes the importance of members being politically responsible and active. In a sermon, Caldwell said, "If you did not vote in the election last Tuesday, please don't let me know. In the past many folks were knocked down by water hoses, bitten by police dogs, severely beaten, and some were killed so that we could have the right to vote. Anyone who does not exercise the right to vote is an abomination to God and a miserable misrepresentation of our foreparents."[7]

Kirbyjon Caldwell's Ten Points for Transformation of the Church

Caldwell summarizes some basic operating principles that are helpful for a transforming church.[8] It is evident that the first five principles deal with spirit and attitude. The second group of five deals with leadership and systems.

1. *Prayer.* Everything begins with prayer and is nurtured by listening for God's leading.
2. *Vision.* The places of pain and struggle for justice give rise to vision for mission.
3. *Kairos.* We must be perceptive of God's time of favor, fulfillment, and purpose.
4. *Questions.* It is important to ask *big* questions and develop a transcendent viewpoint.
5. *Positive Perspective.* Do not dwell on failure. Problems are opportunities for doing new things.
6. *People.* Leaders are people with vision, energy, and commitment who want to do new things.
7. *Real Needs.* Meet urgent needs, know the market, have a broad view of human needs.
8. *Think.* Be imaginative, think outside the box. New situations call for new ideas.
9. *Helpful Structure.* Create a positive, productive, support system. Seek new partnerships.

7. William Martin, "Sunday Best," *The Texas Monthly* (October 1994): 60.
8. Caldwell, interview.

10. *Creative Financing.* Abundant life is the promise of the gospel. Financial resources can be found in surprising places. Explore how your own financial interests and those of others can be combined.

Worship Is the Center

All of the diverse ministries of the Windsor Church are knit together in the rich worship life of the congregation. The multiple services held on Saturday and Sunday provide the dynamic spiritual energy that lifts the people of Windsor Church to a level of life and witness that is a cut above the ordinary. There is a strong participatory spirit. The sanctuary is a beehive of communication. Music and hymns include classical, gospel, and contemporary spirituals. The singing is vigorous. Musical diversity is present in the rich mix of organ and electronic instruments. Members give witness to the transforming power of the gospel in their everyday lives. Intercessory prayer is a vibrant experience. There is a high level of expectation that the gospel will make a difference in the lives of worshippers. There is a strong focus on responsibility in personal and social life. Preaching is the center of worship. Sermons are biblical and practical. Caldwell both assures listeners of the positive power of God's transforming spirit and challenges them to disciplined, responsible life. Sermons deal with relationships; marriage partnership; communication; family life; social, political, economic discipline; and sacrificial giving. Caldwell is a whirlwind preacher. His style is rousing — moving around the chancel, kneeling down, springing up, gesturing energetically, laughing, singing, demonstrating, whispering, and emphatically declaring God's expectations and God's love. Worshippers are challenged to be doers as well as hearers of the Word.

Giving is a means of God's grace being experienced. Caldwell invites persons with financial victories to come to the chancel to thank God for abundant blessing and those with financial concerns to come to the chancel for power to meet financial needs. Many come forward for this affirmation and witness. Blessing is connected to justice and responsibility. Unless there is economic justice there won't be peace in the community. The congregation is challenged to earn, save, invest, and give. "If issues are important enough to talk about, then they are important enough for people to do something about them," says Caldwell. "The days when the church could be high on creeds and low on deeds and expect the pews to be filled are long gone. Churches being led by God to minister among African American people in the twenty-first century must embrace theology, identify problems, and deliver solutions holistically, which is to say, spiritually, economically, and socially."[9]

It is significant to see that the Windsor congregation is made up of a diversity of people who respond positively to the vigorous spirit, style, and social witness of the church. The baby boomers and young professionals are there. The message of strong commitment to family life reaches them. The social activists are there and engaged in the ministries of economic justice and development. The older generation finds fellowship and pastoral support. Youth and children are involved in education programs and are drawn by lively music and the participatory style. There is a cross section of socioeconomic groups, and a multicultural flavor with the presence of Hispanic families. "This is the gift of God," says Caldwell, "and we must press onward as stewards of God's blessing."

The worship services, four on Sunday and one on Saturday, are about ninety minutes in length and that is because of the amount of interaction. Music sets a positive tone. There is an air of relaxed formality. Caldwell does not wear traditional clergy robes. He leads and preaches from a central platform with the congregation, choir, and electronic combo gathered around in a semicircle. There are several prominent focuses in the service. The central focus is the sermon. But intercessory prayer and the witnessing that takes place around the offering are also key centers of worship. The language of Caldwell's sermons is a rich mix of contemporary vernacular, biblical stories retold in modern voice, and pragmatic savvy from the business world. The sanctuary worship space is a plain but comfortable auditorium without much symbolism. The central platform puts the preacher in the middle of the congregation. The public address system is top quality. There are no banners, stained glass windows, or icons. The communion table has only a plain cross and candles. The main focus is on the interaction of people and pastor, and the atmosphere is energy-filled, spiritually alive, and Christ-centered.

9. Swartz, "Race, Religion, and Economic Opportunity," 138.

The Power Center: Thinking Big

In 1994, after Caldwell had been pastor of Windsor Village Church for more than a decade, he was approached by the owners of Houston's Fiesta supermarket food chain about a vacant K-Mart property they owned just a few blocks from the church. Fiesta wanted to lease the twenty-four acres and 100,000 square foot space to the church. Caldwell had a different idea. He proposed that Fiesta give the entire property to the church, a $4.4 million gift, and Fiesta decided to do just that.

The food chain got a tax write-off, a lot of good publicity, and unloaded a vacant building that had become a rat-infested eyesore. Windsor Church got a large property in the parish neighborhood and a big challenge to use it creatively. The vision was for a multipurpose, community-oriented facility that would generate income, provide services for the community, house businesses, and spur further economic development. It was a big challenge and a large risk.

Before this could emerge, the building and property needed a $4.5 million renovation. The church did not have the necessary money. Creative financing was needed, and Caldwell put it squarely up to the congregation. The congregation rose to the challenge. A large banner proclaiming, "The Power Center, It's In Your Hands," was installed across the wall of the sanctuary to visualize the challenge. The congregation raised $650,000 cash as its contribution to the renovation. Another $2.9 million came from issuing interest-bearing bonds, and the final $850,000 came from private grants and government sources.[10] To be in a position to issue new interest-bearing bonds the congregation had to refinance its earlier bond issue (the one used to build the new sanctuary) and then take on the obligation of new debt for the second bond issue. Caldwell sought help from the American Investors Group, Inc., a Minneapolis securities company that specializes in working with nonprofit groups. It was a positive action that resulted in successful financing for the renovation of the Power Center.[11]

The property and buildings were renovated and updated over a

10. Caldwell, interview.
11. Rick Wartzman, "A Houston Clergyman Pushes Civic Projects Along With Prayers," *The Wall Street Journal*, 20 February 1996, 1, 9.

three-year period. The redevelopment of the property was a struggle. It did not always go easily. It definitely tested the congregation's determination. Persuading significant businesses to become renters was not easy. But after the bank agreed to move in and the school began operation, other good elements were attracted. The outcome has been a clear gain in many ways. In the process, over two hundred jobs were created and $25 million in cash flow was generated during the first three years of operation. Now the Power Center houses the IMANI School; a branch of the Texas Commerce Bank, which provides home loans and capital for small businesses; a medical center for family primary care; a large commercial banquet and conference facility; a variety of social service agencies; and a recreation facility. All of these entities pay rent for their space. The cash flow from rent is used to pay off the bonds. Also located in the center is the Evander Holyfield Chapel, created through a gift from the champion boxer and his wife. The Power Center is a demonstration of how private and public, nonprofit and profit-making institutions, local businesses and the church can join forces, serve mutual needs, and build a better community.

What We Can Learn

- A holistic understanding of the gospel and of the church sees every major area of human life as an avenue for ministry.
- Congregational redevelopment calls for new strategies of operation and new approaches to ministry that embrace a wide range of individual and social needs.
- The commitment to let the gospel vision rather than financial resources determine the shape of ministry can motivate the church to create and find the needed financial resources.
- Using new sources of funding beyond congregational giving and beyond denominational resources can provide financial capital needed for exponential growth.
- Selling interest-bearing bonds to raise capital funds is a good strategy for a growing congregation. Bonds can be paid off with income generated by the property acquired and by a growing membership through gifts and pledges. This strategy puts a church more in control of its financial potential and creates less dependence on banks.

- Investment in redevelopment of a community (housing, health, education, jobs) is an investment in church growth and ministry. Without stable communities there will not be stable congregations.
- Leadership that has both vision and technical skills combined in the same person is a blessing. The courage to take risks and the know-how to get things done are both necessary for major projects.
- Ultimately, people with the capacity to see, think, and act beyond the conventional wisdom are the most valuable assets in redeveloping a congregation.
- Thinking big and thinking smart at the beginning of a major project can make the difference between a good idea that becomes drudgery and a good idea that is accomplished with relative ease and in a timely fashion.
- Congregational and community redevelopment always involves risk, struggle, some losses and defeats as well as long-term commitment, hard work, creative thinking, and some providential blessing.

St. John's United Methodist Church

"People who have experienced brokenness and have lost everything they cherish come into the church with a readiness to receive God's transforming spirit," says Pastor Rudy Rasmus. "Our calling is to reach out in every appropriate way to be a community of Christ in which God's transforming Spirit is at work."[1]

Rasmus indicates there are over ten thousand homeless and unemployed people in Houston. Many are on the streets around St. John's United Methodist Church. They are the least likely, in conventional wisdom, to be persons to renew a dying church, and yet they are precisely the group who have become the largest body of new members at St. John's Church over the past five years. How has this happened? The short answer is, by the work of God's spirit through the unconventional, but highly skilled and dedicated leadership of a husband and wife pastoral team — Rudy and Juanita Rasmus. Together with a core group of hardworking members and colleagues they have focused on dealing with the basic, down-to-earth needs of Houston's hungry, homeless, unemployed people in a spiritual community.

St. John's Church is situated in downtown Houston in a commercial district. In 1992 when the new leadership came, the large, old sanctuary, which would seat eight hundred, was in a dilapidated and run-down condition. There were only nine members. The once proud

---

1. All of the quotations in this story of St. John's United Methodist Church are from interviews with Rudy Rasmus, by the author, January 1998.

St. John's Methodist Church had lost its congregation over the years to the suburbs. Decay, decline, and death had firmly taken hold. The only permanent population around the church were the homeless, hopeless street people. The Methodist bishop wanted to use the facility as a base for ministry to street people. The bishop asked the Reverend Kirbyjon Caldwell, the pastor of the highly successful Windsor United Methodist Church in Houston, to take pastoral responsibility at St. John's. Caldwell indicated he would not move to the church, but would be willing to accept oversight responsibility of the church if given the freedom to be creative. The Methodist hierarchy agreed. Caldwell recruited Rudy and Juanita Rasmus from his Windsor congregation to be the pastors at St. John's Church.

Juanita and Rudy Rasmus are local Houston people. She was a professional financial planner; he was a self-employed commercial real estate professional. Neither has the traditional theological seminary preparation for ministry. Rudy says that beyond their experience in the business world, "there were two sources of preparation for answering the call to ministry — the school of hard knocks in life experience, and the spiritual mentoring of the Reverend Kirbyjon Caldwell and the Windsor congregation." Rudy affirms that his life in the Christian faith began about a decade ago when he committed his life to Christ in the Windsor United Methodist Church through the preaching of Caldwell. Thereafter came an intense period of study, prayer, involvement at the Windsor Church, and learning from the Windsor model of ministry.

Resurrection to New Life

In 1992, St. John's as a congregation was dead. The only metaphor that can adequately symbolize its coming to life is resurrection. "At the beginning our biggest asset was the overwhelming array of human needs and a clear focus on making the new church a ministry to rebuild human lives individually and collectively. We had seen this resurrection to new life happen at the Windsor Church and we knew God could do it here at St. John's Church also," says Rasmus. "So with a handful of people, a goal of serving hurting people, and a lot of prayer, we began."

One of the early projects for the new ministry was a renovation of the old parsonage adjacent to the church. With volunteers working for many months, the former pastor's residence was remodeled into a facility designed to serve homeless, hungry, unemployed people. They installed a commercial kitchen to support a feeding program. Called Bread of Life, Inc., the program serves meals in the church sanctuary. Rasmus says, "The sanctuary needed to be 'demystified' so homeless people could feel at ease coming into this space. Furthermore, it was the largest space available and we had a lot of hungry people to serve." Bread of Life now operates a large-scale daily feeding program. Its scope includes securing and preparing food with attention to good nutrition, the operation of a bakery, fundraising, and on-the-job training for a steady flow of people who are learning skills for future employment in the food industry.

The renovated building provides temporary shelter space, laundry equipment to enable homeless persons to wash clothes, and showers to enable them to clean up. The building provides temporary shelter space, facilities for a health clinic, and a community gathering space for prayer and counseling. This renovated facility is appropriately named Daybreak. It is a center in which the light of a new day is dawning for hundreds of people. Fifty to sixty persons per day are served, with a focus on transformation, spiritual recovery, and reentry into meaningful employment. In the beginning Daybreak served one hot meal a week, provided personal counseling, prayer, and employment referral. During the past five years that service has evolved into a more comprehensive and systematic approach that includes a nourishing meal seven days a week, primary health care, personal hygiene, group counseling for recovery from addiction, and a complex program of job training, work preparation, and employment placement in cooperation with a growing network of Houston companies.

After several years of voluntary staffing for occasional medical care, Daybreak now operates a professional health clinic on a regular basis. Medical technicians, working under the supervision of physicians, provide basic health care for over a thousand people a year. This program includes a strong program of HIV screening and AIDS follow-up care. Funding comes in part from the city of Houston, private grants, and congregational giving.

Daybreak knows its limits and does not try to do everything. Its focus is on recovery, transformation, and enabling new beginnings in self-respect and employment. Many of the homeless and formerly

237

homeless become members of the St. John's Church. Resurrection to new life is understood to be a spiritual gift and to require spiritual nurture in the worshipping congregation. Rasmus says that nearly one-third of the total church membership is made up of people struggling for a new beginning. Another third of the membership is among those who are marginally employed. Only one-third of the 2,500 members are securely employed and permanently housed.

Revitalized Worship

The most immediate change at St. John's under its new pastoral leadership team was the complete renewal of worship. There are three Sunday worship services for the congregation, which now numbers over 2,500 members. This is quite a change from the beginning when there was no worship. Rudy Rasmus describes the three worship services as experience-oriented, lively, loud, fast-paced, and sometimes explosive. He says:

> People who come to worship have experienced the depths of life and death. Most of them are here to thank God for recovery and the blessing of new life. The rest are here because they are seeking new life and deeply want the blessing of God's transforming spirit. Everyone comes either in an attitude of joyful gratitude or hopeful expectation. That makes an atmosphere open to the powerful presence and work of the Holy Spirit. People want to sing, shout, clap, and praise God vigorously.

The music is moving, energizing, and emotionally powerful. It is led by a five-piece band with electronic amplification. Although there is a variety of spiritual music, the basic repertoire comes from the current top-forty gospel songs, with some African-American spirituals mixed in. This is not a congregation for the United Methodist Hymnal. Instrumental music is provided by a professional band that includes two electronic keyboards, drums and percussion, brass and saxophone. Congregational singing is the most important vocal music. Emphasis is on congregational praise of God and joyful, rhythmic expression that unites and lifts people.

Preaching is one vital focus of worship. Juanita and Rudy Rasmus alternate Sundays preaching, and they are complemented by a team of six lay preachers — three women and three men — who are also involved each week in worship leadership and preaching. The preaching is highly experiential, relating everyday life struggles of people to the great biblical stories of God's transforming power. The variety of preachers, eight in number, reflects the variety of different people in the church, and affirms its operational theology that gospel preaching is empowered by the gift of God's Spirit, which is not limited to seminary-educated clergy.

Prayer is another powerful focus of worship at St. John's Church. Thanksgiving for the victories which people have experienced in overcoming addiction, unemployment, homelessness, ill health, despair, and family conflict are dynamic witness to God's forgiveness, healing, and spiritual power. The prayers of intercession show the radical openness and great expectations of people who have experienced brokenness and now believe that God restores sight to the blind, health to the sick, vitality and purpose to those who had abandoned all hope.

Sacrificial giving is another key focus in worship. The church teaches that giving one's talents and money is a means of worshipping God and of living the Christian life. The church encourages tithing. This disciplined, systematic giving is one of the keys to the rebirth and continuing rapid growth of the congregation. Rasmus says that members give joyfully and generously because they can see and hear the clear results of their gifts every week in the witnessing that takes place in worship. The needs are so great, so visible, and the feedback from the ministries is so abundant and positive that there is great reinforcement and motivation to support the church.

The significant socioeconomic diversity of the congregation is evident in the three Sunday worship services at 8:00 and 10:00 in the morning and at 12 noon. Each service is about one hour and twenty minutes in length. The early service is the most intentionally ordered and is a bit more moderate in spirit and intensity. This worship event brings the largest number of members from the suburbs, those of middle-class and business orientation, along with less affluent blue-collar, and some homeless, people. Dress is informal. There is a relaxed atmosphere; social mixing and communication are very significant.

The ten o'clock worship service — fondly called The Big Funnel

— brings the largest crowd, the greatest diversity, and the most up-beat spirit. It is the "High Mass" of the morning and the most potentially explosive in emotional terms. The electronic music has a hip-hop tempo. The prayers are longer and the spontaneous participation much greater. The interaction within the congregation is stronger. There may be as many as seven hundred worshippers gathered. The preaching reaches a higher level of fervor and the response of members is more lively, supportive, and vibrant.

The final worship service at noon brings a smaller congregation that is about evenly divided between homeless and housed people. It is the most informal of the three services, with lots of freedom to deal with things that arise in the community or in individual lives. It has the greatest feeling of communal solidarity. There is more non-liturgical communication. The worship is followed by a midday meal in which the positive spirit and supportive communication built up in worship is continued. The worship services are the heartbeat that pulsates through the many weekday ministries, giving them a surging vitality and unusual energy.

Two Forms of New Life: Education and Economy

The two most significant current expressions of new life at St. John's Church are the construction of a new $2.2 million school building and the economic development of new small businesses. These projects are truly amazing when you realize that just sixty months earlier this church was dead. But rapid growth (six hundred new members in 1997) brings the motivation and the capability to do significant new things.

The new school building that is being constructed adjacent to the church will house the St. John's Academy for children age three through twelve. It includes a preschool and all of the elementary school grades. Most of the children who will be served are children at risk who come from difficult family circumstances. For many parents, having their children in the preschool and the academy will provide the opportunity for them to be employed and begin a new life of self-support. The school building will also house the literacy program, GED instruction, computer education, job readiness training, and some health care facilities.

Funding for construction is coming primarily from a capital campaign within the congregation. Again, this is amazing when you consider that perhaps only fifty percent of the members have regular, stable employment and only one-third of the members are in the middle-income level or above. To enable the project to go ahead, a construction loan is in place and will be converted to a mortgage loan upon completion of the new building. The mortgage will be paid off from the member pledges. The capital campaign has secured some gifts outside the congregation and local grants are being vigorously pursued. The fundraising has been successful because the human needs are so clear and the results of the current programs are so evident. Donors can see what their gifts accomplish.

The economic development commitment of St. John's is focused on job creation through small businesses. This emphasis has emerged as the next step in the employment referral program that helps people get entry-level jobs with companies around Houston. The new emphasis is driven by the need to help people become less dependent on temporary, low-paying work; take more initiative; and gain greater self-determination. Current operations have made modest beginnings by putting people to work in several areas — office cleaning, food preparation, the Daybreak bakery, and Harvesters Employment Service. The list for further development is impressive and includes development of several enterprises:

- Commercial bakery
- Fast food restaurant
- Auto repair and filling station
- Bookstore and T-shirts wholesale enterprise
- Large-scale office cleaning service
- House painting, home maintenance, and lawn service.

The entrepreneurial spirit is strong among the leadership in the church. There is a consciousness that thinking smart and working hard can make a vital difference and provide a new economic base for people who have been outside the mainstream economy.

To help fund the creation of small businesses and continue the job training and employment referral network, the staff at St. John's Church are working continuously to cultivate corporate donors, to write and follow up on foundation grant proposals. "To secure grants from local foundations and corporations," says Rasmus, "we focus on the clear needs for recovery and employment; we ask often and with careful preparation; and we show the results of our work over a five-year period." Rasmus emphasizes that St. John's is a regional church serving the wider Houston area (not a neighborhood soup kitchen). Its members live in 140 zip codes of the Houston metropolitan area. Fifty percent of the members are men and ninety percent of the wider constituency served are men.

Underlying all the economic activity is a strong belief in God's blessing. "For personal recovery and productive employment, the time is now; the national climate is positive and we must be good stewards of God's blessing," says Rasmus.

What We Can Learn

- Big things can emerge from very small beginnings in a short time.
- The right leadership is the key to congregational redevelopment.
- The type of support most crucial to redevelopment is support for a big vision, innovative ideas, freedom to make changes, and a commitment to serve basic human needs in the community.
- Worship must be designed to embody the cultural modes of expression that are most appropriate to the people being served.
- The change of music and preaching style are the two most crucial adaptations necessary for congregational redevelopment in areas where there is change of ethnic and racial populations.
- There is no substitute for deep Christian faith that is rooted in first-hand experience of how people's lives can be changed by the work of God's Spirit through worship and other vital ministries of human and social development.
- Often the most sacrificial giving in a church comes from those members who have suffered the most. They have a deep understanding of the human needs that the church seeks to meet. Their selfless giving is a strong motivation for other members and donors.
- Finance follows faith. Creative vision should be the most valued priority in setting goals for finding funds. Sound business and accounting processes are necessary. But vision must drive the

quest for funds and it must be closely related to evident human needs and evident positive results.

- Creating funding sources beyond congregational giving is necessary for implementing long-term and lasting redevelopment.
- To get beyond the limitations of congregational financial resources, churches need to be creative in developing spin-off economic enterprises. The first step is getting the congregation's own financial house in order. But the next step is to go beyond the congregation for capital to invest in economic enterprise that will serve the public good, create jobs, and further strengthen the economic base of the church.
- The time when city-center churches can whine and complain about a lack of financial resources is over. This is the time when the church can move beyond traditional member giving toward new and substantial sources of income outside the congregation.
- Undergirding the success of any strategy for economic development must always be a sound and solid plan to meet urgent human need, put people to work, create more stable family income, and offer hope for a life more in keeping with justice and equity.

First African Methodist Episcopal Church

"Our mission is to make the Word of God incarnate by dealing with personal and social salvation simultaneously," says the Reverend Cecil Murray, senior pastor and spiritual leader for twenty years at First African Methodist Episcopal (A.M.E.) Church in South Central Los Angeles.[1]

This dynamic congregation of over twelve thousand members emphasizes a Christian spirituality of active commitment and involvement in the whole life of the city. The Mission Statement is short and to the point: "First A.M.E. Church of Los Angeles exists to improve the spiritual, social, physical, educational, and economic lives of all those embraced in the earthly Kingdom of God." Making the Word of God become flesh is the focus of the Reverend Cecil Murray, "Chip," as his people affectionately call him, and a deeply devoted and skilled staff of thirty-five ministers. They seek to engage all the members through forty ministry task forces, twenty-seven youth outreach programs, over two hundred related projects with 175 supporting, paid staff.

During the 1992 violence that followed the not guilty verdict for the Los Angeles police officers in the Rodney King beating trial, the Reverend Murray and more than fifty of the men from First A.M.E. Church patrolled the streets in the church neighborhood to protect people and property. They formed a thin line between angry street

1. Cecil Murray, interview with author, Los Angeles, 15 May 1997.

demonstrators and firefighters. They kept the violence and arson from spreading in the Adams and LaSalle Street intersection of South Central Los Angeles. Although there were rocks, bottles, and bullets flying through the air, Pastor Murray spoke to the crowd and calmed them down. It was an act of extraordinary leadership. It is also symbolic of the significant role played by the First A.M.E. Church in directing people and groups toward a constructive future and away from self-destructive behavior.[2]

The congregation has a long history of lively worship and service in the larger community. Organized 125 years ago, First A.M.E. is the oldest black congregation in Los Angeles. Founded in the house of a former slave, the church organized the first black school in the city and has promoted educational and economic achievement throughout its history. As Los Angeles grew, the congregation grew. It moved from its original location in what is now downtown Los Angeles into a larger sanctuary early in the century, and again in 1968 it moved into its present sanctuary, a newly constructed facility which can seat nearly thirteen hundred for worship. Since that time emphasis has been on expanding out into the community. Other property acquired has been for service, education, housing, and economic development.

Worship and Commitment to Justice

When asked what makes this megachurch work, Murray responds without hesitation, "Worship is the heart and it is a celebration of the good news of the Gospel."[3] There are three worship services each week in which the Word of God comes alive in preaching and music. Worship is a high-energy experience that warms the human heart, moves the mind, and stirs the passion to serve. Murray emphasizes that the good news of God's presence and loving spirit creates a vital atmosphere of joyful celebration. He also stresses the expectation that all members will engage in the ministry of service.

2. Brent A. Wood, "First African Methodist Episcopal Church: Its Social Intervention in South Central Los Angeles" (Ph.D. dissertation, University of Southern California Graduate School, 1997), 42-48.
3. Murray, interview.

As the congregation celebrated its 125th anniversary in 1997, it asked each member to serve in at least one of the forty mission task forces. In a letter to the congregation, Murray expressed it this way:

> Today we are convinced that God is calling us beyond ourselves, beyond the usual. We reach out to take you out of yourself into the larger Selfhood of God. . . . We cannot afford the luxury of faith freeloaders. . . . We have too much to do in response to God's call . . . to house the homeless, feed the hungry, teach the unlearned, hire the unemployed, energize businesses, mentor youth, heal the sick, close the race gap, and work for justice.[4]

The 1992 urban strife that broke out in South Central Los Angeles was a catalyst to spur First A.M.E. Church into a much wider and deeper involvement in seeking justice for the people of the city. Previously, there had been a strong emphasis on education and social service. After the rioting, burning, and destruction in April 1992, which expressed the frustration of people following the acquittal of the police officers accused of beating Rodney King, the church made a conscious and well-organized effort to work for economic development. The acronym for the First African Methodist Episcopal Church's larger community-wide ministry, FAME, symbolizes a complex series of interrelated social and economic ministries with strong professional leadership, energetic volunteers, and a vision of faith that goes beyond charity toward a comprehensive plan for the revitalization of South Central Los Angeles. The struggle to bring greater economic justice to marginalized people was built upon the trust that previously existed between the church and community, business, and government institutions of Los Angeles.

Strategic Nonprofit Corporations

To provide the organizational structure for this challenging vision, the church has created six nonprofit 501-C-3 corporations to be in a position to utilize funding from a variety of sources, including local businesses, large corporations, individuals, church members, founda-

---

4. Murray, "Letter to the Congregation," in the First African Methodist Episcopal Church Annual Financial Report, 1996.

tions, and government agencies at the local, state, and federal levels. The corporate structure embodies one of the most important aspects of FAME, which is its entrepreneurial spirit — the willingness to risk — and the conscious intent to grow the financial resources necessary to do big things. The Fund Development Officer is the Reverend Mary Minor Reed. The nonprofit corporations include:

- *FAME Assistance Corporation*, which undergirds social service, youth ministries, recovery programs, and Los Angeles Renaissance Program
- *FAME Housing Corporation*, which plans and develops affordable apartment housing in Los Angeles, nearly three hundred units, with plans for more
- *FAME Good Shepherd Housing Development Corporation*, which does housing renovation and shelter housing for homeless people, in cooperation with city agencies, and serves over five thousand families
- *FAME AIDS Prevention and Education Corporation*, which carries on extensive programs of HIV epidemiology, medical and clinical testing, prevention education, and psychosocial counseling
- *The Cecil L. Murray Education Center Corporation*, which is the support for the church-sponsored K-8 school serving 183 students, with plans to expand through high school
- *FAME Manor Limited Partnership and FAME Gardens Limited Partnership*, which operate several affordable apartment complexes, and manage these properties and the supporting services that go with them.

Building on its long tradition that Christian faith leads believers toward self-development through education and economic enterprise, FAME has a major emphasis on entrepreneurial training and development. The director of economic development, Mark Whitlock, says:

We are on fire for correcting the economic livelihood of communities. We burn the midnight oil managing economic development programs. Our effort focuses on job creation, business development, transportation, legal aid, and environmental protection. The multicultural voice of FAME Renaissance accomplishes its mission via public and private sector collaboration, and through the enabling power of the One who calls all things into being.[5]

Partnerships for Economic Development

FAME Renaissance works cooperatively with the University of California in Los Angeles (UCLA) and the University of Southern California (USC), relationships which have been built up over a period of time. These universities are major partners in providing for educational planning and teaching staff for the Entrepreneurial Training Program. This partnership is a key element in new business development. This church-initiated project trains over eight hundred persons a year in basic business principles, financing, management, business planning, and operation. In addition, FAME provides a Professional Assistance Team which acts as mentor to operators of new businesses and to businesses receiving loans for expansion. A free legal clinic provides legal consultation to individuals and new businesses. A major element in the FAME program is a $1 million Revolving Loan Program that makes loans to inner-city businesses ranging from a few thousand to a quarter million dollars.

Successful new businesses helped by FAME include a shopping center, Prime Tech Electronic Manufacturing, Athletic Apparel Retailing, several restaurants, Pyramid Art Gallery, and housing ventures. Business Resource Center director, Linda Smith, indicates there are two different loan programs: the Micro Loan, up to $20,000, and Financial Restructuring Assistance loans, which range from $50,000 to $250,000. The loan programs have been funded with a $1 million grant from the Disney Corporation and a grant of $300,000 from the ARCO Oil Foundation. The city of Los Angeles and the U.S. Department of Commerce are major sources for business loans.

Entrepreneurial Training Center director, Eddie Anderson, affirms the necessity of sound planning and realistic financing. The center's courses include: (1) Creating a Sound Business Plan; (2) Generating Capital; (3) Planning Realistic Marketing Strategy; and

5. Mark Whitlock, "A Wise Living," *FAME Renaissance Newletter* 1 (Spring 1997): 6.

(4) Business Operation and Management. Instructors are drawn from local universities and business. A commitment to ongoing continuing business education is stressed and the center continues to explore ways to provide further training designed to meet the needs of new entrepreneurs.

Another initiative is the FAME Personnel Services Employment Referral, managed by Nadine Washington. In just two years of existence the service has placed over three hundred persons in jobs with over forty companies. Companies participating include such well-known entities as Warner Brothers Studios, Walt Disney, Metro-Goldwyn-Mayer, Hanna Barbera, the Chubb Group Insurance companies, Metro-Media Technologies, the NAACP, the Los Angeles County Bar Association, and the International Service Employees Union.

Dealing with environmental issues is a key focus for FAME, which has chosen to work on two projects: water conservation and motor oil recycling. FAME promotes the installation of low-water-use toilets, which are available free from the city Department of Water and Power. The low-water toilets save residents about forty percent on their water bills, and saves the city of Los Angeles millions of dollars annually while conserving water, which is one of the most vital resources in California. FAME is promoting the creation of a new business that will locally manufacture low-water-use toilets for sale in a regional market.

The motor oil recycling project also is an income-producing business. Environmental Protection Manager, Sheila Reed, writes: "Used oil from a single oil change (about five quarts) can ruin a million gallons of fresh water, which is a year's supply for fifty people. Do-it-yourself consumers who change their own oil generate over 200 million gallons of used oil per year. Many consumers dispose of this waste oil by dumping it on the ground or pouring it into storm sewers. One gallon of used oil that is recycled can provide 2.5 quarts of lubrication."[6] FAME promotes used-oil recycling collection centers, which are operated by the city. Local businesses and churches — including First A.M.E. — cooperate by providing places for the operation of approved collection centers. An impressive group of compa-

6. Sheila Reed, "The Environmental Corner," *FAME Renaissance Newsletter* 1 (Spring 1997): 6.

nies are participating, including Sears, Anheuser-Busch, K-Mart, Hughes Aircraft, and CBS Studios.

A significant support service sponsored by FAME Renaissance is the transportation program. In partnership with the Metropolitan Transit Authority and the International Institute of Los Angeles, an innovative transportation network has been created that serves over 25,000 persons monthly. The focus is on assisting low-income families, senior citizens, and handicapped persons to travel to employment, medical treatment, and shopping.

There are many more service ministries in which First A.M.E. is engaged, including a prison ministry that extends pastoral care and education to inmates and stays with many of them after prison to help with housing, job placement, and counseling. The Emergency Feeding Program serves over eight hundred families a month. There is also rehabilitation of older housing that has been going on for over fifteen years, including the renewal of a number of former crack houses previously used by drug pushers.

Youth Ministries

There church runs a strong youth program with emphasis on mentoring, tutoring, and scholarship support for college education. Murray says the congregation's commitment to youth begins with birth and baptism, and extends through age twenty-five. The rites of passage for children and youth are clearly identified and affirmed through education, in worship events, and in other symbolic gatherings.

For many youth the church is a surrogate family, an extended network of caring and encouragement. Youth are challenged to make commitments and to give themselves in service and community responsibility. The development of the First A.M.E. School, for children in grades kindergarten through six, is an expression of the congregation's commitment to Christian education. It provides high-quality teaching with focus on reading, math, and science in a spiritual atmosphere. Part of the vision for year 2000 is to extend this school through the senior high grades. Also, in response to the needs of youth, the church brings together over three hundred summer jobs from a variety of sources. Further, the church makes a major commitment to public schools through the ministry of the Reverend Quanitha Hunt, who manages programs for tutoring, mentoring, mediating student disputes in the schools, and bringing knowledge about public school policy into the church.

In the final analysis, "It all comes back to a strong worshipping congregation that is alive and growing," says Reverend Murray. "We believe that if we are faithful the resources will come."[7] At First A.M.E. that means a commitment to worship that is energizing. *It is a commitment to seek and welcome twenty new members every Sunday.* Indeed, the church has been growing by about one thousand new members every year for the past few years. Further, it means having a clear vision for the future and believing that God has given us some definite tasks.

One of the keys to the success of this unusual church is the clear understanding of its leadership, beginning with Murray, that only a well-structured program with clear goals and definite tasks can attract the quality of volunteer lay leadership that is necessary. Murray says, "The people we want are very busy so we must be very focused on what we ask them to do." Another key to the life of this church is its skill for creating "small church warmth" inside a large church structure through over two hundred small groups, projects, and organizations.

What We Can Learn

- Strong, long-term pastoral leadership through which a clear vision is articulated and organized can be very productive.
- The clearly expressed expectation for every member to engage in service to the church and society gets positive results from volunteers.
- Having definite, reasonable goals and well-defined tasks help to attract capable leaders who are busy persons and who want to serve in an efficient manner.
- Worship nourishes and inspires people to go beyond the usual types of service into larger realms of community development and social change.

7. Murray, interview.

- Thinking big — taking the long-range view — attracts able leaders who want to make a significant and lasting contribution.
- The expectation and attitude for growth creates an environment within which people can mature, develop, and grow beyond what many would have imagined.
- Faith and justice go together. Personal salvation and social justice are interdependent. Thinking and acting collectively for a more just society opens persons to inner growth and maturity.
- Small groups of a wide variety of types are important within the large church for personal belonging and support of mission action.
- Generating the capital, cash flow, and income necessary to do big things requires sources way beyond the giving of a congregation. It requires partnership with businesses, foundations, government, and persons of wealth outside the congregation. It requires an entrepreneurial spirit, capacity for risk-taking, and business management skills.
- Clearly identified human needs together with a well-prepared action plan can attract significant funding from surprising sources when presented in a way that allows all parties to benefit.
- The purchase and redevelopment of property for housing and other development purposes is an investment in community building. Cecil Murray has expressed it this way, "We can never afford not to purchase property adjacent to the church."
- The formation of separate, nonprofit corporations enables the use of funds from foundations, government, business, and other sources that cannot give directly to the church as a religious organization. Separate legal incorporation also protects the church itself and greatly extends its systemic outreach.
- The First A.M.E. Church has become a teaching church theologically through its wide-ranging adult education, and functionally through its massive program of entrepreneurial education.
- The drawing power of First A.M.E. includes the whole metropolitan area of Los Angeles. It is truly a regional church within which there is the warmth of a neighborhood church.
- The senior minister possesses the skills of transformation. This includes being a visionary, a motivator, an organizer, and a person whom members respect.

For a much fuller study of this great church, readers are referred to the work by Brent A. Wood, "First African Methodist Episcopal Church: Its Social Intervention in South Central Los Angeles," a 1997 doctoral dissertation, University of Southern California Graduate School, Los Angeles, California 90007.

West Angeles Church of God in Christ

The West Angeles Church of God in Christ in South Central Los Angeles is an outstanding example of how African-American churches have played a vital role in economic development long before this became the popular thing to do. This congregation, led by the Reverend Charles Blake, senior pastor and bishop in the denomination, is taking the tradition of black economic action up to a new level of community development by redeveloping the entire area along Crenshaw and Exposition Boulevards in Los Angeles.

When Charles Blake began his ministry in the West Angeles Church in 1969, there were fifty members in the congregation. In 1997, there were over fifteen thousand members, including a number of high-profile members such as Magic Johnson, Denzel Washington, Stevie Wonder, and Gladys Knight. The church has a big vision of Christian faith and life that encompasses the full range of human activity.

At the center of the struggle to create a stronger community able to deal with the challenges of crime, drugs, poverty, illiteracy, bad housing, and disintegrating families is the church's Community Development Corporation (CDC). The West Angeles CDC is a separate 501-C-3 corporation with a board of directors of twenty-three members and a paid full-time staff of six professionals and many volunteers. The CDC Mission Statement summarizes its calling in this way:

God has called the West Angeles Community Development Corporation to promote justice and peace, demonstrate compassion and eradicate poverty as tangible expressions of the Kingdom of God through the vehicle of community development. The West Angeles CDC subscribes to community development as a liberating process aimed at Economic Empowerment, Social Justice, and Community Transformation.

The Reverend Blake says, "We recognize the need to determine our own future as a community. Standing on God's unchanging Word as our foundation, we are reclaiming our neighborhoods, our cities, block by block and life by life. People thrive where there is respect, opportunity, and hope."[1] Bishop Blake is described by those who know him well as a man of deep faith with a big vision, a strong preacher, and a talented administrator with the gift of attracting intelligent and skilled colleagues for the challenge of transforming a piece of Los Angeles into a community of hope.

Biblical Teaching at the Center

Each Sunday thousands of worshippers crowd into the sanctuary to participate in one of the five services of praise and preaching. The mood is energetic, the spirit is lively, the music is upbeat, and Blake's preaching is solidly biblical with a powerful delivery. The spirit of Pentecost is alive in this congregation. The living Word of God is proclaimed, experienced, affirmed, and expressed with vigor. The congregation is called to a life of righteousness, discipline, faithfulness, and fruitful productivity. "We create a positive atmosphere," says Blake, "of honesty and respect where people and businesses can thrive; we teach people to have respect for life and property, to be the kind of people with whom businesses can deal and around whom they can survive."[2]

Ebony magazine ranks Bishop Blake among the top ten preachers in the large African-American churches across the nation. In part,

1. Charles Blake, "Pastor's Column," *(West Angeles Community Development Corporation) Community News* 4:1 (Winter 1996): 1.
2. Larry Kantor, "Church Seeks to Bring Economic Salvation," *The Los Angeles Business Journal*, 5 May 1997, p. 3.

that high affirmation is related to his ability to see the connections between biblical faith and bold economic action for community development. In the Winter 1996 issue of "Community News," Blake says:

> With the most recent Federal legislation threatening to sentence some in our communities to an indefinite period of economic uncertainty, the value of the West Angeles Community Development Corporation has become more visible than ever before. [Government] programs like welfare have been characterized as a "safety net" to prevent those who are economically disadvantaged from falling into complete despair. However, through the example of Christ, it is clear that the only safety net is the one found in one's relationship with the Lord.[3]

The description of this safety net includes not only biblical faith, but also affordable housing, job placement, and a pilot project in energy-related technology to create new businesses in the area. Blake quotes Psalm 12 as a symbolic statement of the biblical foundation for community development: "For the oppression of the poor, for the sighing of the needy, now I will arise, says the Lord." Part of the meaning of this affirmation is to be found in creative economic development.

Economic Development

The technology for using solar energy — something plentiful in Southern California — can be the basis for the creation of many new jobs in the Crenshaw Boulevard community. The project to develop new uses for solar energy is partially funded by the U.S. Department of Energy. Former Clinton cabinet member, Hazel O'Leary, came to the West Angeles Church to praise this innovative project and give encouragement.

The vision to create new jobs by investing in solar technology, well-suited to California, has great potential for marketing in a number of places around the world. Thinking globally, acting locally to create new and useful products that serve the environmental needs of the world is thinking ahead to the next century. It is an economic vision that can generate a future for thousands of workers. A research

3. Blake, "Pastor's Column," 1.

grant from the U.S. Department of Energy has enabled the West Angeles CDC to begin a feasibility study for the uses of solar energy in relation to disinfecting contaminated water, with a view toward exporting solar water purification products to nations in Asia, Africa, and Latin America.

Another creative use of technology has been adopted by the CDC in its operation of Internet Job Fairs in cooperation with AT&T and Sony Pictures Entertainment. Seventy computer stations were set up for the Job Fair, with AT&T representatives providing technical assistance, designed especially for first-time users. Using the Internet, job seekers were connected to a large array of employment opportunities existing in the greater Los Angeles area. The director of Christian education at the West Angeles Church, Dr. Kenneth Hammonds, has written an introductory manual to help persons learn to use the Internet system. Paul Turner, director of economic development, says, "We are aware that our community must have access to information regarding job and contract opportunities during this time of fast-moving technological advance. Our economic survival is closely tied to our ability to own and apply new computer technologies."[4] Turner sees the church as being in a very favorable position to use new technology since Los Angeles is in the center of a major technology research and development region.

Affordable Housing

West Angeles Church is committed to creating affordable housing and assisting families in becoming homeowners. The CDC has acquired property in the neighborhood on which it will construct forty-four units of affordable family townhouses in 1997-1998. The CDC obtained $2.2 million in low-income tax credits as the start-up money for the $6 million project. The location of the new townhouse complex is across the street from the Los Angeles Manual Arts High School, and the CDC has solicited a partnership to involve students in the construction work. This housing development will not only create highly desirable, affordable living space, but also will provide on-the-job training in the construction trades.

4. Paul Turner, "Internet Job Fair," *Community News* 4:1 (Winter 1996): 4.

When completed, these rental units will serve families and persons whose incomes are below fifty percent of the median income in the area as determined by the city. The CDC will own and manage the property. In addition, CDC will provide social service and family support programs to strengthen and enhance community life. Sandra Speed, CDC housing director, calls this a project in neighborhood revitalization. She says, "During the next eighteen months you will witness the gradual transformation of vacant land into beautiful townhouses. The new West Homes will be safe, affordable and sustainable housing. There will also be programs for residents, including job training, day care, tutoring, and on-site computer televillage."[5]

Beyond rental housing, the CDC sponsors a program to help families become homeowners. This is a significant empowerment initiative. In the past year the CDC helped 150 persons in the community with various aspects of acquiring a home. Twice a year it operates Home Buyers Fairs, which deal with every step in the process of purchasing a home. Cooperative relations have been established with lending institutions and realtors. There is momentum building for rehabilitation and renewal in the neighborhood. The CDC has clear goals for the next year which include: (1) acquiring additional land and financing for a second affordable apartment development; (2) rehabilitating five existing homes for resale under the HUD 203-K program; and (3) helping 250 people buy their first home through two Home Buyers Fairs in the fall and spring seasons.

The Homebuyers Fair is a creative idea that brings together three groups of people: prospective homebuyers, realtors, and lenders. Professional help is given in three areas: solving credit problems and prequalifying the buyer; explaining the mortgage process and the Los Angeles city program that allows low-income households to obtain up to $35,000 for a second mortgage; and how to locate a home and make an offer while staying within one's income limits. The CDC housing event has been growing in popularity and effectiveness, according to planning director Grant Power. One of the helpful services provided is individual consultation for participants. They can get on-the-spot credit reports and analysis. Step-by-step counsel is given so that aspiring homeowners get an accurate and tailor-made outline of

5. Sandra Speed, "Neighborhood Revitalization in Action," *Community News* 4:1 (Winter 1996): 5.

exactly what they need to do to be successful. The goal of the CDC in this event is to promote home ownership. This is a means of developing economic security and community stability by increasing the number of homeowners each year.[6]

Tools for Systemic Change

The church CDC operates a number of self-help programs, the focus of which is to enable people and groups to become more self-determining. The goal is growth and development, not merely adapting to circumstances. These programs can be summarized under the acronym ACT — Adult Education, Community Dispute Resolution, and Technical Training.

Adult Education in the community — called WALET, for West Angeles Literacy Empowerment Team — focuses on reading, writing, and math skills for both school-age youth and adults. WALET trains more tutors than any other organization in Los Angeles. Certified tutors, after receiving training, work with youth and adults one to one and in small classes. Hundreds of adults and even more youth have benefited from the literacy program in improved work skills and better employment.

Another major educational initiative in 1997 was the establishment of a satellite campus of Southern California College in the facilities of the West Angeles Church. Students can now take classes at the church in an accelerated bachelor's degree program for working adults. In addition, the church operates a scholarship fund program to assist persons enrolled in the Los Angeles Trade and Technical School and at the University of California in Los Angeles (UCLA). The church also provides space for the West Angeles Christian Academy and the West Angeles Bible College.

Community Dispute Resolution has four elements that have been built up over a period of years. Each represents important links with significant institutions and demonstrates how the West Angeles CDC works to secure justice through social systems. Dr. Lula Ballton, Executive Director of the CDC, an attorney and previously a lawyer for the California State Justice Department, has given leadership to

---

6. Grant Powers, "Homebuyers Fair," *Community News* 4:1 (Winter 1996): 5.

planning and developing the effective programs in Community Dispute Resolution. The approach is proactive, based on developing strong working relations with key institutions including the public school system, the police department, the court system, and local university law schools. The four distinct components of the Community Dispute Resolution Program are:

1. Community Legal Services, a partnership with the Los Angeles Bar Association, provides legal services to moderate-income families who do not qualify for government-provided legal aid. Help is focused on domestic issues, small business issues, and property ownership.
2. The Peacemakers Project works in partnership with the Conflict Management Services Resource Center, especially in the public high schools, to teach mediation skills. Parents, teachers, students, and administrators are engaged by this program. The goals are: more nonviolent schools, and keeping youth in school.
3. The Court Mediation Project, directed by Dr. Lula Ballton, helps families and individuals who need to use the court system to be proactive in seeking reconciliation between litigating parties. Simultaneous use of the court process and mediation often yields positive results for all parties.
4. The Community Mediation Project provides training for community organizations and nonprofit groups in mediation skills and conflict resolution. This helps to reduce gang violence in the community, teach competing groups how to work cooperatively, and redirect energy toward constructive purposes.

The Technical Training for Community Assistance Project is the systematic approach the church takes to respond to the basic human needs for food, clothing, shelter, and family assistance. The CDC provides technical assistance and management training to other churches and community social service groups in the Los Angeles area. The CDC works as a major player in the Christian Community Development Association (CCDA) to share its expertise and wide-ranging experience with others so as to broaden the base of effective service groups. Special services include preparation and delivery of meals to homebound HIV and AIDS residents; preparation of families for foster care of children; health education and immunization projects; neighborhood clean-up; and the quarterly Community Newsletter widely circulated in South Central Los Angeles. In addition, the church does the usual things frequently done by urban churches — emergency shelter, food bank, utility bill assistance, five thousand meals a month for homeless people, and emergency relief.

The Cathedral Plan

The capstone that will visibly symbolize the total ministry of the West Angeles Church of God in Christ will be the construction of its new sanctuary and related facilities. When it is completed, this will be a $50 million building when it is completed on a seven-acre site at the corner of Crenshaw and Exposition Boulevards. The new 5,000-seat cathedral will be the flagship church for the Church of God in Christ denomination. It will rival the $50 million Roman Catholic Cathedral planned for downtown Los Angeles.

The purpose of the new sanctuary is to expand, enhance, and strengthen the worship of God. It will be the realization of dreaming, planning, and working for more than a decade. However, it is also being planned as a major economic development with a total economic impact of over $100 million. The construction will create hundreds of jobs. Contracts have been let to local, minority-owned businesses, including the architect, consulting engineers, and site preparation companies. The seven-acre site is now ready. The new cathedral, of glimmering glass, steel, and marble construction, is scheduled to open in 1999. Beyond the numerous jobs related to construction, the vision is that this major new building will be the centerpiece to attract other significant development in the surrounding area. Bishop Blake predicts, "Thousands of people will come into the neighborhood to shop, eat, and spend money, creating new economic life. I believe that many new businesses will decide to come into the area."[7]

One project underway that is an early manifestation of the church's commitment to stimulate new business adjacent to the new sanctuary is the rehabilitation of the commercial center on Crenshaw Boulevard. The vision has been translated into reality. It is a first step

7. Kantor, "Church Seeks to Bring Economic Salvation," p. 41.

aimed at attracting at least five new retail franchise stores. There is a new perception and the substance of hope in the South Central Los Angeles community.

Beyond the economic impact, the church sanctuary and related facility will be the home for over eighty small groups — Christian education classes, spiritual nurture, and fellowship programs. The new cathedral will stimulate the growth of the already substantial program of spiritual life.

What We Can Learn

- For church-sponsored community redevelopment and economic enterprise it is important to have experienced, well-educated, and skilled professional leadership.
- Partnership with city, state, and federal agencies can help to take economic development up to a larger scale that benefits a greater number of people.
- The use of tax credit financing for construction of affordable apartments and townhouse homes greatly increases the financial capability of nonprofit church groups to create large-scale projects.
- Developing creative partnerships with major institutions such as universities, the public school system, large corporations, political parties, and business entrepreneurs is crucial for accomplishing substantial community development.
- Developing a business plan with clear goals, financial credibility, and responsible management is essential for church-sponsored economic development.
- For a church in a central urban location to thrive and grow it must be actively committed to promoting development in its locale.
- The leadership of a skilled, long-tenured, visionary pastor is very helpful, even crucial, for large-scale, church-sponsored community economic development. To grow the church is to grow the community.
- It is wise to carefully assess the possibilities for engaging in areas of newly emerging economic opportunity. Seeing what opportunities may be natural to the local area can be significant for

economic development, e.g., solar energy technology in California.

- Make the most of the moment of opportunity. There is no doubt that the riots in South Central Los Angeles after the Rodney King trial led to the emergence of unusual opportunities for redevelopment, renewal, and revitalization. The virtue is in seizing the moment, seeing the possibilities, and taking timely action to move ahead boldly.
- There is no substitute for having a big vision that is powerful enough to attract investors, inspire workers, generate energy, mobilize institutions, and draw them into creating a positive future.
- For an urban church to sustain a broad range of ministries it must create substantial income from enterprise beyond member giving.
- Vital spiritual life and the struggle for justice are interdependent.
- The leadership of professional staff who are Christians and work from a spiritual motivation to enable peacemaking, reconciliation, and the creation of community is a powerful witness to the Gospel.
- The involvement of hundreds of church member volunteers in the community programs is a major factor in the growth of the congregation.

Ingleside Presbyterian Church

The Ingleside Presbyterian Church in San Francisco has a long and proud history of community involvement. But when Roland Gordon began his ministry there in 1978, the congregation had declined to four members in a large building. Like so many mainline churches situated in changing neighborhoods of major cities, Ingleside Church had lost its older members and not gained new ones.

The three assets that Roland Gordon had to begin with were, in order of importance, a strong faith in God's calling; a large building with a gymnasium; and the traditional commitment of the church to serve the diverse Ingleside community.

Today, twenty years later, the church is a clear example of evangelical witness moving with a sense of compassion beyond charity toward social justice. How did the present congregation become the heartbeat of the Ingleside area?

Seven initiatives stand out as crucial in the redevelopment of the church: (1) establishing the Ingleside Church Basketball League; (2) revitalizing the Ingleside Senior Center; (3) establishing the Ingleside Community Center; (4) reaching mature adults through revitalized worship; (5) refurbishing the church building; (6) engaging the broader Oceanview, Merced, Ingleside community through "Vision 2000" and the campaign for construction of affordable housing; and (7) creating the Thad Brown Boys Academy.

Focus on Youth

It all started with basketball. Roland Gordon grew up playing basketball in Gary, Indiana. He was a star player at Roosevelt High School and at Baldwin Wallace College (Berea, Ohio). From his own experience with and love for basketball he saw the Ingleside gym as an opportunity to bring youth from the surrounding neighborhood into the church. He reopened the gym. His love for the game, boundless energy, and enthusiasm for youth led him to organize the Ingleside Church Basketball League. This program brings youth and young adults into the church the year around. There are clear expectations that youth who play basketball in the gym will also be involved in at least one church activity. Mentoring in faith and in the sport go hand in hand. Relationships are formed that have positive, lasting significance for life.

One of the most striking symbols in the Ingleside Church gym is the Black History Collage that covers the walls of the gym from floor to ceiling. Images of historic black leaders, religious figures, sports heroes, and contemporary black cultural and political personalities surround the room and project a positive spirit to all those who enter the gym. The gym is also a multipurpose facility used for many church functions beyond basketball. So the Black History Collage speaks to many people attending church dinners, task force meetings, and numerous community gatherings.

Revitalized Senior Program

The Ingleside Senior Center was established by the church in 1964 as a service outreach into the surrounding community. There is a substantial older population in the area. When the congregation was in decline in the early seventies, the senior program also was at a low ebb. One of the first actions of Roland Gordon when he became pastor was to encourage the renewal of this area of ministry. Previously, the program just used space in the church building. With new leadership the connection between the church and the program has become a vital link. The senior program was an early avenue for securing outside funding to support outreach services. This successful experience helped the church to see the possibilities of further funding from nonchurch sources in the public and private sectors.

Revitalizing and expanding the senior services was a visible sign to the community that the church intended to continue its long tradition of active advocacy for people in the neighborhood. A director and volunteer staff now guide and promote the senior program. The program includes daily activities, a drop-in center, hot lunches, health services, a network of communication, and computer training for seniors. Through the initiative of the senior program, participation in VISION 2000 community planning by older citizens has been enhanced. The senior program has been active in lobbying for new apartment housing for seniors that is now being planned for the area.

Ingleside Community Center

With energetic leadership from their pastor, the congregation established the Ingleside Community Center and incorporated it as a nonprofit 501-C-3 entity. The center has its own separate board of directors that connects the neighborhood with resources in the wider metropolitan area. The full-time director of the center, Gil Gordon (no relation to Reverend Gordon), is an experienced community organizer. The director and board have been assertive in finding and using the financial and leadership resources of city agencies, private foundations, and friends of the center.

The Ingleside Community Center is a vehicle for a variety of education, advocacy, and employment programs for youth and young adults. Under the leadership of Gil Gordon, the center developed the first community-based computer literacy program in the area. A job referral service enables youth and young adults to connect with employment opportunities in the San Francisco Bay area. There is computer training and work skill orientation. The staff of the center are funded through grants from public and private sources, and they serve all who come from this diversely populated area.

The Ingleside Community Center has been a key player in the VISION 2000 community survey and planning sponsored by the San Francisco Foundation. Center staff and volunteers have been active advocates for expanding educational and economic opportunity in the area.

Lively Worship and Fellowship

The Sunday morning worship at Ingleside Presbyterian Church is a moving experience of music and powerful preaching. The congregation is modest in size — ranging from 100 to 150 people — and is warm, welcoming, and winsome in spirit. The sanctuary has been refurbished. There is a center pulpit and communion table in the chancel. Colorful banners reflect the joyful and praise-oriented spirit of the people. Hymn singing is vigorous. The choir is a major force in the worship atmosphere of praise and spiritual energy. "Not by might nor by power, but by my Spirit says the Lord" (Zechariah 4:6b) describes the moving force in this worshipping congregation which has taken for its motto, "We walk by faith, not by sight" (II Corinthians 5:7).

In the middle of the worship service there is a time for greeting, welcoming, and reaching out to embrace one another. It is a high-energy time in the morning service. Members mingle throughout the sanctuary. The choir joins in the mixing. Old and young, members and guests move freely about the whole worship area. This precedes the preaching and clearly creates an atmosphere of energy and positive expectation. Roland Gordon's preaching invites a lively response. The sermon is biblical exposition lifted up by high-energy delivery, and congregational responses punctuate the pastor's preaching. There can be no doubt the people are actively listening. Worship is at the heart of the renewal at Ingleside Church.

Worship is followed by dinner served to members and visitors in the church gym. There is friendly visiting — a hubbub of conversation — and family gatherings around the Sunday noon tables. Visitors and inquirers are especially welcomed as guests, and members invite the visitors to sit with them and get acquainted. There is a lot of church committee work and member consultation that gets done at this time. There is a continuation of the positive spirit generated earlier in worship. As families, friends, and visitors break bread around the tables, the body of Christ is being knit together with an inner strength that enables members to go out and serve in the wider community.

Church Building Redeveloped

The rehabilitation of the church building and the facilities that house the Ingleside Community Center took place over an extended period of years. Funding came primarily from the mayor's Office of Community Development as a result of the many community programs housed at the church facility. The gym was restored and this enhanced the youth program. The public spaces used by the senior citizen program — parlor, kitchen, restrooms — were renovated, and many groups benefited from this improvement. Office space was redeveloped to create facilities for city-sponsored job training and employment referral operations. A major addition was the construction of an elevator entered at street level and reaching all floors, making the building accessible to people with disabilities. These improvements helped to make Ingleside Presbyterian Church much more functional and appealing to the community. They also helped demonstrate that the church had a commitment to a useful future in the neighborhood.

The church building is a striking structure with an impressive white stone exterior. It is in a good location on a busy street, Ocean Avenue, and has high visibility. The building is a strategic asset. The church's physical location has helped to create the possibility for the congregation to be at the center of community activity. The congregation thinks of their church as "the heartbeat of the Ingleside community." In addition to the Community Center and Senior Center, the building houses a number of Alcoholics Anonymous groups, which are important to the well-being of the Ingleside community. The church is also the site for most special community meetings.

Action for the Community: VISION 2000

In the mid 1990s, the San Francisco Foundation organized and conducted a community survey in the Ingleside-Oceanview-Merced neighborhoods which identified both the resources and the problems of the area. People from the church were prominent in this community project. The survey, not surprisingly, identified the Reverend Roland Gordon as one of the key leaders and community facilitators in the area. This affirmation has helped the congregation to move more into the mainstream of community organizing and planning for future development. It also has helped to confirm the church's role as a strategic center for city-sponsored programs of education, housing, and employment services.

The foundation survey led to a community planning project, called VISION 2000, which has organized people into six working groups: (1) business and economic development, (2) education and culture, (3) health and human services, (4) environment, (5) public safety, and (6) children-youth-young adults. The director of Ingleside Community Center, Gil Gordon, and Pastor Roland Gordon have played key roles in the Coordinating Council of VISION 2000, and on the committees for Education and for Public Interpretation. This project brought together representatives of twenty-two community organizations and seven agencies of city government. Six major goals for the area were established with thirty-three specific objectives. Emerging from this community planning process were the following priorities (to name just a few):

• construction of affordable senior housing
• creation of a comprehensive health care clinic
• establishment of a job training program linked to industry
• improvement of public parks and recreational facilities
• establishment of a community policing program.

One of the most substantial outcomes of this effort has been the establishment of agencies in the Ingleside neighborhood to make available hundreds of small loans for upgrading, renovating, and improving individual family-owned homes in the area. The church has encouraged and lobbied for this renewal program, which has strengthened the parish neighborhood.

The Thad Brown Boys Academy

Perhaps the most ambitious and visionary project of the Ingleside Presbyterian Church ministry is the planning now going on to create a school for boys. The Thad Brown Boys Academy (TBBA) is a direct response to an overture passed by the 1990 General Assembly of the

Presbyterian Church, USA, proclaiming African-American males an "endangered species." Roland Gordon says:

> My charge is to lead in the creation of a school devoted to developing African-American boys into outstanding leaders and role models. TBBA is developing well-educated, spiritually-grounded leaders committed to helping restore the endangered African-American male children, and improve their community. We will focus on training our boys to become self-sufficient leaders who will in turn find their God-given mission to their community. Training the boys from an early age is critical. Thus, our long-range goal is a school with grade levels of preschool through high school graduation.[1]

At Ingleside Church, as is true in many new church-sponsored schools, the planning is being done in close communication with the public school system. Both state and city standards must be met, and only certified teachers will be employed. In addition, there is a vital role for volunteer and parent participation, which enriches the educational culture and creates a stronger sense of linkage with the community.

The conception of the church-sponsored private school is a challenge for the Presbyterian denomination, which abandoned church-operated schools in the 1870s in favor of public schools exclusively. Now, in a different time and in the face of urban challenges, a new policy and innovative action seem to be needed. The Ingleside Presbyterian Church is moving ahead to do this new thing. The Thad Brown Boys Academy is part of a trend toward church-sponsored education, especially in the African-American communities in urban areas. This movement is in part an affirmation of the church's historic role as a pioneer in education. It reflects the theological fact that education is integral to full human maturity and that quality education is a matter of social justice.

The Importance of Focus

Working with limited staff and modest resources, the church needed to focus on the most crucial areas of mission. One of the reasons for

1. Roland Gordon, interview with author, 19 May 1997.

the decline of congregations is their failure to engage children, youth, and young adults. Realizing this, the Ingleside Church chose to concentrate their efforts toward reengaging the younger generation of the community. With the reorganization of the Community Center, the creation of the basketball program, formation of the Job Training Program, and especially in the planning for the Thad Brown Boys Academy, the church has taken a cluster of positive steps to engage children, youth, and their families in the church.

What We Can Learn

- Strategic location is one significant factor in determining success in church redevelopment.
- The building and physical facilities of a church can be another positive factor in redevelopment when they have spaces that can be used to serve the community.
- Long-term pastoral leadership is very important, especially when the pastor is energetic and has the skills to help the congregation create a positive vision of the church.
- Partnership with community institutions and agencies can bring needed financial resources and skilled leadership into the parish program.
- Identifying one or two vital needs of the community and focusing effort on a few specific areas helps the congregation learn they can make a positive difference.
- Building on part of an already existing tradition makes it easier for a congregation to change. In this case it was the history of community service that was revitalized.
- Lobbying to get public and private institutions into action to fulfill their responsibilities is a major contribution that an urban church can promote. In this case it was helping to get urban planning, city improvements in housing, community policing, and employment services.
- The movement toward church-sponsored schools in the inner-city areas is an idea whose time has arrived. Major Protestant denominations need to reassess their policies of exclusive support for public schools and develop a more creative policy for education in the inner city.

- Reengaging children, youth, young adults, and their families is crucial for any congregation that wants to have a significant long-term future.
- Allocation of resources to benefit children, youth, and young adults is significant in helping a church move from being in decline (feeling like a victim) toward creating a positive future.
- The Ingleside Presbyterian Church is an example of how a small church with visionary leadership and entrepreneurial skills can develop a variety of financial resources beyond member giving to become self-supporting.

San Francisco Network Ministries: The Personal Is the Pastoral Is the Political

Glenda Hope and Penny Sarvis

The personal is the pastoral is the political. This lesson is repeatedly taught to us in our ministry in a poverty ghetto near the major up-scale tourist/shopping center of San Francisco. In November 1972, Glenda Hope resigned as assistant pastor in a downtown congregation and sat down in her own living room with eight venturesome people to begin ministry with young adults who were not coming to traditional forms of church.

That house church shaped itself as a faith community, meeting weekly for two to four hours, sharing a meal, singing, doing Bible study on the meaning of the Scriptures for our individual, communal, and political lives, and celebrating Holy Communion. Word about this house church spread through the San Francisco Bay Area, attract-

---

This story was originally published in *Church & Society* magazine, in the November/December 1995 issue, under the title, "We Are All Sparrows." It is reprinted here in revised and updated form by permission of *Church & Society*, published by the Presbyterian Church (U.S.A.), National Ministries Division, Louisville, Kentucky.

The Reverend Glenda Hope is a Presbyterian minister and the Director of San Francisco Network Ministries. She is an author and serves as an adjunct faculty member at the Pacific School of Religion. She is the recipient of the Woman of Faith Award of the National Presbyterian Women's Association.

The Reverend Penny Sarvis is a United Church of Christ minister and the former Associate Director of San Francisco Network Ministries. She is a member of the Network's Board of Directors, a leader of renewal retreats and spiritual life conferences.

ing Christians wanting face-to-face engagement and worship with other Christian political activists.

Very quickly, San Francisco Network Ministries was drawn deeply into the Tenderloin district, a ghetto of poverty populated by disabled people, the homeless, the frail elderly, the unemployed or underemployed, and a diverse racial/ethnic population. In the 1980s the Tenderloin experienced an explosion in the numbers of homeless people; Southeast Asian families; those buying, selling, and/or using illegal drugs; prostitutes; and poor people diagnosed as HIV-positive. It became the area with the highest crime rate in the city. Newspapers called it the "Kill Zone" due to the high rate of homicides and aggravated assaults. San Francisco Network Ministries was willing and able to respond to the great human needs of the district. If someone on the board or staff came with a vision believed to be God's call, the response was not "Can we?" but "How can we?"

The Ambassador Hotel is a 150-room residential hotel sitting tiredly in the Tenderloin. The building is old, the elevator breaks down regularly, and pest control is a constant problem. The hotel and the neighborhood seethe with drug traffic and violence in spite of valiant efforts to combat them. In the midst of all this, the hotel manager became dismayed by how many people with HIV were homeless. He decided that the Ambassador would become a center for people with HIV/AIDS unable to find housing elsewhere because they were so poor, so devoid of connections, so encumbered with other problems such as chemical addictions or mental illness. He called Network Ministries, inviting us to join him in providing support for these people, although neither of us knew what "support" would look like.

Initially, support meant acquainting the residents and ourselves with available services in the city, none of them in the Tenderloin area. Eventually, people moving into the hotel came already linked to health and social work systems. What they did not have was personal contact with someone who would simply listen with love. We became hotel chaplains, opening a daily drop-in for everyone in the hotel who just wanted to talk, staffing it with Penny Sarvis, Glenda Hope, and a Catholic priest.

Now it is open seven days a week, staffed by volunteer men and women — gay and straight, Roman Catholic, Presbyterian, United Church of Christ, Lutheran, Episcopal, and Methodist. What unites us is a call to take ministry beyond church walls, especially to places and people often forced outside of these walls by the church. We listen. We also walk with people through General Assistance and Social Security lines. We accompany them to the doctor, the hospital, and the pawnshop. We wait with them in waiting rooms. We write letters for those who are illiterate, make phone calls for the one who is deaf, stand beside those who can make their own phones calls but are scared stiff. We contact relatives for someone who is dying or has died. We deliver donations from local churches of towels, sheets, pillowcases, lamps, and plants, pictures, television sets, and radios.

We train and support the residents to be caregivers for one another. Such a one was JoAnn, a heroin addict and sometime prostitute. Anthony came into the hotel, friendless and very ill, to be surrounded by loving care from our group of people who might be passed by as bums on the street. Quickly this became his home and family, and he wanted to die "at home." His greatest fear was of dying alone. So JoAnn took him into her eight-by-ten-foot room and gave him her bed, organizing a twenty-four-hour vigil so that Anthony could die within sight of a loving face. She was a principal mourner at the memorial service held in the office of the hotel manager. Penny Sarvis mentioned in prayer that not a sparrow is forgotten by God who made and loves us. Later, as people remembered aloud Anthony, their new old friend who had died, someone said, "He was a sparrow. We're all sparrows."

"Tell the Mayor We're Dying Out Here"

Memorial services are a major part of our ministry, averaging one a week. "Come over into this hotel, that alley, our agency, and help us. Bring the Word of God in prayer and scripture to those who mourn. Dignify the deaths of the poor and the outcast." Wearing clerical collar, cross and stole, we respond. How moving it is to stand in some dirty doorway or dreary residential hotel, joining with the believers in saying, "The Lord is my shepherd . . . green pastures . . . still waters . . . goodness and mercy all the days of my life." At a service held in Golden Gate Park for a Vietnam vet, one man cried out, "He was my friend. We shared everything. Tell the mayor, Reverend. Tell the people. We're dying out here."

And tell them we do. San Francisco Network Ministries people write letters, participate in neighborhood organizing efforts for everything from sidewalk clean-up to increased detox programs to providing public toilets. We lead prayer vigils, testify at City Hall in meetings of city commissions and the City Council, confront the mayor, break into long-abandoned buildings to rehab them for homeless housing, strategize with others to impact decision-making at all levels of government, challenge more Tenderloin people and church people to become informed and involved in political processes working for justice, dignity, preservation of God's good creation, health care, and much more. The Bible studies, the worship, the personal face-to-face ministry drive us into the political. And the direct political advocacy we do gives this ministry a credibility that draws people hungry for spiritual nurture. The personal is the pastoral is the political.

A Special Type of Church

The Tenderloin Community Church (part of the San Francisco Network Ministries) holds weekly worship that includes sharing of our faith and lives, singing, Bible study, prayer, laying on of hands for healing, celebration of Communion. One who joined us was Doug, whom we first met at the Ambassador Hotel. He dropped in, high on speed, reading the Book of Revelation, and convinced that he had the mark of the beast and was damned. Gradually Doug began to believe that God loves him. Eventually he knelt on the bare floor and we baptized him into the church of Jesus Christ.

Another is Andy, also an Ambassador Hotel resident. We had spent many hours with Andy, yet he persisted in his self-destructive ways. Andy suffered a cardiac arrest in the lobby but was revived by paramedics. He said, "God brought me back to life for a purpose. I think it is to try to get others to stop doing the things I was doing. I want you to commission me to do this work in God's name." Challenging Andy to "serve the people with energy, intelligence, imagination, and love," we laid on our hands, praying, "God, give him special gifts for his special work." A year later, still clean and sober, he is a volunteer outreach worker for a substance abuse program.

We have begun a spiritual direction program for staff of service-providing agencies in the Tenderloin. Also, we're introducing a monthly gathering for people who grew up in the church but drifted away, and people working for justice and longing for a faith community combining face-to-face engagement with others like them with prayer, Bible study, and sharing stories of faith journeys. In collaboration with an African-American congregation, we also hold a weekly service of prayer, scripture, and gospel music.

The church is open five days a week as a street chaplaincy, with volunteer staff. We do not offer food, clothing, money, or even a cup of coffee — only ourselves, our love, our listening. One woman said, "This is my sanctuary." A man, functional but struggling with mental illness and a feeling of worthlessness, found that a place of healing. Using his own money, he placed ads inviting elderly and disabled persons to become part of a telephone Friendship Network. He now engages in his own style of ministry, operating from the phone in his tiny studio apartment.

Not all is such good news. Some people simply disappear. Some slide back into substance abuse. Some go to jail. Some die. Volunteers grow weary and leave. The *Network Journal,* an occasional publication with an international subscription list, carries the human stories of and by them all. "We are all sparrows, none are forgotten."

Renewing a Congregation

In 1979, Seventh Avenue Presbyterian Church, a small congregation with an aging membership and dwindling financial base, contracted with San Francisco Network Ministries for half-time pastoral leadership. It was a courageous, visionary act on their part — and it worked. The original few welcomed the staff's Bible-based preaching with a strong emphasis on contemplative prayer and political action, a goal shared by those who joined through the years. Seventh Avenue became a Sanctuary Church, providing shelter for refugees from Central America; a More Light Church, offering leadership responsibilities whatever one's sexual orientation; a sponsor for a nine-member family of boat people; an original member of the AIDS Interfaith Network, offering pastoral care to those infected with HIV — all while continuing their historic support of a senior center and reestablishing their Sunday school.

Tenderloin people came to Seventh Avenue Church for worship and special events. Church members joined Network Ministries in the Tenderloin, working with homeless people and the frail elderly poor, becoming politicized in the process. Church members went out to volunteer for work and witness in Latin America and Africa, commissioned by prayer and laying on of hands. Returning, they told inspiring stories of faith and resistance to tyranny, challenging us all to increased prayerful action.

As this handful of faithful disciples gave themselves to mission, not maintenance, to serving, not surviving, we learned that "those who lose their life for my sake, and for the sake of the gospel, will save it" (Mark 8:35) applies to institutions as well as individuals. A study by Howard Rice of San Francisco Theological Seminary documented that when San Francisco Network Ministries stopped sponsoring the Seventh Avenue Church after eleven years, the congregation had increased six-fold, the average age of the membership was twenty years younger, and the budget was two-and-a-half times larger. The personal is the pastoral is the political.

Reinventing Seminary Education

San Francisco Network Ministries persuaded Pacific School of Religion to join in a bold venture in *contextual theological education*, eventually attracting three other seminaries — Church Divinity School of the Pacific (Episcopal), American Baptist Seminary of the West, and San Francisco Theological Seminary (Presbyterian) — to the Network Center for Study of Christian Ministry. With Network Ministries as the organizer and the base, students were placed for nine months in parishes ranging from affluent to those barely hanging on, in racial/ethnic ministries, and in street ministries.

For two semesters they worked half-time in their ministries, gathering together twelve hours a week for four classes, including theology, Bible, Spiritual discipline, Christian ethics, pastoral care, church history, and community organizing. Some classes were taught by full-time seminary professors, others by urban practitioners named as adjunct faculty by the seminaries. All classes fully integrated active ministry experience with high-quality academic work. Spiritual directors were provided for those students desiring this special mentoring. The program ran for eight years. A small book, *Mending Severed Connections*, by Lynn Rhodes and Nancy Richardson, records the insights gained from this program of contextual theological education. This book is available from the San Francisco Network Ministries.

From Pastoral to Program

A Catholic sister on the Network Ministries staff met an elderly disabled woman after Mass. Learning that Ruth lives in a tiny room with no cooking facilities in a run-down Tenderloin hotel, Sr. Clare began visiting her regularly. From this grew the vision that became one of the Ministries' largest programs — *Tenderloin ElderFriends.* Volunteers from the Tenderloin, from churches, from wherever, are trained to be pastoral caregivers and are matched with seniors wanting a friend.

Seniors living in the Tenderloin are afraid of the streets that oftentimes can be mean and dangerous. They live as virtual prisoners in their residences, their only crime being that they grew old and also poor. Family members are distant, uncaring, dead, or beset with problems of their own, so our ElderFriends take their places, visiting, going for walks or drives, taking the elders to church, chatting, reading aloud, helping balance bank accounts — bringing the love of God to those who are ending their lives feeling abandoned and alone. Strong bonds form between older and younger (although some volunteers are over seventy). It becomes a relationship of trust, which is mutually rewarding.

A nonprofit housing developer asked us to provide programming for the residents, mostly Chinese immigrant families. We teach English as a Second Language there, help people prepare for citizenship, provide individual and family counseling, give tutoring and recreation for the children. Most recently, we began a wildly popular program in which children sign up for blocks of time to read aloud to adult volunteers. The roles are reversed — the adults listen, the children read.

Affordable Housing Excellence

In 1990, Network Ministries was operating on a budget of $125,000 in rented space for office and church, as well as on the streets, in the hotels, on the steps of City Hall. A staff member, returning from a spiritual retreat, reported a clear call from God to construct apartments for low-income and poverty-level families in the Tenderloin, and developing on-site programming to aid them in building strong, healthy families and in breaking the cycle of poverty. An initial grant of $475,000 in 1992 from the Creative Ministries Offering of Presbyterian Women (national level) proved enough to leverage the funding for a five-story, $7.2 million, 38-unit apartment building complete with counseling rooms, meeting rooms, reference and lending library, landscaped backyards where people may sit in peace and children may play in safety, a computer lab, a rooftop garden, and a bigger office from which we work. How did this happen?

It was clear that banks and major funding groups would not have the faith in the Network Ministries displayed by Presbyterian Women, since we had no collateral for such a building development. We interviewed seven established nonprofit housing developers and found Asian Neighborhood Design our clear choice. It was a marriage made in heaven. Their staff put together the thick applications for public funds, and then put up their one housing complex as collateral. We won grants for $2.4 million from the city of San Francisco, and $3.2 million from federal tax credit funds. The Presbyterian Women's money played a key role in securing these funds, as well as an additional $400,000 in gifts from foundations, churches, corporations, and individuals for equipping and furnishing a place whose beauty affirms the beauty of our residents. We have won two awards for "design excellence in affordable housing." We are now also on the World Wide Web with other buildings recognized as setting a high standard for low-income housing. The highest award came from a single parent living in the building who said, "This building was designed by people who know how families live and who care about them." We are thrilled at the beauty and usefulness of the new apartment building for thirty-eight families. But, we are sad at the knowledge that over two thousand families applied to live there, and that Congress was at the same time cutting off funds to create affordable housing while reducing capital gains taxes for the wealthy. The personal is the pastoral is the political. Our work at the personal and the systemic levels continues.

Expect a Miracle

In 1996, we were forced to vacate the space we had used as our store-front church and center for street chaplaincy. A space five times larger was available across the street, but the rent was quoted as being $1,600 a month. Despondent, we said we could only afford $500 a month. The next day the call came: "Its yours for $500." Now, twice weekly worship, daily 8:30 a.m. Alcoholics Anonymous and Narcotics Anonymous groups (so needed in this high drug use area), street chaplaincy, marriages, and memorial services are held there. An old friend came to us with his dream of opening a computer-training center in the Tenderloin district as a way of helping people escape poverty. His generosity made that possible. We partitioned off about one-third of the storefront space, installed state-of-the-art machines, hired staff, and were soon busy with regular classes and drop-in instruction times six days a week. At our opening, one woman, learning that everything in the computer lab is free to Tenderloin residents and homeless persons, said in a tone of wonder, "Thank God there are Christians doing something like this." We affirm the wisdom of Francis of Assisi, "Proclaim the Gospel at all times. Use words if necessary."

Transformation: Overcoming Prostitution

God does not let us rest. The Tenderloin district is a major area for street prostitution arrests. We felt called to act for and with prostituted women. Our zeal for this was intensified by three memorial services our clergy led for prostituted women who were murdered. We formed a planning committee to begin development of a Safe House for Women Leaving Prostitution. We planned for appropriate counseling, education, health care, and other services. Believing our most difficult task would be securing a building, we experienced another miracle when a near-perfect facility was given to us a scant three months after our first committee meeting. Less than a year later, we had refurbished the building, secured three years of funding, selected staff, and begun receiving residents. We are engaged in pressing for changes in punitive and nonproductive laws that result in an estimated six thousand prostitution arrests annually in San Francisco at a cost of over

$7 million. We are also educating the public and the churches to re-search study findings, such as: 70 percent of prostituted women suf-fered long-term incest; at least 90 percent suffered some form of child abuse; fewer than half are high school graduates; over 90 percent are drug-addicted; 88 percent have never held a regular job; the average age for women entering prostitution in the United States is fourteen. Many, we believe, suffer posttraumatic stress disorder just like com-bat veterans and victims of torture. Leaving prostitution involves a massive, exhausting, painful life makeover. Yet there are only four safe houses for women leaving prostitution in the entire country, all of them begun by Christian women. Long-term work in this area in-volves radical change in those political, economic, gender, and eccle-siastical structures that foster exploitation of women. The book, *Casting Stones*, by Susan Thistlewaite and Rita Nakashima-Brock, available from Augsburg/Fortress Press, is a good resource for under-standing this tragedy. The personal is the pastoral is the political.

Fiscal Freedom and Responsibility

Network Ministries began with the simplest of structures, a gathering of like-minded people of faith, with no funds. It now has a board of di-rectors from many churches and the larger community, as well as a second nonprofit organization, San Francisco Network Ministries Housing Corporation, for the purpose of building, rehabbing, and op-erating residential buildings. Only the Housing Corporation accepts public funds, and only because of the large amount of money needed for the operation of the apartments and the Safe House. San Francisco Network Ministries has never sought public funds due to the restric-tions accompanying them, preferring to live frugally on gifts from in-dividuals, congregations, judicatories, and occasional foundation grants.

The freedom accompanying such frugality enables us to move into ministries as we are led by people, prayer, and the Holy Spirit, unencumbered by government agencies which always try to shape the policy and forbid overt religious symbols and actions. We know that to do the work of advocacy, to confront injustice, and to nourish the spirit we must be creative and develop new sources of funding. The needs are so great. We are now forming a partnership with the Sisters of the Presentation, a community of Roman Catholic religious women, as part of a long-range plan to privately fund the Safe House for Women Coming out of Prostitution. After all, we are a network. A basic source of our strength is in unity with others. The personal is the pastoral is the political.

What We Can Learn

- Thinking big, having a large vision — the apartment building for affordable family housing, the Safe House for Women — can attract support from unexpected sources.
- Enabling people to be open to the transforming power of God can lead to many surprising redemptive outcomes that go beyond our imagination.
- It is often the marginalized and alienated people who have suffered deeply who understand most fully what needs to be done to heal and renew human life.
- Ministries of compassion and service, when pursued to the sources of human need, tend to lead to engagement with the larger structures of society, as in the case of the Safe House for Women Coming Out of Prostitution.
- Moving beyond the local church tendency toward preoccupation with private life and finding a balance with engagement in the public sector is the calling of the church. The personal and the public are always interrelated. The church is the middle-level institution that provides the connecting link.
- New church development needs to have a reason for being that goes beyond merely creating a new congregation in order to preserve the church. New congregations that are rooted in living out the gospel in response to great human need tend to develop much more vigorous and vital worship and ministry.
- The challenge of developing new sources of funding from the private sector is worth the effort, often very rewarding, and is a means of experiencing the grace of God. To give people the opportunity to share sacrificially is part of the church's ministry. We dare not do less than challenge people to give courageously beyond what they think they can do.
- The importance of women as visionaries, leaders, and pastoral

ministers in the most difficult life situations is clearly visible in the San Francisco Network Ministries. This is a great asset, which the church-at-large needs to embrace, utilize, and celebrate.

- "Always proclaim [live] the gospel. Use words [only] when necessary." The call to do justice is the call to live the love of Christ in the world creatively, and when we do that, very few words may be necessary. This advice from St. Francis of Assisi speaks to the church today.

First Presbyterian Church of Portland

Founded in 1854, First Presbyterian Church of Portland is a congregation with a long and significant history of accomplishments. By the end of its first fifty years of life it had grown to over one thousand members; built a large sanctuary seating thirteen hundred; given birth to or helped sponsor thirty new churches, including seven Native American mission churches; built a hospital in Korea; initiated medical work with women in China; and sent the first missionary, founded the first mission schools, and organized the first church in the Territory of Alaska.

In the 1950s the church, like many congregations in that post–World War II era, grew rapidly. It reached a peak membership of over four thousand. It was filled with families and large numbers of children, youth, and young adults. It carried on a vigorous program of local mission and public service. It played a significant role in the founding of Lewis and Clark College. It acquired and developed a Retreat and Conference Center in the Columbia Gorge, and expanded the Friendly House, a neighborhood center owned and operated by the church since the 1930s. The congregation renovated and updated its historic building (constructed in 1887), operated a large Sunday school, and sponsored numerous candidates for theological education and preparation for the ministry. One of its outstanding pastors, Paul Wright, was elected Moderator of the Presbyterian Church, U.S.A.

General Assembly. After several decades of growth and prosperity, things began to change.[1]

Thirty-five years later, in 1985, the situation was very different. The church, located in the center of downtown Portland, was negatively impacted by a number of factors. A ring of new freeways cut up the downtown area. There was an outward movement of families to newer housing, decline of older buildings, and a change of population toward more transient residents. An older hotel contiguous to the church had become living space for drug dealers, prostitutes, and marginally employed people. Street crime around the church was significant. The neighborhood was not safe at night. Petty theft, vandalism, panhandling, and drug dealing were common occurrences in broad daylight.

The decline of the church happened right along with the deterioration of the downtown neighborhoods. The congregation steadily lost members. Many families with children and youth moved to suburban congregations. The average age of the membership rose to sixty-eight. Church finances were in significant decline. Long-term maintenance of the large, old, church building was deferred for lack of funds. Program and education space did not meet prevailing standards for light, heat, and ventilation. The elderly members were dying at a rate of approximately fifty per year. Memorial services and care for the grieving were the most common pastoral functions. People were reluctant to come into the downtown area in general, and to the church in particular. Its program and spirit were at a low ebb.

At that point the congregation began to realize that its future was bound up with the need for a younger constituency, and with the redevelopment of the downtown area. With that challenge in mind the church called a new pastor, the Reverend William Creevey, who had served urban congregations in Seattle and Sacramento. His coming to First Presbyterian Church was the beginning of a new era of redevelopment for the church and the surrounding area.

---

1. William Creevey (pastor of First Presbyterian Church), interview with author, 20 May 1997.

Downtown Renewal

Bill Creevey led the church in joining with other religious groups, businesses, and civic organizations to work as partners in efforts for the redevelopment and revitalization of downtown Portland. He helped the church understand the interdependence of the congregation and the community. He worked in the church to renew and update the congregation's historic sense of public responsibility in ways appropriate to the changing needs of the city and the church. At first it seemed like an overwhelming task because the needs were so great. Downtown Portland was engaging in much-needed:

- new urban planning and development policy
- commitment to revitalize the city center
- tax incentives to attract investment
- new transportation system
- new apartment housing and housing rehabilitation
- new business and employment opportunities
- redevelopment as a cultural center
- social services for transient, chronically mentally ill, and homeless persons
- community-based police and street safety.

The church, under Creevey's leadership, joined with other congregations to organize ecumenically to support the adoption of a new downtown development policy and plan. Over a period of years a number of significant improvements were achieved by the city, including: new and remodeled housing in the residential ring around the business district; redevelopment of downtown business; new, light rail transportation; increased employment; community-oriented safety programs; and a more proactive social service program. The churches, including First Presbyterian, played an important role in helping to develop the support necessary to accomplish these changes. These efforts helped to create a more positive climate and environment within which religious congregations could be renewed in the downtown area.[2]

2. Creevey, interview with author, 16 September 1997.

Church and Community Interdependence

With leadership by the new pastor and a core group of members, the congregation began a forward movement in five areas: (1) revitalizing spiritual life; (2) rejuvenating the congregation through membership enlistment; (3) refurbishing the church building; (4) rehabilitating the church neighborhood; and (5) renewing the congregation's wider mission. An early symbol of the church's dual commitment to revitalize the congregation and the community came in the 1987 Centennial Celebration Fund Campaign. This capital campaign effort raised one million dollars for new programs to reach people who were not members of the church. The church's vision was to serve both church members and people in the community. The church became a creative partner for community redevelopment in a number of ways that will be described more fully later. At this point, we briefly indicate the following:

- Purchase and renovation of the Hub Building, across the street from the church, into the Julia West House (a neighborhood center housing an ecumenical street ministry called Operation Nightwatch); the Food Box Hospitality program for homeless and low-income people; and initial housing for arriving refugee families.
- Renovation of the church-owned Danmore Hotel, adjoining the church building, into quality, low-income housing in cooperation with the city.
- Sponsorship and construction of Alder House, with 130 units of new, single-room occupancy housing for low-income residents, in the air space above the church parking lot across the street from the church.
- Transfer of ownership of the Friendly House property (a multiservice center founded by the church in the 1930s) in 1989 to the Friendly House Corporation, to enhance its eligibility for grant funds, while continuing to provide leadership and annual church financial support. This social service program includes a preschool, a senior center, transportation program, personal counseling, emergency food and housing, a day-care program serving one hundred children, a drop-in center for youth, and a support group for persons in the downtown area who are recov-

288

ering from mental illness. One-third of the board members of Friendly House are from First Presbyterian Church.[3]

- Creation of Community Housing, Inc. to sponsor low-income housing. Two projects, including Alder House, have been completed and a third was underway by 1998.
- Funding of social services and an artist-in-residence in Alder House as a community-building activity, and sponsorship of a community Art Festival, with residents' leadership and involvement, to change the cultural climate of the neighborhood. This was in addition to the year-round program of exhibits in the church art gallery.

We will return to these themes later after seeing how the congregation was active to renew its own spiritual life and inner strength.

Congregational Renewal

William Creevey helped the church session to understand that its first priority was to attract a new, younger constituency and that planning, staffing, and funding must reflect this top priority for congregational development. The centennial celebration of 1987 was to commemorate the laying of the cornerstone of the present sanctuary in 1887. But the real emphasis was on the consideration of how the church could lay a foundation for another century at its historic downtown location. The central question addressed by the congregation was, does God want a church here in the decades ahead? Sermons were preached, discussions were held in church groups and organizations, and dialogue was carried in the church media. The result was a positive affirmation that God was calling First Presbyterian Church of Portland to remain downtown in its historic location, and to be renewed for another century of ministry of faithful, prophetic, mission-oriented life and witness. With new commitment and a sense of God's calling, the work began. Many revitalizing actions were taken:[4]

---

3. "First Church Supports Friendly House," *The Spire Monthly* 2:2 (February 1989): 1.

4. Creevey, interview with author, 3 March 1998.

- Worship was strengthened as the empowering center for spiritual renewal.
- A strategic element in the revitalization and outreach of the church was an expanded music program. A children's choir was organized when there were few children in the church. This choir grew into a multiple-choir program with six choirs for children and youth. Families were recruited by mail, newspaper ads, and calling. Radio spots announced the choir program on classical music stations.
- Preaching was biblical, faith-filled, and prophetic. It addressed personal life and public policy issues from a biblical perspective.
- The Parish House renovation featured a state-of-the-art nursery for infants and toddlers in a highly visible central location. Classrooms for young children were remodeled to be more attractive to young families.
- Outside ushers were organized to move the presence of the congregation onto the streets outside the imposing stone walls of the sanctuary, to welcome worshippers on the sidewalks and at the parking places near the church, and at the same time provide greater security for those coming to worship.
- The church building was cleaned up, refurbished, and brightened into a warm and welcoming place where people wanted to be, to complement the beauty and dignity of the historic sanctuary. The city helped to clean up adjacent streets, and installed new streetlights.
- Sunday worship with great music and strong preaching was broadcast on a local radio station to reach both the large number of shut-in members and other listeners in the wider metropolitan area.
- The culture of worship was diversified through the participation of the new children's and youth choirs, the introduction of a gospel choir, and the use of music both from the growing global, ecumenical repertoire and the strong traditional, classical heritage of the church.
- Visitors were warmly welcomed and received a follow-up contact from the church on the same day. Visitors were invited into involvement, membership, and leadership quickly. They were called to become part of a congregation with an obvious challenge and a long history that was engaging in unfinished work to get ready for the next century.

- A new singles ministry quickly grew into a strong program attracting over seven hundred persons per month. Quarterly divorce recovery groups had long waiting lists. Some singles joined the church to participate in the emerging music, education, and outreach programs.
- The walls and lighting in the small chapel of the church were enhanced for exhibition of art. The monthly openings of adjudicated and invitational art exhibits drew crowds of nonchurch members. Chamber music performed by church musicians and the presence of church greeters provided points of engagement with the congregation for city residents interested in the arts.
- Gay and lesbian people in the congregation were affirmed. Newcomers were welcomed into the diverse church family in spite of the struggles both in the Presbyterian denomination and in the state of Oregon over gay and lesbian rights and ordination. The divergence and polarity of attitudes on this matter were a challenge. The session led the way in creating opportunities for careful listening to each other's stories in the diverse membership of this city congregation.
- A long-dormant youth program was renewed with special staff and volunteers. The major effort was to "grow" a youth program by attracting a constituency of young families who would become involved in creating a program for children growing into adolescence over the years. This proved to be effective in the long term.
- Adult education was enriched with spiritual life groups and retreats. The church's conference center, Menucha, outside of Portland, was more fully developed and utilized for education, spiritual formation, and leadership training events.

Everything was permeated with a new spirit of positive expectation and undergirded with prayer and dedicated hard work. There was a quicker, stronger heartbeat in the church. The motto of the congregation became "A Heart for the City." The church was growing. Infant baptisms and new members became more plentiful. The average age of the membership moved toward thirty-eight instead of sixty-eight. Now the congregation had growing pains instead of dying pains.

A Heart for the City

Parallel to the renewal of the congregation was the redevelopment of the downtown region and especially the transformation of the neighborhood around the church. At the heart of the church renewal was the leadership of the pastor, the church session, and many hardworking staff and volunteers. Now we ask, what made the "heartbeat" for redevelopment in the city successful?

After the church had made a clear commitment to its own renewal and had acknowledged that its own future was interdependent with that of the city center, then positive things began to develop.[5] An early victory was the Danmore Hotel. This older, three-story building sharing the city block with the church was a center of drug traffic and prostitution. Two businessmen and a third member of the congregation bought the hotel and gave it to the church. This gave the church the opportunity to reorient the use of this deteriorating hotel. The church rose to the challenge by creating the Committee on Replacement Housing. The committee's commitment was to serve the needs of low-income people with replacement housing of better quality at affordable rent. The chairman of the committee was a church member and professional with redevelopment experience in urban planning. The committee included professionals with experience in Portland and other cities, and leaders in the Portland business sector.

The Committee on Replacement Housing did research and study of the church's neighborhood. They led the way in planning for the renovation and redeployment of the old Danmore Hotel for low-income housing on the upper floors and social service agencies on the first floor. This process gave the new committee experience, helped establish connections with city agencies, and showed that the church was serious about neighborhood redevelopment.

A second major project was the design and construction of Alder House as efficiency apartments with a safe and stable environment for low-income people ranging in age from twenty-one to seventy. This 130-unit apartment building, seven stories tall, with 43,384 square feet of floor space, built above the parking lot across the street

---

5. The description that follows of the successful neighborhood development by the church is based upon a memorandum written by William Creevey to the author, dated 3 March 1998.

from the church, was the first single-room-occupancy, low-income housing to be constructed in Oregon in over fifty years. This project was developed in airspace over a parking lot owned by the church, sponsored by the church's Replacement Housing Committee, and constructed by an independent developer. The apartment building was planned with the needs of single-occupancy residents in mind, and included common area facilities such as a library, lounge/meeting room, storage area, large laundry, and a sun deck. Financing was a combination of federal low-income housing tax credits sold to corporate buyers, and bank construction loans converted to a longer-term mortgage.[6]

Through these two substantial housing projects the Replacement Housing Committee of the church was developing connections with city planners, neighbor churches, and other people and groups interested in downtown redevelopment. The city of Portland was moving ahead to deal with its city-center problems, developing its own plans and welcoming participation from the private, nonprofit sector. It is within that climate that the Replacement Housing Committee worked with other groups to help create the Downtown Housing Corporation, Inc. (DHCI) as a larger, broader-based, non-profit entity to deal with some of the housing needs in the inner-city ring around the business district. First Presbyterian Church formed DHCI, with a minority of its own members on the board. It shows the evolution of vision and effort from compassion toward the larger-systems level of justice.

The congregation, drawing younger members and growing in membership and commitment to public service, surrounded the low-income housing with a number of places where people can get help to lift themselves up to greater stability. The church created an indoor play park in the renovated Danmore Hotel for children of the neighborhood, and welcomed the community. The Alder House Child Development Center — a child-care program catering to single-parent families, with a sliding fee scale and scholarships — offers a professional staff and a cosmopolitan experience for children of working parents. The center is beneath the sanctuary of the church and is subsidized by the Christian Education Program of the church.

6. "Replacement Housing Project Receives Session Approval," *The Spire Monthly* 1:2 (20 April 1991): 2.

Another notable human effort to surround people of the neighborhood with compassion is Operation Nightwatch. The church purchased a small commercial building across the street, named it the Julia West House, and converted its ground level into a nighttime center for ecumenical ministry to homeless and lonely people. This ministry is called Operation Nightwatch. Volunteers from First Presbyterian Church and other Portland congregations staff Nightwatch. Volunteers are trained to relate to people on the streets at night. There is food, recreation, companionship, referral information, and a safe gathering place at night. Some of the volunteers provide a foot care ministry, washing and tending feet, providing clean socks and better shoes to people who walk the streets.[7]

The same space is used in the daytime for the church's emergency Food Box and hospitality program that ministers to chronically mentally ill, homeless, and addicted people who seldom find their way into established social assistance programs. Some spend the night in shelters and come to Julia West House in the morning. From 75 to 125 persons per morning find enough help to make it through the day. They are welcomed with kindness, given hot snacks, trustworthy hospitality, and informal referrals.

Both Nightwatch and the Food Box/Hospitality Center commonly serve capacity crowds each day they are open. The upper floors of the Julia West Building serve as initial housing for refugee families sponsored by First Presbyterian or other downtown churches. These ministries have provided a window of learning for many volunteers to more fully understand the lives and needs of homeless people. It is a point of contact through which some persons come to see the need for action at the systemic level. At First Presbyterian Church there are constantly emerging opportunities for those who are willing to move beyond one-on-one charity toward justice through public policy involvement.[8]

7. Gary Vaughn, ed., *Operation Nightwatch Newsletter* (September 1997): 1-4.

8. "Hub Building Purchase Enhances Mission," *The Spire Monthly* 2:1 (January 1989): 1.

What We Can Learn

- The essential investment must be in congregational development. Staffing, marketing, and funding programs for prospective new members must have first priority. The renewal of a vital spiritual life and the recruitment of a growing body of new members must come first if the church is to be able to lead and fund social justice programs and mission outreach.
- Long-term, creative, skilled pastoral leadership is one of the keys to creative downtown church redevelopment.
- Strengthening worship with strong preaching, and the development of children's choirs, are major resources for helping a mainline downtown church attract families and increase membership.
- A downtown mainline church with a strong tradition of ministry to families and a strong tradition of social justice and public service can thrive and grow.
- The vitality of a downtown mainline church is interdependent with the vitality of the city center.
- The self-interests of the congregation and the community are linked and it is unlikely that one or the other can be healthy for very long while the other is in steady decline.
- Creative redevelopment of existing older buildings in the downtown area to meet real human needs and serve the public interests can contribute significantly to a congregation's own well-being and expanding mission.
- A positive policy of engaging the surrounding community with a vision for transformation can help attract leadership to a congregation that is committed to redevelopment.
- Making a commitment for community redevelopment, taking some risks and investing money and human resources can help attract other churches and allies into the effort.
- Engaging the business community through pastoral care and preaching can be a helpful factor in community revitalization and congregational growth.
- Preservation of endowment for the maintenance and/or development of buildings will not guarantee continuing vitality or necessarily contribute to the future strength of a city congregation.
- Funding and implementing future-oriented efforts to attract and

involve new, younger constituencies and leadership are essential ingredients in developing parish-funded social ministry at the center of the city. Planning and funding priorities must reflect this fact.

- Strengthening the spiritual life of the congregation through small groups and the teaching ministry contributed significantly to membership growth and to ministry in the public sector.
- Some of the weekday service programs in the community provided points of entry for persons to come into the congregation's worship and fellowship.
- The excellent quality of programming and preaching in the church made a key contribution to the redevelopment of a younger, more active membership.

Beyond Charity Toward Justice

The theme which runs through this book may be expressed like this: In a growing number of urban churches there is a positive movement beyond individual acts of Christian charity toward more organized, collaborative action for justice. This movement is very much related to the revitalization of urban congregations and surrounding communities. Acts of charity, service, and justice overlap. They all have positive value as well as limitations. They are not mutually exclusive, yet each has distinct and defining qualities. They are interrelated and can best be understood on a continuum of complexity and levels of influence. In the past decade, many urban churches have moved beyond charity toward justice. They have acted to form networks and collaborative partnerships to change public policy and structures to create new and more just conditions in urban communities. From our experience in studying twenty-eight urban congregations, we can now bring together in a summary our insight into charity, service, and justice.

Charity

From a Christian theological perspective, charity is rooted in sacrificial love as seen in the life, ministry, death, and resurrection of Jesus Christ. In its ultimate meaning, charity is the unconditional love that God freely gives to humankind, as expressed in Jesus Christ. Over the centuries the church has taught that charity is the greatest Christian virtue. In some traditions, it is understood to be the preeminent empowering divine spirit for human social life — a gift of God's grace, which makes it possible for people to live in community. Christian theology came to understand charity in two ways. On the one hand, it is God's gift, which enables sinful humankind to be forgiving, put the best interests of others first, and live together in true community. Here the emphasis is on living in community, suffering with one another in mutual burden bearing, supporting one another without counting the cost. On the other hand, charity is understood to be works of love, acts of mutual aid, the duty of Christians, as in the great commandment, "Love God with all your heart, soul and mind; and love your neighbor as yourself" (Matt. 22:37, 39). This perspective emphasizes personal deeds of mercy and acts of compassion within the local community. In summary, charity is understood as the central virtue for Christians, modeled in Jesus, and as the spiritual power that motivates persons to acts of compassion at the individual and social level. We are able to love because God has first loved us. The motive power of love to enable individuals and groups to act unselfishly for the common good is the meaning we must keep in mind.

There are significant limits to what charity can do. Ordinarily, charity deals with personal needs of an immediate nature, and does not deal with the root causes of injustice and human suffering. Sometimes charity can become a barrier to doing the more difficult work of justice. In some churches, there is pride in giving financial support to charitable organizations that serve poor people. Often this is done with little or no thought about its unintended consequences. It may be done without any intention of becoming involved with the people for whom the aid is intended. Sometimes charity is given as a means of intentionally avoiding involvement with people who are different from one's own group of people.

To have a vital Christian witness, urban congregations must go beyond acts of charity. They must go beyond the need to feel good about giving. What is most valuable is active partnership between oppressed people seeking to change the conditions of injustice, and other people who are willing to join in a common effort so that equity can be established. The most important gift urban churches can give is the creation of relationships within which people of different backgrounds can learn to trust, respect, and work together. The creation of such a community is the foundation for the redevelopment of the church and the neighborhood. The enormous challenges of urban neighborhoods belong to all the people in the whole city. Bringing people together from different sectors of the city, partnering for redevelopment, collaborating for justice, that is the calling of Christians. Such a calling moves people beyond charity toward greater commitment, wider vision, and more systematic action for justice.

Social Service

As society grows more complex, the uncertainties of socioeconomic life play a more powerful role in shaping the quality of individual and social life. In response to a more institutionalized society, more organized patterns of Christian compassion have developed. At first, churches and governments responded to the growing needs of large numbers of people, primarily in cities, by creating agencies to do the works of charity. What persons could no longer do individually or in small groups would have to be done through larger, better-organized, more dependable structures. Social work agencies were slowly developed. In the context of religious denominations there was still a measure of personal responsibility, a caring for persons as individuals, an expectation that those who were helped would give something in return, and a personal connection between the giver and the receiver.

Gradually, there was a transition toward charity meaning simply the giving of money to support organizations, which were expected to provide aid to those who needed it. In this process, services — food, shelter, clothing, counseling, health care — were provided to people in need, who became clients, by social workers, who became professionals. This developed on a massive scale in the public sector through government bureaucracies, and on a smaller scale in church-sponsored social service agencies. The operative motivation became service. Religious communication was reduced or prohibited even though many social workers were motivated by religious values. The goal became the providing of social services to needy people on a regular basis in an efficient, coordinated manner.

In social service, there is a tendency to create dependent clients, who learn to make a career out of "working the system" for all possible benefits. There is a strong tendency toward establishing a permanent underclass of alienated, marginalized, apathetic people. This is not true of all social service. In fairness, it must be acknowledged that social service helps millions of people cope with immediate emergencies, and provides helpful short-term assistance to people struggling with urgent problems. In a complex modern society a social safety net is a real necessity. Its major limitations are that it focuses on aiding people to adjust, adapt, and cope within the existing conditions. It does not challenge root causes of human misery and social injustice. It tends to create dependency and dehumanization and encourages the mentality of victimization. It becomes a central component in the welfare culture. It does not adequately emphasize a sense of responsibility for changing basic conditions.

Systemic Justice

Changing policies, structures, and behaviors that are at the root of injustice is the focus of systemic justice. Efforts to change the large-scale systems that have great influence on the lives of persons and groups involve the conscious use of political and economic power. The emphasis is on distributive equity, and empowering groups of people to take charge of their own lives. At this level, consciousness shifts from being a victim to becoming a participant in shaping society in a more humane fashion. In the religious frame of reference, love operating as justice at the societal level helps to unveil the pretensions and social fictions by which injustice is maintained. It can be the motivating spirit that enables new and more just structures to be created and put into operation. Justice is understood to move beyond the purely personal realm into the institutional realm where people power can be mobilized over against entrenched institutional power.

Social justice focuses on basic causes of oppression, inequity, and disenfranchisement. It seeks to change public policy and public priorities. It works to empower people to take initiatives in ways that are positive and constructive. The movement for systemic justice understands that oppressed people have strengths, skills, cultural assets, and the responsibility to act corporately for their own common good. It works for long-term goals and more permanent solutions that create more just social arrangements. Systemic justice by its nature involves political action, mobilizing voting power, creating common interest alliances, and building cooperative coalitions. We see this exemplified in the Baltimore story about BUILD, the Chicago Resurrection Project, and in the Los Angeles FAME development projects.

The limitations of working for systemic justice are many in number. Justice work takes time. It seeks large-scale goals, which do not come quickly. It does not deal directly with immediate, urgent needs. It involves risk-taking, and the investment of large amounts of human and financial resources. It involves political processes and almost always involves conflict and stress in the community. It deals with institutional power that is located outside the neighborhood and not easily subject to direct citizen influence. It often fails to deliver. Nevertheless, the work of seeking justice is necessary to create a democratic society that works for the good of all the people. The chart (pp. 302-3), the Charity — Service — Justice Continuum, shows the differences and commonalties of the three forms of Christian social responsibility.

From my experience in visiting urban churches in major cities and gathering information on the work they are doing, the contemporary understanding of justice that emerged is the concept of *equity*. Equity, as I see it embodied in the work of these urban churches, has a broad meaning that includes shareholding, fairness, and community.

- *Shareholding* is a commitment to enable every citizen to participate in the political processes through which social policy and public priorities are determined. It means that every citizen can have ownership, invest in the larger society, and share in the managing of goods, services, and property. It means the opportunity to enjoy the blessings of life.
- *Fairness* is a commitment to a reasonable distribution of the goods and services that are essential to make human life humane. It means access to quality education, opportunity to develop one's potential, to learn, earn, and prosper. It means access to employment, health care, and affordable housing. It means curbing wasteful excesses and seeking to enable all citizens to be productive and contribute to society.

301

THE CONTINUUM OF
CHARITY — SERVICE — JUSTICE

	CHARITY	SERVICE	JUSTICE
REALM	Private: personal acts of compassion; individual deeds of assistance; voluntary aid organizations.	Private and public: organized delivery of assistance to families, individuals, and groups.	Public: public policy-making based upon equity; fairness, shareholding, community.
TIME	Quick response to urgent, emergency needs; can meet immediate needs.	Intermediate timeliness: can be fast response; but tends to be more deliberate, slow paced.	Long term: does not produce a quick fix; does not serve urgent, immediate needs.
WHO BENEFITS	Direct help to individuals, families, small groups, neighborhood communities.	Direct help to individuals, families, small groups, and can provide long-term aid to large, diverse populations.	Can bring long-term improvement to large sectors of society; challenges oppressed to change basic conditions.
RESPONDS TO	The secondary effects of injustice, social crisis, people in pain and need — food, shelter, clothing.	The secondary consequences of unjust conditions, social upheaval, groups in pain, and emergency disaster situations.	Basic causes of injustice, the roots of injustice, socioeconomic and political sources of suffering, group oppression.
PATTERN	Requires repeated responses to meet individual need after repeated requests.	Can deliver dependable, stable, continuous supply of goods and services efficiently.	Changes basic public policy and priorities; changes structures and institutions.

	CHARITY	SERVICE	JUSTICE
BIBLICAL MODEL	The good Samaritan helps a person who has been robbed and beaten, giving emergency treatment, rescue, short-term hospitality, and personal compassion. (Luke 10:30-37)	Early Christian Church appoints six deacons to care for the widows, orphans, and the poor. Food and shelter provided with prayer and support community. (Acts 6:1-7)	Moses leads the entire Hebrew nation out of slavery in the Exodus. Appoints leaders to organize self-government under law. (Exodus 12:37, 13, 14, 18)
CURRENT MODEL	Soup kitchen feeds hungry people; Salvation Army sells used clothes to individuals; shelters give overnight housing; donor gives aid to the homeless.	Government welfare program gives aid to unemployed person; aid to dependent children; food stamps for family living in poverty; public housing; emergency health care. Can be a base for recovery.	Community Development organizes people to create affordable housing, develop jobs, train workers, develop community health care, advocate legislative change.
STRENGTH	Personal, simple, quick, deals with immediate need; involves volunteers; promotes giving; provides tax deductions.	Organized, prepared in advance, provides accountability; public tax supported, provides social safety net; serves large numbers of people. Can promote new beginnings.	Engages people in self-development; empowers people to meet their needs, take charge of their lives, form partnerships, take political action.
LIMITS	Does not deal with the basic causes of human problems; is reactive, sporadic; promotes one-way giving; may inhibit responsibility.	May create dependency, apathy; does not deal with basic causes; often expensive/wasteful, and can be dehumanizing.	Requires time, risk-taking, hard work, compromise, financial resources; can cause conflict; may fail; no guarantee of success.

- *Community* is a commitment to interdependence, mutuality, responsibility to one another, and engagement in seeking the common good. It means willingness to balance the rights and responsibilities of competing groups within loyalty to a larger public good. It means affirmation of diversity, social inclusiveness, participation in the democratic decision process, and creative tension between individual aspirations and social priorities. It means accountability within the larger society.

Equity means being a shareholder in the common good with a fair distribution of goods and services within the bonds of mutual responsibility for the larger community. The experiences of people in urban churches working together with others from the neighborhood and with institutions beyond the local area have often produced a community within which there is a strong sense of equity. This positive experience is a life-affirming, motivating spirit that is at the heart of the movement in urban church redevelopment. It is a significant part of the good news to be shared and celebrated.

One significant instrument for seeking systemic justice is community organizing around public issues. Neighborhood leaders are assisted in gathering people of an area to identify their most urgent issues and then trained to take appropriate action. Local people learn to use political and cultural processes to engage government and to use other resources to respond to the needs of the community. In community organizing, local leadership is in charge. Local people decide what needs to be done and take responsibility to get things accomplished for the benefit of the wider community. In doing this work of justice, partnerships are formed, new resources are discovered, leadership is developed, the social fabric of the community is strengthened, and more equitable conditions are created. Many urban churches that are being revitalized have learned that community organizing is an essential part of redeveloping a vital congregation and neighborhood.

Barriers to Urban Church Revitalization

In conversations with pastors and people in urban churches in fifteen cities across the country, a number of difficulties encountered in doing the work of revitalization were described. Among the many barriers identified, a few were indicated more often than others:

- unwillingness to try new approaches designed to involve new groups of people, and resistance to becoming more inclusive
- resistance to changing worship patterns, especially music, and reluctance to accept a more participatory style
- anxiety about survival and reluctance to think beyond internal problems of leadership, membership, and finance
- lack of vision, inability to see a larger picture of potential opportunity beyond immediate circumstances
- holding on to worn-out traditions, inability to let go of past history, and unrealistic expectations
- difficulty overcoming a victim mentality; being ruled by experiences of poverty and oppression
- impatience with developing new grassroots participation, reluctance to do the hard work of community organizing and becoming more welcoming
- difficulty seeing real assets in depressed urban neighborhoods, such as vacant land, old buildings, strategic location, and the skills of people
- neglect of worship, spiritual life, and nurture of members in favor of too much engagement with external mission
- urban problems such as street crime, poor police protection, inadequate trash pick-up, bad housing, changing population.

Clearly, the revitalization of an urban church is a struggle that requires overcoming formidable barriers, persistence over a long period of time, and vision to see beyond the immediate short-term issues. It takes courage to act with positive expectations and the ability to find or create new resources. Again and again, pastors indicated that the most important factor in eventual revitalization success was having a vision, helping the congregation embrace a new vision, and staying with it, not getting sidetracked. The words of one pastor are very much to the point, "A dream is having a vision with goals and a timetable." Not every urban church that has a vision for revitalization succeeds. It takes more than vision.

Positive Factors in Urban Church Revitalization

What factors do urban church pastors identify as important in the positive accomplishments of the congregations? From interviews with pastors, a number of influential factors were evident. These factors can be loosely categorized as internal and external. The internal factors have to do primarily with strengthening the congregation and its inner spiritual life. The external factors have to do primarily with carrying out the mission of community redevelopment and justice.

The internal factors most often mentioned by urban church pastors as influential in strengthening the congregation were:

- the centrality of worship — strong preaching, appropriate music, interaction of members
- strong Christian education — positive programs for adults, families, and children
- community building — creating a network of positive relationships and effective partnerships
- holistic approach to ministry — integrating personal and social mission in supportive community
- pastoral leadership — vision, goal setting, spiritual motivation, skilled organizing.

There were other frequently mentioned internal factors, including the following: becoming proactive; taking initiative; moving away from a reactive posture; emphasis on transformation; reconfiguration of church building space for new uses; clarifying purpose; setting priorities; gaining new financial resources; gaining new members; and strengthening youth ministry.

The external factors most often mentioned by urban church pastors as influential in creating and sustaining mission in the community were:

- identifying indigenous leadership — connecting with and involving new leaders
- asset-based development — seeing the potential in land, people, buildings, local culture
- forming partnerships — linking with groups, donors, foundations, government, other churches

- creating new income-producing enterprises
- developing community culture — affirming, celebrating, promoting, creating events and local symbols
- community redevelopment — empowering people to rebuild neighborhoods, both physically and socially.

Other frequently mentioned, positive external factors were: clear focus on justice issues; community organizing emphasis; getting positive media coverage; visible accomplishments in the community; being action-oriented; and taking initiative to gain support among community leaders.

Learning About Pastoral Leadership

The leadership of the pastor is crucial in any lasting revitalization, and in ministries of systemic justice. There are a number of insights that we can report from the pastors of the twenty-eight congregations in our study.

Overall, the value of long-term pastoral tenure far outweighs negative limitations. In urban churches where there is instability in the surrounding community, the stability that can come from a long pastoral tenure is very important. Further, in difficult urban church situations, it often takes a long gestation period to establish trust, develop new lay leadership, and create the conditions that are essential for redevelopment. Good examples of this can be seen in St. Pius V Roman Catholic Church in Chicago, Luther Place Memorial Lutheran Church in Washington, D.C., Windsor Village Methodist Church in Houston, and First African Methodist Episcopal Church in Los Angeles.

In the churches we studied, a variety of leadership styles can be seen. There is no predominant formula. Contextual factors definitely play a role. In some urban churches there is a straightforward, strong, direct, and authoritarian style of leadership. In other churches there is a more relaxed, team-oriented, nondirective style of leadership. In still other situations, there is a mix of styles with modes of leading changing as circumstances change. There are several generalizations we can make based upon observation. The pastor in urban churches usually is the number one symbol of the message. That is to say, the pastor becomes the representative of whatever the congregation's focus may be — whether it is revitalization, spiritual renewal, justice, or community redevelopment. This may come about more or less intentionally. It has to do partially with the pastor being at the center of communication and action. It also has to do with the faith commitment and symbolic meaning of pastoral functioning. There is an important interaction between the personality strengths that a minister brings to the office and the contextual norms and demands that arise in the situation.

There is a continual balancing act going on for most urban church pastors between the demands of internal leadership in the congregation and external leadership in the community. Successful pastors are the ones who manage to do the right things at the right time most often. The pastor is the spiritual leader for the inner life, for worship, nurture, and care of members. In most urban churches, the pastor is also the most visible leader of the congregation's participation in neighborhood redevelopment and social justice activity. The rhythms of religious life in the congregation do not always synchronize neatly with the rhythms of life in the surrounding community. This is especially true in communities that are socially diverse. Pastors who have the personal strength to set limits, determine priorities, say no to multiple demands, and avoid burn out, survive longer. Some pastors use the opportunities for travel to out-of-town meetings to rest, get a break, and keep at arm's length the unceasing demands for their presence and service.

Attending to the human needs within a sizable urban parish is a never-ending stress. No matter how well organized the parish may be with lay volunteers, the demand for pastoral services is a constant pressure. Pastors who are able to work out an understanding with the congregation about their availability, schedule limitations, and overall priorities tend to be more able to provide the most positive leadership overall.

A key factor in pastoral leadership seems to be spiritual and personal authenticity. Ministers whose personal and pastoral identities are rooted in mature faith and personal stability seem to be able to lead with greater ease. Being a symbol of positive, hopeful faith and generating trust, commitment, and energy within the congregation seem to go together. In strong urban churches, this is both visible and real. Most of the pastors we interviewed had been strengthened by significant religious experiences prior to and during their present ministry.

Developing a strong, talented, loyal team of colleagues to staff the variety of professional needs in urban churches is one of the most important tasks of pastoral leadership. There is a wide variety of ways to accomplish this important leadership function. Most of the urban pastors we visited seem to have attracted other capable people to serve on the staff of their churches. Having a big vision that challenges persons, providing opportunity to engage in meaningful relationships, and seeing positive, often tangible, results are key factors that we observed in urban church staff retention. There is a new generation of highly motivated, skilled, and dedicated ministers currently engaged in serving many of the churches we visited. They have intentionally chosen to be involved in urban ministry. Most are well educated and prepared for the challenge. Such staffs are crucial to meeting the intense human and technical demands of contemporary urban ministry.

In smaller and medium-sized urban churches, pastors were often successful in attracting capable help from seminary interns, urban corps volunteers, mid-life second career people with business skills, retired clergy serving as parish associates, and persons wanting to work part-time, but willing to do a lot for modest compensation. The creation of several nonprofit 501-C-3 corporations eligible for public funding is a helpful strategy for obtaining specialized staff for community projects. Often, the excitement of participating in projects that clearly are doing important things for community redevelopment attracts capable volunteers who are willing workers for an important cause.

Leadership in the crucible of city-center churches is always a mix of special talents, skills, and abilities together with the mystery of spiritual calling, faithful devotion, and disciplined ministry. The tides and times of local culture and national events are also factors beyond individual control that can sometimes play a significant role. In the 1990s, the federal government's trend toward decentralization of authority and power is a factor. The growing realization that if things are to get done, more initiative at the local level must be taken, is a powerful trend influencing urban church leadership. This may well be a time of special opportunity when many factors seem to come together to promote and encourage vigorous development within the life of urban congregations.

Group Study Materials

Discussion Questions

Thinking about Christian Faith in Relation to Urban Life

1. Jesus conducted most of his ministry in cities. The Christian church grew up in the cities of the Roman Empire. Christians have always lived in urban centers and worked in various ways to transform them. Make a list of ways in which that long tradition of Christian witness continues in urban communities today.

2. The Old Testament prophets called people to build up the city and work for its welfare (Jer. 29:7; Isa. 58:12). To what extent do you believe this is our calling? List some ways in which your church is actively seeking the transformation of the city.

3. What do you think the prophet Amos was saying to the religious people of his day in these words: "I hate, I despise your festivals, and I take no delight in your solemn assemblies. Take away from me the noise of your songs; I will not listen to the melody of your harps. But let justice roll down like waters, and righteousness like an everflowing stream" (Amos 5:21, 23-24). In what ways does this text speak to your church?

4. Jesus counsels us not to think of our faith as a matter of ritual worship — prayer and tithing (see Matt. 23:23) — while ignoring the

more important matters of justice, mercy, and compassion. In your church, how are you seeking to engage the important matters of justice, mercy, and compassion in the city?

5. Christians are part of the body of Christ, knit together by the Holy Spirit into a community of worship and witness, within the world created by God and for which Christ gave himself. How is your church present as Christ's body in the world, doing the work of reconciliation and transformation? Make a list of ways in which your congregation seeks to be the body of Christ in the urban world where you live, work, and worship.

6. We are all children of God, and we are all citizens of the political community. Beyond paying taxes and voting, what does your Christian faith motivate you to do in order to build up the common good of our society?

7. Realizing that seeking justice requires working in and through public institutions, what institutions could your church become involved with for the increase of justice in your urban community?

Thinking about Factors of Justice in Your Urban Community

1. Who owns the businesses, service companies, factories, retail stores, food shops, and lending institutions in your community? What degree of local ownership is there in the community? In the church?

2. To what extent does the income from goods and services produced in your urban community get reinvested within the community? Does it largely leave the area as profit for absentee owners who are not invested in the community? Think of specific businesses.

3. What is the level of unemployment and underemployment in your community? What is the level of good-paying jobs that can provide adequate financial support for a family? How does this affect the community? How does it affect your church?

4. To what extent do the people of your community have open access to good quality, affordable housing as owners or renters? Are some groups more able to secure good housing than other groups?

5. What is the attitude and action of the city government toward your urban community? Who are the city council members from your area? What is the quality of the relationship between the state gov-

ernment and your community? What are some ways in which this affects your area?

6. What is your own attitude toward and involvement with local and state government in relation to your urban community? Can you think of some ways in which the church has affected how you think and act in relation to local government?

7. How do the issues of crime, safety, police protection, and community participation in local street safety affect your community?

8. Over the past decade, what significant changes have taken place in your urban community that affect quality of life and levels of opportunity?

9. What major losses have taken place in your community that tend to create inequity, insecurity, and a sense of injustice? To what extent has the church responded to these losses?

10. Are there significant ethnic, racial, religious, or social conflicts in the community? To what extent are these openly recognized? Are these conflicts related to the operation of public and other institutions in your community?

Thinking about Positive Assets
and Resources in Your Urban Community

1. What are the physical assets within your community — for example, parks, schools, open land, commercial buildings, hospitals, colleges, sports facilities, church buildings, community centers, shopping centers, and libraries? What are some ways in which some of these assets might be resources for helping to solve some of the challenges facing your community?

2. What human resources are in your community? Who are some of the key leaders, talented and skilled people, persons with special experience, long-time residents who know the community's history, younger persons with energy, middle-aged persons with useful connections, political figures, clergy, local business owners, school principals and teachers, leaders of voluntary organizations and service clubs? Make a list of five or six persons in the community who might be helpful in engaging the challenges facing your area.

3. What are some of the service and information resources within your urban community — for example, school librarians, city librarians, city government agencies, social welfare agencies, police

department, fire department, college faculty and research institutes, federal census reports, city planning documents, clergy, regional planning bodies, computer internet, local and regional newspapers? To what extent has your church used these information resources to promote adult education, mission planning, and thinking about assets?

4. What potential partnerships, locally or regionally, might your church be able to create in the wider metropolitan area? Who might have knowledge, skill, experience, financial assets, political connections, and a willingness to join with you in doing new things to meet human needs? Make a list of five or six such persons or institutions where such persons might be found.

5. What foundations, corporations, government agencies, and other voluntary organizations can you identify that could be invited to become partners in working for positive change and greater social justice? Make a list of at least ten such potential partners.

6. What agencies of your own church denomination and its regional bodies might consult with you and assist with financial or other resources in your initiatives for the common good? Make a list of at least five. What other churches might want to be partners in such initiatives?

7. Whom do you know who could help seek new financial resources necessary for initiatives in your urban community? Who could study the foundation directory at the local library? Who would be willing to consult with the pastor, Presbytery executive, college fund-raiser, foundation development officer, local banker, or local businessperson to get information?

For more insights and information, consult the many useful resources listed on pp. 319-25.

Selected Biblical Texts

(Quotes are taken from the New Revised Standard Version of the Bible)

The churches discussed in this volume found the following texts particularly helpful in expressing their vision for mission.

Nehemiah 2–3

> "Jerusalem lies in ruins. . . . Let us rebuild the walls of Jerusalem."
> (Neh. 2:17)

Nehemiah organized the people into forty units for cooperative, community work to rebuild the walls of Jerusalem and much of the city. He also instituted reform and renewal.

Psalm 46:4-5

> There is a river whose streams
>   make glad the city of God,
>   the holy habitation of the Most High.
> God is in the midst of the city;
>   it shall not be moved;
>   God will help it when the morning dawns.

This psalm is a song of Zion, the city of God. It is a celebration of God's steadfast love for and presence in the city of Jerusalem. It is also the biblical basis for Martin Luther's great hymn, "A Mighty Fortress Is Our God."

Isaiah 58:12

> Your ancient ruins shall be rebuilt;
>   you shall raise up the foundations of many generations;
>   you shall be called the repairer of the breach,
>   the restorer of streets to live in.

Justice, mercy, and compassion are the offerings that God requires — freeing the oppressed, feeding the hungry, sheltering the homeless. Then shall the people be able to rebuild the city and repair the ruins.

Jeremiah 29:4-7

> Thus says the LORD of hosts, the God of Israel, to all the exiles whom I have sent into exile from Jerusalem to Babylon: Build houses and live in them; plant gardens and eat what they produce. Take wives and have sons and daughters; multiply there and do not

decrease. But seek the welfare of the city where I have sent you into exile, and pray to the LORD on its behalf, for in its welfare you will find your welfare.

This passage forms part of the letter the prophet Jeremiah wrote to the people of Israel living in exile in the city of Babylon.

Amos 5:21-24

> I hate, I despise your festivals,
>> and I take no delight in your solemn assemblies.
> Even though you offer me your burnt offerings and grain
>> offerings,
>> I will not accept them;
> and the offerings of well-being of your fatted animals
>> I will not look upon.
> Take away from me the noise of your songs;
>> I will not listen to the melody of your harps.
> But let justice roll down like waters,
>> and righteousness like an everflowing stream.

With these words the prophet confronted the king and the people with the emptiness of their worship and called them to do justice and be righteous.

Micah 6:8

> He has told you, O mortal, what is good;
>> and what does the LORD require of you
> but to do justice, and to love kindness,
>> and to walk humbly with your God?

This is the covenant of the people with God; this is the basis for rebuilding the life of the city.

Matthew 23:23

> "Woe to you, scribes and Pharisees, hypocrites! For you tithe mint, dill, and cummin, and have neglected the weightier matters of the law: justice and mercy and faith. It is these you ought to have practiced without neglecting the others."

Jesus exposed the hypocrisy of the powerful religious leaders of his day, many of whom had misused power, exploited the weak, laid heavy burdens on the poor, and ignored justice.

Matthew 23:37

"Jerusalem, Jerusalem, the city that kills the prophets and stones those who are sent to it! How often have I desired to gather your children together as a hen gathers her brood under her wings, and you were not willing!"

Jesus lamented the sinfulness and destructiveness of the city of Jerusalem, conditions that apply all too well to urban centers today.

Luke 4:18-19

"The Spirit of the Lord is upon me,
    because he has anointed me
        to bring good news to the poor.
He has sent me to proclaim release to the captives
    and recovery of sight to the blind,
        to let the oppressed go free,
to proclaim the year of the Lord's favor."

When Jesus spoke in the synagogue in Nazareth he read these words taken from Isaiah 61:1 to announce the great needs on which his ministry would focus.

Romans 8:35-39

Who will separate us from the love of Christ? Will hardship, or distress, or persecution, or famine, or nakedness, or peril, or sword? . . . No, in all these things we are more than conquerors through him who loved us. For I am convinced that neither death, nor life, nor angels, nor rulers, nor things present, nor things to come, nor powers, nor height, nor depth, nor anything else in all creation, will be able to separate us from the love of God in Christ Jesus our Lord.

Christ empowers us to transform urban strife into new life.

Guidelines for Going Beyond Charity Toward Justice

The following are some of the positive principles derived from the twenty-eight church stories in this book. Discuss how some of these guidelines might be useful in the urban ministry of your church.

1. **Be guided by Christian faith** in identifying your mission, not by your fears or sense of limitations. We do not work alone. God is doing new things through the church in the world. The challenge is to see what God is doing and join in his work of transformation.

2. **Have a big vision** challenging enough to attract new members, participants, friends, allies, and partners. Many urban churches are plagued by thinking only of survival.

3. **Worship is central to urban ministry.** Vital worship will affirm, spiritually empower, and strengthen persons and call them into action for transformation. Keep balance between nurturing faith and justice.

4. **Define your mission positively** by what you believe in and what you are in favor of, not by what you are against. There is a difference between being realistic and being negative.

5. **Reach out and seek partners** — new allies who want to be part of your positive vision for creative change and purposeful mission. Constructive change and social justice require making new alliances and involving new participants.

6. **Focus on one or two basic human needs** in your community and don't try to do too many things at one time. Creative change and social justice require strong, continuing commitment.

7. **See the positive assets in your community** that could be resources for development instead of being preoccupied by the negative. There are valuable resources even in the most deteriorated areas.

8. **Form new partnerships** with people and institutions outside your local area. Think and act within a wide region. The challenges of urban neighborhoods belong to all the people of a metropolitan region. Having a wide network of support is important.

9. **Seek financial resources outside the church,** both locally and also at the city, state, and national levels. There are many more avenues of money available today than there were even a decade ago. Foundations, corporations, service organizations, and government agencies are all investing in church-sponsored, faith-based community revitalization projects.

10. **Create new income producing enterprises** that serve people, meet basic human needs, and also generate a stream of money. The day is gone when urban churches could minister effectively using only the income from member giving.

11. **Make a long-term commitment.** Expect progress; celebrate the small victories along the way. Realize that significant change takes time and involves struggle, difficulty, defeats, and hard choices. Don't dwell on defeats. Look for new partners and new resources, and keep going. Long-term pastoral leadership is very important.

12. **Stay focused.** Don't give up. Leaders' most important roles are in communicating a big vision and in generating commitment and participation. Leaders must give strong affirmation, appreciation, and reinforcement, especially at moments of difficulty. Others can give energy, money, labor, skills, and hard work. Leaders must help everyone keep their eyes on the prize, take the long view, and stay focused.

13. **Tell your story widely.** Tell your story beyond the local community — in regional and national publications and through organizational networks and church channels. This is sharing the good news of the gospel in action. It is one important way to find new partners and secure new resources. Telling your story offers others the opportunity to be part of the gospel in action.

14. **Redevelopment of urban church ministry is interdependent with the redevelopment of the surrounding community.** The vital elements include strong worship, effective education, creative vision, and engagement with basic needs such as quality schools, affordable housing, economic development, health care, and strengthening family life.

15. **Undergird everything with prayer.** Spiritual reformation is ongoing. God's grace shared in the community of prayer is the ultimate source for healing discouragement and despair. In moving beyond charity toward justice, the formation of new hearts and minds is crucial. By the grace of God all things are possible.

Resource List

Books and Periodicals

Theology

Berger, Peter L., and Richard John Neuhaus. *To Empower People: The Role of Mediating Structures in Public Policy.* Washington: American Enterprise Institute for Public Policy, 1987.

Brueggemann, Walter. *Biblical Perspectives on Evangelism.* Nashville: Abingdon Press, 1993.

———. *The Prophetic Imagination.* Philadelphia: Fortress Press, 1978.

———. *Using God's Resources Wisely: Isaiah and Urban Possibility.* Louisville: Westminster John Knox Press, 1993.

Calvin, John. *The Necessity of Reforming the Church.* Audubon, NJ: Old Paths Publications, 1994.

Coalter, Milton J, John M. Mulder, and Louis B. Weeks. *Vital Signs: The Promise of Mainstream Protestantism.* Grand Rapids: William B. Eerdmans Publishing Company, 1996.

Conn, Harvie M. *The American City and the Evangelical Church: A Historical Overview.* Grand Rapids: Baker Book House, 1995.

Evans, James H. *We Shall All Be Changed: Social Problems and Theological Renewal.* Philadelphia: Fortress Press, 1997.

Harris, Maria. *Proclaim Jubilee! A Spirituality for the Twenty-first Century.* Louisville: Westminster John Knox Press, 1996.

Lutz, Charles P., ed. *A Reforming Church . . . Gift and Task: Essays from a Free Conference.* Minneapolis: Kirk House Publishers, 1995.

Lincoln, C. Eric, and Lawrence H. Mamiya. *The Black Church in the African American Experience.* Durham, NC: Duke University Press, 1990.

Meeks, Wayne A. *The First Urban Christians: The Social World of the Apostle Paul.* New Haven: Yale University Press, 1983.

Ottati, Douglas F. *Reforming Protestantism: Christian Commitment in Today's World.* Louisville: Westminster John Knox Press, 1995.

Palmer, Parker J. *The Promise of Paradox.* Washington, DC: The Servant Leadership School, 1993.

Rasmussen, Larry L. *Moral Fragments and Moral Community: A Proposal for Church in Society.* Minneapolis: Fortress Press, 1993.

Schaller, Lyle E. *The New Reformation: Tomorrow Arrived Yesterday.* Nashville: Abingdon Press, 1995.

Tillich, Paul. *Political Expectation.* New York: Harper & Row, 1971. See especially chapters 1 and 2.

Wallis, Jim, and Joyce Hollyday, eds. *Cloud of Witnesses,* Third printing. Maryknoll, NY: Orbis Books, 1993.

Westerhoff, John H. III. *Inner Growth/Outer Change: An Educational Guide to Church Renewal.* New York: The Seabury Press, 1979.

Wuthnow, Robert. *The Crisis in the Churches.* New York: Oxford University Press, 1997.

Urban Life

Cisneros, Henry G. *Higher Ground: Faith Communities and Community Building.* Washington, DC: U.S. Department of Housing and Urban Development, 1996.

———. *Interwoven Destinies: Cities and the Nation.* New York: W. W. Norton Company, 1993.

Eade, John, ed. *Living the Global City: Globalization as a Local Process.* New York: Routledge, 1997.

Etzioni, Amitai. *The Spirit of Community: The Reinvention of American Society.* New York: Simon and Schuster, 1993.

Evans, Thomas. *Mentors: Making a Difference in Our Public Schools.* Princeton: Peterson's Guides, 1992.

Green, Constance McLaughlin. *The Rise of Urban America.* New York: Harper and Row, 1965.

Royal, Robert, ed. *Reinventing the American People: Unity and Diversity Today*. Grand Rapids: William B. Eerdmans Publishing Company, 1995.

Robertson, D. B., ed. *Voluntary Associations: A Study of Groups in Free Societies*. Richmond, VA: John Knox Press, 1966.

Rusk, David. *Cities Without Suburbs*. Washington: Woodrow Wilson Center Press, 1993.

Sennett, Richard, ed. *Classic Essays on the Culture of Cities*. New York: Meredith Corporation, 1969.

The American Prospect, November-December 1997. See especially the articles: Isaac Kramnick and R. Laurence Moore, "Can the Churches Save the Cities?" pp. 47-53, and Robert Geddes, "Metropolis Unbound," pp. 40-46.

Wachter, Mary, with Cynthia Tinsley. *Taking Back Our Neighborhoods: Building Communities That Work*. Minneapolis: Fairview Press, 1996.

West, Cornell. *Race Matters*. Boston: Beacon Press, 1993.

Wilson, William Julius. *When Work Disappears: The World of the New Urban Poor*. New York: Alfred A. Knopf, 1996.

Yeo, Frederick L. *Inner-City Schools, Multiculturalism, and Teacher Education: A Professional Journey*. New York and London: Garland Publishing, Inc., 1997.

Urban Ministry

Claman, Victor N., David E. Butler, with Jessica A. Boyatt. *Acting on Your Faith: Congregations Making a Difference*. Boston: Insights Incorporated, 1994.

Cully, Kendig Brubaker, and Nile Harper, eds. *Will the Church Lose The City?* New York and Cleveland: The World Publishing Company, 1969.

Dudley, Carl S. *Basic Steps Toward Community Ministry: Guidelines and Models in Action*. Washington: The Alban Institute, 1991.

————. *Next Steps in Community Ministry: Hands-on Leadership*. Washington: The Alban Institute, 1996.

Elliott, Michael. *Why the Homeless Don't Have Homes and What to Do About It*. Cleveland: The Pilgrim Press, 1993.

Evans, Alice Frazer, Robert A. Evans, and William Bean Kennedy. *Pedagogies for the Non-Poor*. Maryknoll, NY: Orbis Books, 1987.

RESOURCE LIST

Green, Clifford J., ed. *Churches, Cities, and Human Community: Urban Ministry in the United States, 1945-1985.* Grand Rapids: William B. Eerdmans Publishing Company, 1996.

Hartley, Loyde. *Cities and Churches: An International Bibliography: 1800 to 1991,* 3 vols. ATLA Bibliography Series, 31. Metuchen, NJ: Scarecrow Press, 1992.

Klein, Joe. "Can Faith-Based Groups Save Us?" *The Responsive Community* 8:1 (Winter 1997/98): 25-52.

Linthicum, Robert, Douglas Edwards, and Roy Schlobohm. *Are We a Church of the City?* Temple City, CA: Urban Ministry Planning Group, 1997.

Palmer, Parker. *The Courage to Teach: The Inner Landscape of the Teacher.* San Francisco: Jossey-Bass, 1998.

Pasquariello, Ronald D., Donald W. Shriver, Jr., and Alan Geyer. *Redeeming the City: Theology, Politics and Urban Policy.* New York: The Pilgrim Press, 1982.

Perkins, John M. *Beyond Charity: The Call to Christian Community Development.* Grand Rapids: Baker Books, 1993.

Perkins, John M., ed. *Restoring At-Risk Communities: Doing It Together and Doing It Right.* Grand Rapids: Baker Books, 1995.

Progressions, a Lily Endowment Occasional Report 5, issue 1, February 1995.

Roof, Wade Clark, and William McKinney. *American Mainline Religion: Its Changing Shape and Future,* fourth printing. New Brunswick, NJ: Rutgers University Press, 1992.

Schaller, Lyle E., ed. *Center City Churches: The New Urban Frontier.* Nashville: Abingdon Press, 1993.

Wood, Brent A. "First African Methodist Episcopal Church: Its Social Intervention in South Central Los Angeles." Ph.D. dissertation, University of Southern California Graduate School, 1997.

Justice

Baumgartner, M. P. *The Moral Order of a Suburb.* New York: Oxford University Press, 1988.

Bellah, Robert N., Richard Madsen, William N. Sullivan, Ann Swidler, and Steven M. Tipton. *The Good Society.* New York: Vintage Books, 1991.

322

Branch, Taylor. *Parting of the Waters: America in the King Years 1954-63.* New York: Simon and Schuster, 1988.

———. *Pillars of Fire: America in the King Years 1963-65.* New York: Simon and Schuster, 1998.

Brueggemann, Walter. *A Social Reading of the Old Testament: Prophetic Approaches to Israel's Communal Life.* Edited by Patrick D. Miller. Minneapolis: Fortress Press, 1994.

Gutiérrez, Gustavo. "The Irruption of the Poor in Latin America." In *The Challenge of Basic Christian Communities,* edited by Sergio Torres and John Eagleson. Maryknoll, NY: Orbis Books, 1981.

Meeks, Wayne A. *The Origins of Christian Morality.* New Haven: Yale University Press, 1993.

Niebuhr, Reinhold. *Love and Justice.* Edited by D. B. Robertson. Louisville: Westminster John Knox Press, 1957.

———. *Moral Man and Immoral Society: A Study in Ethics and Politics.* New York: Charles Scribner's Sons, 1932.

Olasky, Marvin. *The Tragedy of American Compassion.* Wheaton, IL: Crossway Books, 1992.

Villafañe, Eldin. *The Liberating Spirit: Toward an Hispanic American Pentecostal Social Ethic.* Grand Rapids: William B. Eerdmans Publishing, 1993.

Wallis, Jim. *The Soul of Politics: Beyond "Religious Right" and "Secular Left."* New York: Harcourt Brace and Company, 1995.

Technical and Financial Resources

United States Department of Housing and Urban Development (HUD)

Post Office Box 6091
Rockville, MD 20849
1-800-245-2691

Ask for the Religious Organization Initiative:
Anna Towns, (202) 708-2046 Ext. 5553

Local Initiatives Support Corporation

> 733 Third Avenue
> New York City, NY 10017
> Telephone: (212) 455-9800
> Fax: (212) 682-5929

Helps groups rebuild deteriorated housing, mobilizes financial resources, organizes partnerships, assists grassroots community groups, works with community development corporations, provides funding.

The National Equity Fund (NEF)

> 547 West Jackson Boulevard
> Suite 601
> Chicago, IL 60661
> (312) 360-0400

> 1055 Wilshire Boulevard
> Suite 1660
> Los Angeles, CA 90017
> (213) 250-9550

Assists community development corporations with funding for the creation of housing in low-income areas — rehabilitation and new construction.

National Congress for Community Economic Development

> 875 Connecticut Avenue N.W. #524
> Washington, DC 20009
> (202) 234-5009

Network for technical information and resources.

Christian Community Development Association

> 3827 West Ogden Avenue
> Chicago, IL 60623
> (312) 762-0994

Offers conferences, publications, consulting, and training.

Urban Ministry Planning Group

9642 Live Oak Avenue
Temple City, CA 91780-2522
(818) 292-1951
e-mail: umpg@earthlink.net

Offers urban church leadership training and consulting.

Seminary Consortium for Urban Pastoral Education (S.C.U.P.E.)

200 N. Michigan Avenue
Chicago, IL 60601
Telephone: (312) 726-1200
Fax: (312) 726-0425
e-mail: scupe502@aol.com

Continuing education for urban pastors.

The Enterprise Foundation

10227 Wincopin Circle, Suite 500
Columbia, MD 21044
(410) 964-1230

Economic development assistance.

The Lilly Endowment for Religion

Dr. Craig Dykstra, Director
Post Office Box 88068
Indianapolis, IN 46208
(317) 924-5471

Ask for publications from the Religious Institutions as Partners in Community Based Development.

The American Investors Group

Burnsville, MN (612) 892-1222
Minnetonka, MN (612) 945-9455

Works with nonprofit organizations to plan and manage the sale of investment bonds for construction.

The Foundation Center

79 Fifth Avenue
New York, NY 10003-3076
Contact: 1-800-424-9836

Offers The Foundation Center's Guide to Proposal Writing (1993); The Foundation Directory and Supplement, 15th ed., which includes information on 6,300 larger foundations and many other directories. Call for their catalog and information about their libraries in various cities.

The Taft Group, Rockville, MD

1-800-877-8238

Offers a directory listing foundations and others that donate to religious organizations: Fundraiser's Guide to Religious Philanthropy (1994).

Research Grant Guides, Margate, FL

(407) 795-6129

Offers: Directory of Building and Equipment Grants; Directory of Operating Grants; and Directory of Grants for Organizations Serving People with Disabilities.

Urban Church Research

Nile Harper, Director
2828 Seminole Road
Ann Arbor, MI 48108
(734) 971-6177

Research and education for urban churches.

People of Faith Network

David Dyson, Director
85 South Oxford Street
Brooklyn, NY 11217
(718) 625-7515

Action resources for justice in the workplace.

Index

Abel, Earl, 193, 196

African-American churches, 19, 30, 74, 83, 101, 110, 138, 157, 193, 223, 235, 244, 254, 264

Allen African Methodist Episcopal, New York: and action for racial equity, 36-37; as an African-American church, 30; and alternative schools, 35; and economic development, 39; and economic enterprise, 39-40; and family ministry, 35; and improvement of education, 35; and pastoral initiatives, 38-40; relationship with public schools, 35-37; and social service, 33; theological vision of, 36; worship empowering mission, 32

Ballton, Lula, 260

Barstow, Ann L., 55

Bernardin, Joseph Cardinal, 177

Big Bethel African Methodist Episcopal, Atlanta: as an African-American church, 83; and church redevelopment, 85; and creative funding, 86-89; and economic development, 86; and economic enterprise, 86; and economic justice, 86; and health care, 88; and social service, 88; and transforma-tion of church and society, 85-89; worship empowering mission, 89

Blake, Charles, 255-56, 261

Caldwell, Kirbyjon, 223

Cearley, Cynthia, 213, 215

Central Presbyterian, Atlanta: and child care, 95; and economic justice, 98; and family ministry, 95; and health care, 94; and pastoral initiatives, 93; and social service, 96; theological vision of, 93

Charity: defined, 297-99

Child care, 13, 21, 80, 95, 177, 196, 216, 224, 240, 293

Church of St. Edmund (Episcopal), Chicago: as an African-American church, 157; and affordable housing, 160; and alternative schools, 163; and church redevelopment, 158; and community organizing, 157-58; and creative funding, 161-63; and economic development, 161; and economic enterprise, 160-63; and economic justice, 158; and improvement of education, 163; and mentoring, 158-60; and pastoral initiatives, 157-59; relationship with public schools, 164-65; theological

About the Author

Dr. Nile Harper was educated at Ball State University in Muncie, Indiana; at McCormick Theological Seminary in Chicago; and the Union Theological Seminary in New York City. He earned the master's degree in sociology at the New School of Social Research in New York and the doctorate in education at Columbia University, New York City.

Harper is an ordained Presbyterian minister and served churches in New Jersey, Iowa, and Michigan. He served the ninety churches of the Presbytery of East Iowa as Associate Executive, with responsibility for the development of congregational life.

For eight years he was Professor of Church and Society and Director of Field Education at New York Theological Seminary. He served as Professor of Sociology of Religion at the Schools of Theology in Dubuque, Iowa (Presbyterian, Catholic, Lutheran) for eight years.

Harper was the Presbyterian Campus Minister at the University of Michigan and Director of the Ecumenical Center in Ann Arbor, Michigan, for ten years. He has served as adjunct lecturer in the urban ministry program of the Ecumenical Theological Seminary in Detroit. He is currently Director of Urban Church Research doing consulting, research, and writing.

Harper's previous publications include the following titles: *Social Conflict and Adult Christian Education*, *Will the Church Lose the City?*, *Social Power and the Limitations of Church Education*, *The Dubuque Freeway: A Case Study in Urban Power.*

333